SPORT AND TRAVEL IN THE NORTHLAND OF CANADA

BY

DAVID T. HANBURY

NEW YORK
THE MACMILLAN COMPANY
LONDON: EDWARD ARNOLD
1904

Publishing Statement:

This important reprint was made from an old and scarce book.

Therefore, it may have defects such as missing pages, erroneous pagination, blurred pages, missing text, poor pictures, markings, marginalia and other issues beyond our control.

Because this is such an important and rare work, we believe it is best to reproduce this book regardless of its original condition.

Thank you for your understanding and enjoy this unique book!

PREFACE

IN this narrative I have endeavoured to give a plain and unvarnished account of twenty months' journeying through the Northland of Canada. The book deals with sport and travel, no attempt having been made to accomplish elaborate geographical or other scientific work. I have written of the Eskimo as I found them, having, with my two white companions, lived their life, sharing their habitations, clad in deerskins, and subsisting on caribou and musk-ox meat in winter, or on fish in summer. Of the Indians, with whom I have been much longer acquainted than with the Eskimo, I have also written without prejudice.

To the natural features of the country it would be difficult for any writer to do justice. They require the artist's pencil rather than the pen of a wanderer. The photographs will give the untravelled reader but a poor idea of the character of the country which for many years has, with scant justice, been called the "Barren Ground." The Northland must be lived in to be understood and appreciated, for its constantly changing aspect baffles description.

That such an enormous tract of territory should remain untrodden by the foot of the white man is to me a matter of surprise. Africa and Central Asia have attracted many explorers, while the men of European origin who have passed through the Northland of Canada can almost be counted on one's fingers. To the geologist, especially to the student of glacial phenomena, this region offers a field of exceptional interest. The sportsman, the naturalist, the artist, the ethnologist, even the prospector, will find abundant interest in these northern wilds which hitherto have been so severely avoided. If I succeed in directing some attention to this neglected region, and, in so doing, assist in whiling away an idle hour for those into whose hands the book may fall, my modest pretensions will be accomplished.

The map showing my route was prepared, in collaboration with the late Mr. W. Shaw, by Professor Logan Lobley, F.G.S., who also revised my geological notes, and prepared the geological map. The geological specimens were determined by Dr. J. S. Flett of the Geological Survey of England, and the botanical specimens by Mr. R. A. Rolfe, A.L.S.

The Historical Sketch of Exploration in North Canada was written by Mr. J. P. A. Renwick.

To Mr. H. J. Elwes, F.R.S., I am indebted for the description of the Arctic coast butterflies shown in the coloured plate in the Appendix.

Most of the photographs reproduced were taken by myself, but my acknowledgments are due to Captain Deville, Surveyor-General of the Dominion of Canada, for permission to reproduce a few taken by Mr. J. W. Tyrrell, C.E., and to Mr. C. E. Mathers of Edmonton, Alberta, for permission to reproduce a few others.

In the endeavour to represent the sound of Eskimo names and other words, both in the text of the book and in the vocabulary given in the Appendix, the system of spelling adopted by the Royal Geographical Society has been followed so far as it was found practicable, but, to avoid the frequent duplication of consonants, the quantity of vowels has in many cases been indicated by the usual signs.

D. T. H.

CONTENTS

CHAPTER VII

CHAPTER VIII

CHAPTER IX

CHAPTER X

CHAPTER XI

CHAPTER XII

CHAPTER XIII

CHAPTER XIV

CHAPTER XV

CHAPTER XVI

APPENDIX

LIST OF ILLUSTRATIONS

COLOURED PLATES ·

MAPS

HISTORICAL SKETCH OF

EXPLORATION IN NORTH CANADA

THAT portion of continental Canada with the exploration of which this sketch is concerned is the region which lies between the north-western coast of Hudson Bay on the one side, and Great Slave Lake and Great Bear Lake on the other. Its northern boundary is the coast line from the mouth of the Coppermine River to the mouth of Back's River, and its southern, the course of the waters which flow respectively eastwards to Chesterfield Inlet and westwards to Great Slave Lake from the watershed between Artillery Lake and the head-waters of the western branch of the Ark-i-linik. This region forms a large part of the so-called "Barren Ground." It is neither barren nor uninhabited; but the conditions of life within its borders are too severe for Europeans. Exploring parties and hunters have visited it, but it contains no European settlement, not even a Hudson Bay Company's trading post. Its exploration was begun, not for the sake of gaining a knowledge of the country, nor for the development of its resources, but in the hope of finding a passage through it to the Western Ocean. Henry Hudson was engaged in the search for a North-West Passage when, on August 3, 1610, he rounded the north-western shoulder of Labrador and entered the Bay which now bears his name. He sailed along its eastern side and wintered on its south coast, but, in the following summer, soon after leaving his winter quarters, he, his son (a mere boy), and seven sick men were seized by the mutinous crew and sent adrift to perish in an open boat.

The search for a passage westwards from the Bay was taken up by a succession of navigators, some of whom were appointed to the task by Government and others by merchants. These discoverers were in general skilful as well as daring, but, as they only touched at points on the coast, making no attempt at inland exploration, brief mention of their work will here suffice. In 1612 Captain (afterwards Sir Thomas) Button entered the Bay with two ships, and, holding on his westward course, encountered land at about 60° 40′ N. lat. He called the place "Hopes Checkt," and turned southwards. Being a Welshman he called the land "New Wales," a name which afterwards gave place to "New North Wales" for the northern part, and "New South Wales" for the southern; but all three designations, as applied to the Hudson Bay coast, are now only of historic interest. Button wintered at Port Nelson, which he so named in memory of a shipmaster who, with many of the sailors, died there. When the ice broke up he went northwards past Cape Churchill and a place in about 60° N. which he called "Hubbart's Hope." On July 23, 1613, he reached "Hope's Advance," now taken to be Marble Island, and on July 29 he was in 65° N. lat. Farther he did not go, but, turning south-eastwards, shaped his course for the homeward voyage. "Button's Bay" is the name by which our Hudson Bay is distinguished on old maps.

In 1619 a Danish expedition, comprising 64 men in two ships under the command of Captain Jens Munck, reached the Bay, and, on September 9, laid their vessels in winter quarters at Churchill. By June 18 of the following year all the men had died except Munck and two others, who were just able to make their way back to Denmark.

In 1631 two notable voyagers, Captain Luke Foxe and Captain James, in separate expeditions, searched the coasts of the Bay both north and south. The former, on July 27, reached the western shore at a point in 60° 10′ N. lat., and to a small island there he gave the name of "Sir Thomas Rowe's Welcome," a name which now denotes the channel at the south end of which the island stands. Turning southwards he passed, on July 29, "Brooke Cobham," the island which a hundred years afterwards received the name of Marble Island. Two days later he reached the group of small islands which he called "Brigges his Mathematics"; on August 2 he was opposite "Button's Checks," and next day at "Hubbart Point." On August 6 he passed the mouth of the Churchill River, and two days later he entered Port Nelson, where he found remains of Button's expedition. He then searched the coast eastwards and southeastwards, calling it "New Yorkshire" after his own county. He went as far south as Cape Henrietta Maria, and then, having gone northwards to Foxe Channel, he explored as far as 60° 47′ N. lat. When this was accomplished he returned to England without having been under the necessity of wintering in the Bay. The investigations of Captain James were carried out chiefly in the bay which now bears his name, where he wintered, and in Foxe Channel, and they require no further mention here.

The next expedition with which we have to do was prepared in 1719 by the Hudson Bay Company, mainly for the discovery of a North-West Passage. Samuel Hearne, in the Introduction to the Narrative of his own remarkable journey, tells the story of this expedition. The command of it was given to Captain James Knight, a man who had had experience in the Company's service, but who, being nearly eighty years of age, was presumably unequal to the task he undertook. Two vessels were fitted out in the Thames, and, being provided with supplies and all the articles and appliances which were considered necessary for a successful voyage, sailed in June 1719 under the command of Captain Barlow and Captain Vaughan. By the end of the following year they had not returned to England, and in 1721 the Company's officials in London sent orders to Churchill that search should be made for them. These orders could not be carried out till 1722, and then John Scroggs, who was entrusted with the search, and who sailed as far as 64° 56′ N., could find no evidence that the vessels were lost. In these circumstances many conjectured that they had

found the North-West Passage and had sailed to the South
Sea by way of California. The truth was not known till
1767 (forty-eight years after the vessels had sailed). In
that year some whaling-boats belonging to the Company
discovered a harbour near the east end of Marble Island,
and at the head of it they found guns, anchors, cables, and
other articles too heavy for the Eskimo to remove. Sunk
in the harbour were the hulls of two ships, and the figure-
head of one of them was identified as belonging to one
of the missing vessels. In 1769 some particulars were
gathered from Eskimo of the region respecting the fate
of the crews. The two vessels had reached the island in
1719, and the natives had seen the crews, who, they said,
numbered about fifty, setting up their wooden house with
iron fittings. The Eskimo visited them in the following
year, and observed that their numbers were much smaller
and the survivors unhealthy. When winter set in there
were not more than twenty left alive, and in the summer
of 1721 only five survived. They purchased from the
natives seal's flesh and whale's blubber, which they ate;
but three of them died in a few days. The remaining two
were often seen going to the top of an adjacent rock and
looking earnestly to the south and east as if in expectation
of relief. At length one of them died, and the other, in
attempting to dig a grave, fell down and died also. These
details, which were supplied by an aged Eskimo, were
supported by the position of the bones and other remains
found about the harbour.

Still the search for a passage to the west of the Bay was
continued. A ship, despatched from Churchill in 1737 for
discovery in the north, was used merely for purposes of
trade. In 1741, however, two vessels, under Middleton and
Moore respectively, sailed from England, and on August 10
reached Churchill, where they wintered. Next year they
went northwards and discovered Wager Inlet and Repulse
Bay. Rankin, one of Middleton's officers, entered the
harbour near the west end of Marble Island, and his name

is given to the large inlet on the neighbouring mainland coast. Middleton's expedition was highly successful, for he had showed that there was no outlet from the Bay to the north. But this result was not satisfactory to those who had employed him; his statements were discredited, and suspicion was cast on his motives. He was, in fact, an ill-used man, and, after spending what money he had in repelling the attacks made upon him, he died in distress. With the idea of correcting Middleton's misrepresentations, another expedition, with two ships under Moore (Middleton's former colleague) and Smith respectively, sailed from England in 1746. In the following year they did much useful work, examining the bays and inlets from Cape Esquimaux to Wager Inlet, but they supplied no evidence that Middleton had been wrong. Narratives of this expedition have been left by Henry Ellis and by Drage, both of whom took part in its work. Of interest here is the exploration of Chesterfield Inlet. This opening was entered by the long-boats of the two ships, which advanced for eighteen leagues, or about half its length. The water, however, "from being salt, transparent, and deep, with steep shores and strong currents, grew fresher, thicker, and shallower at that height," so that the officers were discouraged from proceeding farther.

The search for a passage was now restricted almost exclusively to an examination of Chesterfield Inlet. In 1761 Captain Christopher sailed up the Inlet, till, from the water losing its saltness, he concluded that he was on a river, not a strait. Next year, being ordered to repeat the voyage, he found that the Inlet ended in a freshwater lake (Baker Lake), closed up on every side except the west, where it was entered by a little rivulet. Norton, Christopher's companion, ascended this rivulet, and saw "that it soon terminated in three falls, one above another, and not water for a small boat over them" (Cook's "Third Voyage," Vol. I. p. XLV). A perplexing fact in view of this statement is that the Doobaunt, a large river, flows without a single break which could be described as a "fall" into the north-west corner of Baker Lake. How could an explorer have missed seeing it? There was, at all events, room for further investigation.

In 1791, Captain Duncan, in a brig from the Thames, explored the head of Corbett's Inlet, and in 1792 he was sent to examine the head of Baker Lake. He left his brig in Lake's Harbour, and went in a boat to "Norton's Falls." Thence he followed, not a rivulet, but "the course of the river, by land, till he found it came from the north-ward, in which direction he traced it near thirty miles." Then he desisted, convinced that to follow it farther could lead to no useful discovery. (Goldson's "Observations on the Passage between the Atlantic and Pacific Oceans." 1793.)

The Hudson Bay coasts became familiar not only to voyagers sent specially to explore them, but also to captains of the vessels which in the summer months were employed in the Hudson Bay Company's traffic. Such a sailor was Captain Coats, who, after having been engaged in this service from 1727 to 1751, wrote a book called "Remarks on the Geography of Hudson Bay" (published by the Hakluyt Society in 1852). These "Remarks" are pronounced by competent authorities to be surprisingly accurate. They are roughly put together, but some of his kindly thoughts respecting the natives may be set down here. "It will be necessary," he says, "before I quit these parts, to set down my own sentiments and that of others, in regard to the Usquemows, the naturall inhabitants of all the northern borders of Hudson's Bay and Streights, which swarms with robust, hardy fellows, fitt for the severest exercise, and indeed, with such dispositions, as if God's providence in fullness of time had prepared them to receive the yoke of civility. And I do assert of my own knowledge that these people are nothing near so savage as is represented by our early voyagers, and that their confidence is in their innocence, not in their numbers, which I have often experienced when one or two has put themselves into my hand without reserve or caution." Elsewhere he describes them as "bold, robust, hardy people, undaunted, masculine men, no tokens of poverty or want, with great fat, flatt, greazy faces, litle black percing eyes, good teeth, &c.," and he propounds a pious scheme whereby those tribes "may be made useful to us, and acquire salvation to themselves."

The first European to traverse the region with which we are concerned was Samuel Hearne, an officer of the Hudson Bay Company. The Indians who visited Churchill for the purpose of trade had reported that, far to the north, there was a large river, the banks of which abounded with copper, and with animals of the "fur" kind, and it was clearly desirable to ascertain what truth there was in their statements. The difficulty of exploration was great, for the region, bare, bleak, and frozen for the greater part of the year, was known only to roaming tribes of Indians. The task, however, was undertaken by Hearne, who, though not a man of masterful character, had quiet, persistent energy. An Indian guide was appointed, and, on November 6, 1769, Hearne set out westwards with heavy-laden sledges hauled by Indians. He had not gone far when he found reason to distrust his guide. This rogue began by trying to discourage his companions, suggesting that they should turn back; next he took measures to starve the party into compliance; then he induced several men to desert, and finally, on November 30, he, with the rest of his countrymen, packed up their belongings and went their own way towards the south-west, making the woods ring with their laughter. Hearne of course turned back, and reached Churchill on December 11.

His second attempt had little better success, though its failure was not brought about by treachery. He set out from Churchill on February 23, 1770, directing his general course towards the north-west. He travelled slowly, making long halts lest he should outstrip the birds and beasts on which his party depended for supplies, and on August 11, after he had reached a point somewhere to the north of Doobaunt Lake, his quadrant was blown down and shattered. As this instrument was indispensable for the determination of his position from time to time, he resolved to turn back, and, on November 25, he for the second time entered Churchill an unsuccessful explorer.

Having been provided with an old and cumbrous Elton's quadrant, he, on December 7, 1770, set out for the third time, accompanied by a party of Indians. His course is not easily followed, for many lakes and rivers which he crossed are now unknown by the names he gave them; their shapes and their distances from each other, as laid down on his map, do not agree with those on recent maps, and, in short, his determinations of latitude and longitude were all wrong. A stalwart geographer of those days, Alexander Dalrymple, pointed out Hearne's errors, and Hearne did not take his remarks in good part; but no one in our time blames this indefatigable traveller for defects which were inevitable in his circumstances. He did excellent work with the poorest equipment, and his descriptions of the country, of the Indians who roamed over it, and of its animal and vegetable life, are full of interest.

At first he held westwards, and, on April 8, 1771, reached a lake, "The-lewey-aza-yeth" (apparently about 106° W. longitude). His party had gradually increased by the addition of Indians, and now it contained seventy persons. Holding northwards he reached "Lake Clowey" on May 3, and here he was joined by about 200 Indians from different quarters. The Indians had a deadly hatred of the Eskimo, and Hearne discovered that the volunteers who now thronged about him were eager to accompany him to the Coppermine River for the purpose of slaughtering their hereditary enemies. He tried to dissuade them, but finding that his remonstrances only gained him the reputation of a coward, he thought it prudent to desist.

However, when the time came for resuming the journey, many of these volunteers, with characteristic Indian fickleness, changed their minds and remained behind.

Continuing northwards Hearne crossed "Catt Lake" (Artillery Lake), and then "Thoy-noy-kyed Lake" (Aylmer and Clinton Colden Lakes), and on June 20 reached "Cogead Lake" (Rum Lake). A few days later he crossed, in canoes lent by Copper Indians, the stream which still has the name of "Conge-ca-tha-wha-chaga." Here the women of the party were left behind, and, on July 2, Hearne and the men went forward, guided by Copper Indians. On July 14 he reached the Coppermine River, probably in the neighbourhood of the Sandstone Rapids, and the Indians lost no time in setting about their murderous purpose. Three scouts were sent to look for the enemy, and in two days they returned with the news that there were five Eskimo tents on the west side of the river. Hearne's Indians were simply savages whom he could not control. They at once resolved that the occupants of the tents should be slaughtered during the night, and, having put their weapons in good order, they crossed the river. Each man painted his shield with red or black figures, and then they marched under cover of hills and rocks to a spot about 200 yards from the Eskimo tents. Here they lay in ambush, smearing their faces with war-paint, tying or cutting their hair, and making their dress as light as possible. Then, at about one o'clock in the morning of July 17, they rushed forth and fell on the unsuspecting creatures. After the first attack about twenty men, women, and children rushed from the tents, but not one of them escaped the spears of the savages. A young girl ran towards Hearne, who looked on in horror, and when the spear struck her she fell at his feet, twisting round his legs. He begged the two pursuing Indians to spare her life, but they transfixed her to the ground and then asked him if he wished an Eskimo wife. The slaughter was followed by mutilation, the search for more victims, and the plundering or destruction of the property of the slain. There were Eskimo at the farther side of the river, beyond the reach of the Indians, and they escaped to tell the tale of murder which is remembered by their descendants to this day.

After the massacre the whole party had a good meal of fresh salmon, and then, at about five o'clock in the morning, Hearne, accompanied by Indians, proceeded to survey the river to the sea. This survey, after such a night's experience, was obviously hastily begun and perfunctorily carried out, and from its defects Sir John Richardson concluded that it was merely imaginary; that, in short, Hearne only surveyed the river from the hill overhanging Bloody Fall. Hearne, it seems, under-estimated the distance from the Fall to the sea, and at the mouth of the river he found marks indicating a tide 14 feet high. How Franklin regarded such mistakes we shall see in due course.

The limits of space forbid the attempt to follow Hearne on his homeward journey. His return route lay at first farther to the west, but later almost coincided with his out-going route, and it was not till June 29, 1772, that, after undergoing numberless privations, he re-entered the fort at Churchill.

The more important of Hearne's errors were corrected by Captain (afterwards Sir John) Franklin, who, fully equipped by Government for scientific work, and accompanied by Richardson, Back, and Hood—men of distinguished ability, set out on August 2, 1820, from old Fort Providence, on the north side of Great Slave Lake, to ascend the Yellow Knife River. His party comprised Canadian voyagers and Indians who were inclined to insubordination, for there were rapids, cascades, and portages to be passed, and very often only scanty fare could be procured; but on August 20 he reached Winter Lake, near which he established his winter quarters. Here wooden houses, dignified with the name of Fort Enterprise, were erected, and, after various exploring excursions in the region, the party settled down for the long winter.

On June 14, 1821, Franklin resumed his march; on June 20 he crossed the ridge separating the waters flowing south from those flowing north; then he reached Point Lake and the Coppermine, down the rapids of which he passed, portaging at times. On July 7 he gained the portage leading to Great Bear Lake, and found the river narrower, with banks sometimes precipitous like stone walls, from 80 feet to 150 feet high. On July 12, when approaching the Eskimo country, he sent forward two Eskimo interpreters to negotiate, keeping his Indians well in hand. But the natives were suspicious, and, though in several interviews they seemed not unfriendly, on noticing (July 15) some of Franklin's men on the hill tops, they turned and fled. The place answered exactly to Hearne's description, and, even then, several human skulls, bearing marks of violence, and many bones were lying about. Next day the Indians were surprised to meet a band of Eskimo, who seemed equally surprised. Both parties made signs of peaceful intentions, but neither had confidence in the other, and they separated. One old Eskimo remained, and his description of the ways of his countrymen agrees with those given by travellers in our own day.

On July 18 Franklin descended the river to the sea, which he found to be decidedly salt, and he observed a rise and fall of 4 inches (not 14 feet) in the water. He found his position in latitude to be 67° 47′ 50″ N., and in longitude 115° 36′ 49″ W. Hearne's determinations here had been 71° 54′ N., and 120° 30′ W. Notwithstanding these differences, Franklin says, "the accuracy of his description, conjoined with Indian information, assured us that we were at the very part he visited." He makes no reference to Hearne's statement that here, on July 21, he saw the sun at midnight, but only records, on July 19, that "the sun set this night at 30 minutes after 11, apparent time."

From the mouth of the Coppermine River Franklin turned eastwards and paddled along the coast, well pleased to quit the "fresh-water navigations," though a voyage on the "Hyperborean Sea" was alarming to his Canadian companions. Setting out on July 21, he kept inside the crowded range of islands; sometimes he was impeded by ice; sometimes assisted, sometimes retarded by the wind. Here and there he found traces of Eskimo. On July 25 he rounded Cape Barrow, and on July 30 found, at the foot of Arctic Sound, the mouth of Hood River. Thence he explored round the head of Bathurst Inlet, and on August 13 and 14 passed along the southern and northern coasts of Melville Sound. Turning northwards he proceeded as far as the north-west corner of Kent Peninsula, where, as the season was now far advanced, it was necessary to halt. The point where he stopped he called Point Turnagain, and on August 20 he set out for Bathurst Inlet. On August 24 he reached Barry Island, and next day passed to the head of Arctic Sound, and up Hood River as far as the first rapid, where the Canadians were delighted to be again on fresh water. On August 27 he camped beside Wilberforce Falls, the height of which he estimated, the one at over 60 feet, and the other at over 80 feet, the whole descent at the place being over 250 feet.

The water above the falls being too shallow for the large canoes, it was resolved to strike overland to Fort Enterprise, about 149 miles distant. Two small canoes for crossing lakes or rivers were made out of the material of the large ones, superfluous baggage was left behind, and on August 30 the party set out, each man carrying about 90 lbs. weight. Their march proved a long course of suffering. Supplies were soon exhausted, and they travelled through a country where game was scarce, and where there were no berries, only grass and lichens, with sometimes Labrador tea. Heavy rain and snow with violent wind sometimes made travelling impossible. One canoe got broken, and the other was not always serviceable

when required. Now and then a few partridges were shot;
one day a musk-ox, and afterwards some deer were killed,
which kept the party in hope. On September 13 they
reached Rum Lake, where, to lighten their loads, they
deposited several instruments and books; a week later
Richardson had to leave his specimens of plants and
minerals. The men had to satisfy their hunger by eating
the skins, bones, and horns of deer which had been devoured by wolves, many of them adding their own old shoes
to the repast. They had thrown away fishing-nets and other
needful articles, and now they abandoned the canoe. On
September 24, however, they killed five small deer and
fared sumptuously. To cross the Coppermine at Point
Lake, they built a raft which proved unmanageable. Dr.
Richardson volunteered to swim across with a rope, but
his limbs became benumbed and he was hauled back to
land half dead. A second raft proved as useless as the
first, but at length, on October 4, a canoe, made of canvas
on a willow frame, was found sufficient for the transport of
the party one by one. Back and three Canadians were
now sent forward to obtain help while the rest trudged
slowly onward through the deep snow. Soon Richardson
and Hood, with Hepburn (a Scotch sailor) to attend to
them, had to be left behind. Then several Canadians
dropped away from Franklin's band, but only one, Michel,
joined Richardson and Hood.

Franklin reached Fort Enterprise on October 12, and
found it desolate, but a note left by Back stated that he
had gone further south in search of Indians and supplies.
Soon, however, a messenger from Back brought word that
no Indians were to be found; whereupon Franklin sent
forward two men to join in the search, he himself remaining behind at the Fort, where the best fare consisted
of deerskins, bones, and lichens.

One day Richardson and Hepburn entered, and announced that Hood was dead, and Michel dead. They
told a painful tale, which may be summed up thus. In the

direst extremity of hunger, Michel had become refractory ;
Hood, in the depth of physical weakness, had rebuked or
remonstrated with him, and then Michel had shot him
through the head. Of this there could be no doubt. Then
Michel had assumed an offensive attitude towards Richardson, and had used threats towards Hepburn, so that, being
armed, he was clearly a dangerous companion. Hepburn,
the first time he and Richardson were alone together, offered
to shoot Michel, but Richardson took that responsibility on
himself, and, when Michel approached, shot him through
the head with a pistol.

In the meantime Back, in desperate circumstances, was
making his way towards Fort Providence, accompanied by
two Canadians, the other having been frozen to death. On
November 3 they found Indian footprints, which one of the
Canadians followed up, and in the evening an Indian boy
came to Back with meat and a letter, which Franklin had sent
by the messengers already mentioned. The Indians at once
set about the work of relief, and, early next morning, three
sledges with supplies were on their way to Fort Enterprise.
On November 7 these stores arrived, and by November 16
Franklin and the others were able to begin the journey to
Old Fort Providence. The Indians treated them with the
utmost kindness, and on December 11 they reached the
Fort.

Franklin, having been successful in surveying a long
stretch of coast to the east of the Coppermine River, was
appointed to the command of an expedition to explore the
coast to the west of that river. The exploring party spent
the winter of 1825–26 at Fort Franklin, at the west end of
Great Bear Lake, and on June 22, 1826, set out along Bear
River and Mackenzie River for the coast. When they
reached the head of the Mackenzie delta they separated,
Franklin and Back descending the western arm, and
Richardson and Kendall, a capable young naval officer,
the eastern. The coast surveys of both parties were
successful, but were mostly outside our sphere. On

August 4 Richardson and Kendall, in two boats, the *Dolphin* and *Union*, reached the Dolphin and Union Strait; on August 7 they rounded Cape Krusenstern into Coronation Gulf, and next day, having entered the mouth of the Coppermine River, camped within a hundred yards of Franklin's old camping-ground. On August 9 they ascended to Bloody Fall, where they left their boats and superfluous stores, taking, however, a canvas boat, which might prove useful. They soon found that the Coppermine could not be navigated in a canvas boat, and, abandoning this craft, with other encumbrances, they worked their way over the difficult ground near the river. On August 13 they breakfasted at the place where the Coppermine is at its nearest to Great Bear Lake, and then they struck westwards. Next day they were stopped by a stream (afterwards named Kendall River) at a place where it issued from a chain of lakes (afterwards called the Dismal Lakes), but just above the outlet they found a shallow bar, along which they passed, and, on August 15, reached the height of land between the Coppermine and Great Bear Lake. Here they fell in with Indians, who led them to Dease Bay, whence there was an easy passage to Fort Franklin.

In 1832 fears were entertained for the safety of the Arctic expedition which had sailed in 1829 under the command of Captain Ross, and a search expedition was organised at the cost of the Hudson Bay Company and Captain Ross's friends, with Government assistance. At the head of the search-party was Captain (afterwards Sir George) Back, who had instructions to descend the Thlew-ee-cho-dezeth or Great Fish River to the coast. That river, which, for brevity, we shall call Back's River, was then totally unknown, and Back, on reaching Great Slave Lake in August 1833, at once began to look for its headwaters. On August 18 he entered the mouth of Hoar Frost River, which flows from the north into the lake about thirty-four miles from its eastern end. From this river, which was merely a series of cascades and rapids, he passed to Cook Lake, Walmsley Lake, and Artillery Lake. Following up Lockhart River he reached Clinton Colden Lake on August 25, and next day he entered Lake Aylmer, not far from the north shore of which he found a small lake, Sussex Lake, which proved to be the source of the river he was in search of. He descended the stream as far as Musk-Ox Lake, and this was his limit till next year. In returning to Great Slave Lake he passed down Artillery Lake, and, avoiding the rapids and cascades of Lockhart River (known to him as Ah-hel-dessy), walked in a straight course to the east end of Great Slave Lake. Here he built a wooden house, Fort Reliance, which served for quarters till June 7, 1834. At that date he resumed his journey, and, proceeding to Artillery Lake, found the two boats which he had instructed his carpenters to build for the expedition. He had heard that Ross was safe, and there now remained only the work of exploration to complete.

Taking only one of the boats, the party, ten in number, went forward, usually dragging it over the ice on runners, but sometimes towing it on open water. An expert officer of the Hudson Bay Company, MacLeod, preceded them to Lake Aylmer, and here and there left caches of deer which he shot for the party. Thus there was little difficulty about supplies, and on June 27 they reached Sandhill Bay, on Lake Aylmer, where the portage to Back's River was only about a quarter of a mile. The boat was safely launched, but there was no prospect of an easy passage to the sea. The river and lakes were still mostly frozen, though the ice was not always practicable, and there were many portages. On June 30 they crossed Musk-Ox Lake, and reached the limit of their autumn journey. On July 2 they made a portage of four miles, then ran a series of rapids, and then dragged their boat on runners over a frozen lake. Farther down the rapids were frequent and violent, and the weather became boisterous, but on July 8 the prospect somewhat brightened. The men pushed from the shore and went down with the current, which sometimes surged among rocks and boulders, sometimes broadened into lakes still beset with ice. On the banks they saw musk-oxen which gazed stupidly at them, and deer which scampered away. As they descended, they left here and there caches of meat for their upward course. On July 13 they reached Beechey Lake, where the river bends suddenly to the south-east. Back had hoped the stream would carry him to Bathurst Inlet, but now he feared that his destination would be Hudson Bay. Then they came on more difficult rapids, down which the boat had to be manœuvred with the utmost caution. They passed the mouths of many tributaries flowing in from east and west. Now and then they saw piled stones and traces of circular encampments which indicated that Eskimo frequented the region; at Buchanan River these marks became more numerous. On Pelly Lake the travellers were involved in a labyrinth of bays and islands, and, when they found an outlet and reached Lake Garry, the passage was obstructed with ice, through which they had to break or cut a way, and often to portage, till, on July 21, they reached open water. In crossing Lake MacDougall they were guided to the outlet by the noise of the rapids, and the descent to Lake Franklin was a long series of cascades which taxed the skill of Mackay and Sinclair, two boatmen whose praises Back was never weary of repeating. In this region they found deer, musk-oxen, wolves, and geese, and below Lake Franklin they came on a band of Eskimo, who took them to their tents, gave them information concerning the coast, and helped them with their boat at the one remaining cascade. Before long the river banks changed, on the east to cliffs, and on the west to low flats, while the channel opened out into an estuary with headlands and islands. They explored the eastern side, crossed to Montreal Island, went northwards as far as Ogle Point, and from neighbouring heights viewed and named the principal features of the region.

The return journey began on August 16; they reached the river mouth on August 21, the head of the river on September 17, and Fort Reliance on September 27.

The long stretch of coast from Point Ogle to Point Turnagain still remained unknown, and its exploration was undertaken by Warren Dease and Thomas Simpson, officers of the Hudson Bay Company. These men had already done excellent work in exploring to the west of the Coppermine, when, on June 6, 1838, they moved from their winter quarters at Fort Confidence on the north-east corner of Great Bear Lake to make their way eastwards along the coast as far as might be practicable. In their boat voyage they did not reach Point Turnagain, but Simpson went on foot about 100 miles beyond it. The expedition added little to what was already known, and the travellers returned to Fort Confidence in the hope of proceeding farther in the following year.

Setting out on June 15, 1839, they reached on July 20 their boat limit of 1838, and then coasted round the Kent Peninsula. They passed the Minto Islands, sailed between the mainland and Melbourne Island, crossed Labyrinth Bay, "a perfect maze of islands," and on August 1 camped near the mouth of Ellice River. At White Bear Point they were detained till August 5. Then they passed to Ogden Bay, and on August 10 opened a strait (Simpson Strait) running to the southward of east. Following its south shore they went far to the east, and, without suspecting it, landed on Ogle Point. On August 16 they went to Montreal Island, where Mackay directed them to a cache which Back had left. Thence they passed north-eastwards, and, on August 20, gained their farthest east at Castor and Pollux River. Then, hastening westwards, they reached the Coppermine on September 16, and Fort Confidence on September 24. Two days later they left the fort to ruin and the Indians.

The last voyage of Sir John Franklin is not within the range of this sketch, but several expeditions in quest of the missing voyagers visited the rivers and islands of our region. Richardson, accompanied by Rae, searched the Coppermine region in 1848, and Rae continued the search in 1849 and 1851. Dr. John Rae, who gained a place in the front rank of explorers, was the first to obtain news of the fate of the Franklin expedition. In 1846–47 he had traversed the isthmus between Repulse Bay and the Gulf of Boothia, and in 1853, when no trace of Franklin could be found elsewhere, he again turned his steps in that direction. First he sought a short cut to the mouth of Back's River by Chesterfield Inlet and the Quoich River, which he ascended in a boat for two-and-a-half degrees of latitude (up to 66° N.), but, finding the river full of rapids and impracticable for his purpose, he returned and hastened north to Repulse Bay. In 1854 he crossed the isthmus, and while searching the coast found in Pelly Bay some Eskimo, from whom he gathered tidings of Franklin, who, as is otherwise known, had died off the north of King William's Land on June 11, 1847, the command of the expedition then devolving on Captain Crozier. The information which Rae acquired, when put together, amounted to this. In the spring of 1850 about forty white men were seen travelling southwards; at a later date about thirty of their bodies were found on the mainland (near Point Ogle), and five on an island (Montreal Island), a day's journey north of the mouth of a large river (Back's River). From the Eskimo Rae purchased articles (spoons, forks, &c.), bearing the initials of the names of Captain Crozier and other officers of the *Erebus* and *Terror*. The men had marched 250 miles dragging boats on runners and sledges over the ice, falling from the drag ropes, and dying where they fell, their track being marked by a line of dead bodies. One boat they had dragged to Montreal Island, where it was broken up by the Eskimo for the wood and nails. Traces of it, with other relics, were found by John Anderson, a factor of the Hudson Bay Company, who in 1855–56 descended Back's River and visited Montreal Island and Ogle Point.

The last of the explorers of our region is Warburton Pike, who in 1889 travelled by a new route northwards from Great Slave Lake to Mackay Lake, Lac-de-Gras, and the head-waters of the Coppermine to hunt musk-oxen, and in 1890 descended Back's River to Lake Beechey. In these journeys, which he has described in a lively narrative, he discovered a number of important features in the geography of the country.

Important researches were carried on in 1893–94 by J. B. Tyrrell of the Canadian Geological Survey, and in 1900 by J. W. Tyrrell over areas adjacent to and sometimes overlapping the southern boundary of the tract dealt with in this sketch.

SPORT AND TRAVEL IN THE NORTHLAND OF CANADA

CHAPTER I

FROM WINNIPEG TO HUDSON BAY, AND FROM HUDSON BAY TO GREAT SLAVE LAKE

MY first attempt to reach the unexplored tract lying between Chesterfield Inlet and Great Slave Lake was made in the summer of 1898. That attempt was baffled at the outset, but the experience I then gained contributed to the success of subsequent efforts. I had travelled by canoe from Winnipeg *via* Norway House, Oxford House, and York Factory, and had reached Churchill on July 6, only to find that my projected journey was impracticable for that year. There would be no open water towards the north for at least a fortnight. The Hudson Bay Company's trading boat would not start for Marble Island before July 20; the voyage would take about ten days, and I would be landed sixty miles from the mouth of the inlet, too late to commence a long journey through an unknown country. I therefore quietly changed my plans, and decided that, after spending the summer on the Hudson Bay coast, I would make preparation for an early start in the following year.

I found the country about Churchill not without attractions; in some places the scenery is pretty, and, now and then, caribou are to be found not far off. The men employed by the company are of various races, many

A

of them being Eskimo or Huskies, as, in accordance with local usage, I shall call them. I had many opportunities of becoming acquainted with Huskies and of taking photographs of scenes to show their appearance, mode of life, dress, habits, and amusements. Some of those who belonged to the crew of the trading boat were clad partly in white men's clothing; but Huskies, as a rule, adhere both to their native costume and their native habits. They produce fire with great dexterity by rubbing two sticks together. They are fond of sports, wrestling, and feats of strength and skill, and they enjoy games and dancing. One evening I entertained some Huskies and Chipewyan Indians at a feast. For the former the viands consisted of oatmeal and sugar, followed by plenty of tobacco; for the latter, tea, sugar, flour, bacon, and tobacco. The feast was followed by dancing and games, and the entertainment was most successful. Early next morning I was awakened by a knocking at my door, and George Oman, the interpreter, entered with two Huskies. They had come on behalf of all the other Huskies to thank me for the feast; they said they were sorry to wake me up so early, but must thank me, and could wait no longer. From the Indians I neither received nor expected thanks.

I may here remark that, in general, less confidence can be placed in Indians than in Huskies. Two Cree lads (to give one instance) who, after signing contracts at Oxford House, had come with me to Churchill, now left me, pleading sickness as an excuse for wishing to return to their homes, when in fact they dreaded the prospect of privation. A Husky never disappointed me without sufficient cause.

After a time a whale-boat with a crew of Huskies put into port. The boat was their own, having been " traded " to them, or perhaps given to them by one of the American whalers which visit the bay. They had caught an ūgyūk or large seal, and on coming ashore they cut it up, so that each man who had helped to kill it received a slice.

In summer the Company's servants, using large nets, catch many white whales from ten to sixteen feet long. The whales, being retained by the nets till low water, are easily lanced by the men in boats. Their flesh is cut up and kept to feed the dogs in winter, the blubber is boiled down at the factory, and the hides are shipped to England, where they become the " porpoise hides " of commerce.

Harpooning whales from a boat affords excellent sport, and several can be killed in this manner on any suitable day. I found that the more successful plan was to sail down on to them. With a shoulder gun, firing a light harpoon, one could kill large numbers of them, but I am told that this has the effect of making the whales leave the place.

The Company's trading boats, small craft of about ten tons, are usually open, but some have a small cabin aft. They sail well off the wind, but not when close hauled. I made a voyage in the first that sailed for the north. At Eskimo Point, half-way to Marble Island, we found Husky families in deer-skin tents, and saw men engaged in the construction of kyaks. For kyaks on the Hudson Bay coast deer-skin is used ; on the Arctic coast seal-skin, which is heavier but more durable. These cranky vessels are managed with great skill and boldness by the Huskies, who feel perfectly at home in them so long as they are under way, but exercise great caution when at rest. I observed that they invariably landed when they wished to light their pipes, or even to take a cup of water. If a kyak turns over, its occupant is almost certainly drowned. They do not trust their women in them unless they are lashed together so as to form a raft. Kyaks are usually constructed out of the material of old sleighs, the ribs being simply tied together with deer-skin thongs. They are skilfully made, and are never seen lop-sided. It is not every Husky who can build them ; in fact, most have to seek the assistance of a master-builder. From the Huskies at this place I procured dogs, and at the next place we visited I obtained a few more, all of which were to be sent on to Churchill.

Our next port of call was at Term Point, where there is an excellent harbour for small craft. Here we met many Huskies trading "furs," mostly of the musk-ox, wolf, and fox. Then we ran up to Marble Island, and on the mainland coast opposite I deposited my canoe in cache to be ready for future operations. It was near the end of August when we got back to Churchill with our cargo of "furs," which were at once hung out to dry in preparation for shipment to England.

Having resolved that, for my next year's journey, I should not wait for the breaking up of the ice, but set out from Churchill for the north in spring, and haul as far as possible with dogs and sleighs over the ice, I now ordered two sleighs to be made, engaged Huskies to meet me, and gave directions that such articles of outfit as could be procured at Churchill should be ready on my return in spring. Having made all the arrangements which were necessary, I set out for Winnipeg with dogs and sleighs on September 5. Difficulties, however, beset me at the start. I had twelve excellent Husky dogs, but I was almost a total stranger to them, and they would not follow me. They had for weeks been revelling in meat and blubber and were unwilling to leave their comfortable quarters. Coaxing was of no avail, so I coupled them two and two together. Some of the couples were led and the others were expected to follow but would not. The dogs were in the worst temper, and before we had travelled a dozen yards, they were engaged in a sanguinary battle, blood and hair flying in all directions. Those which, being apparently well disposed towards each other, had been selected to run in couples, became the bitterest enemies, and, though I changed the couples in my efforts to suit tempers if possible, there was no improvement, and, in the excitement, one dog went quite mad. I then muzzled the most aggressive animals and made another start, but a hotly contested running fight was kept up till we reached Ribboos Bay, where we camped for the night.

On September 7 we camped near Cape Churchill, and in that neighbourhood we spent the next ten days. I had abundant supplies for myself and the men, but required food for the dogs. Polar bears were said to be numerous here, and no doubt frequently are so, but though I went in search of them every morning I had no success. I came on the fresh tracks of a large bear, but he had gone inland to seek out winter quarters in the woods, for in this region polar bears as well as black bears "hole up" in the winter. At York Factory I remained six weeks waiting for the "freeze up," and during this time, snow having fallen, I broke in my dogs, several of which had never been in harness before. The white fish at York Factory are very small (four or six to the pound), and are caught with sweep nets of one-inch mesh a few miles up Hayes River. By November 8, Hayes River was frozen solid, and, as a large amount of snow had fallen, I started for Oxford House, distant about 240 miles. I had a guide, for there was no trail and the country is one vast moss swamp, or muskeg, with only a stunted, scattered, and useless growth of spruce and larch, scarcely fit even for firewood. As there had been a heavy fall of snow before the hard frost set in, the swamps were soft, so that the dogs' feet passed through the snow into the slush below with the result that they "balled up." On the lakes the deep snow had submerged the ice so that they had to be skirted. We, however, were travelling very light, and with two excellent trains of dogs, and did not exceed the twelve days usually allowed for the journey. The Hudson Bay Company have abandoned the use of dogs for this stage, the mail being now hauled by an Indian on a hand sleigh.

At Oxford House we remained two days to rest and feed the dogs. In Oxford Lake, which is 30 miles long, many fine white fish are caught, fishing in winter being carried on through the ice. The soil of the surrounding country (notwithstanding the assertion of a young missionary who, in a written report, stated that it is a " country where nothing will grow") is exceedingly fertile and produces fine potatoes, turnips, and other vegetables. The journey with dogs from Oxford House to Norway House, at the foot of Lake Winnipeg, takes about six days, and from Norway House to Winnipeg about eight days. At Norway House the temperature of −30° Fahr. had already been registered.

Reaching Winnipeg in the early days of December, I had leisure to complete my preparations. A fresh outfit which I had ordered from England had duly arrived, and I engaged two trustworthy Red River half-breeds for the journey. In February the Manitoba hotel ,where I was staying was completely destroyed by fire, but I fortunately saved my instruments, cameras, rifles, and other equipment for the journey.

On February 26 I set out from Selkirk and went with horses and sled as far as Berens River, about half-way down the Lake, and here my dogs and drivers from Norway House met me. At this place I had the novel experience of riding in a sleigh drawn by a team which included a wolf. This animal was muzzled, and, though rather savage, worked well. I was told that a pure wolf does not retain its stamina in captivity, but a half or quarter cross makes a most useful animal. In this region sleighing with dogs forms the subject of never-ending talk, and tales of notable journeys (some of them not well authenticated) are frequently told. One such tale, which I heard, there is no reason to doubt. John Sand, a pure Indian, travelled with dogs· from Little Grand Rapids to Norway House, a distance of 250 miles, in three days (probably including portions of the night), thus covering over 80 miles a day. He did not drive the dogs, but ran in front of them.

Of the dogs used in "tripping," the Husky dog with his pricked ears, shaggy coat, and tail curled close over his back, looks like the gentleman of his profession, and his disposition is attractive, in spite of his love of a fight. At work he seldom tires, his feet are tough, he seldom requires the whip, and he can stand hunger marvellously. Though he is slow, going only about five miles an hour, he can keep up this pace the whole day if the weather is cool and he is not overloaded. The Indian dog is usually a non-descript sort of animal, but I have seen good Indian dogs. Crosses have been tried with the Scotch deer-hound, the mastiff, the setter, and the wolf. The mastiff cross seems the most successful, notwithstanding the weight and the short hair, but few are agreed on this subject. Consider-ing the importance of the dog in this region, it seems strange that so little trouble has been taken for the im-provement of the breed. These animals are hard worked. The usual load for one dog is about 100 lbs., a train of four dogs drawing 400 lbs., and 80 miles is not an unusual day's journey when weather and ice are favourable. In some years mange is prevalent, but it is not severe, and the dogs at work seem little incommoded by it. The animals never have fleas.

From Berens River I made a rapid run to Norway House, and then to Oxford House and York Factory, short delays being made at each of these posts. In the first week of April, 1899, I reached Fort Churchill, to the surprise of my friends there, and also to their de-light, since I had brought the mail with their letters.

This was the last store-house from which supplies could be obtained, and there was no need to hurry away, for the spring was very late, the thermometer frequently registering from $-10°$ to $-30°$ Fahr. Here I spent five weeks, the monotony being broken by the arrival of Huskies with loads of caribou, which were reported to be abundant all along the coast. Chipew-yan Indians also came in with tales of starvation during the winter months. One Husky who had pro-mised to accompany me did not turn up, so I engaged another, Milük by name, who agreed to go with me as far as I pleased, and was able to act as guide as far as Marble Island. My company, including myself, consisted of four men, and we had two sleighs with twelve dogs. I had left (as already stated) a canoe near Marble Island, but, lest it should have been destroyed by bears, I provided another. We had dried meat for ourselves and the dogs, but only in sufficient quantity for several nights, as we expected to kill caribou and fish in abundance. We were provided also with tea, tobacco, and trade articles, such as knives, files, beads, thimbles, awls, &c. We had the indispensable rifles, guns, and nets, but did not burden ourselves with bacon or flour.

On May 12 we left Churchill, and on June 5 reached Marble Island, where, finding the canoe safe in cache, we speedily broke up the spare canoe for fuel." The ice had been fairly good for travelling, but the deer had gone inland, and we found only their tracks. Except for one blizzard, we had had glorious weather, the air clear and cold, and the surface of the ice as dry as in mid-winter, but we were in straits for supplies, and I bitterly regretted having brought such a small quantity of dried meat. At one time it seemed as if we should have to fall back on Churchill, where I should hardly have dared to show my face after being baffled a second time. Fortunately, we found and killed a few deer, the mainstay of the traveller on the "Barren Ground," just in time to save us from an ignominious retreat. We held on our way and reached the entrance to Chesterfield Inlet on June 8, the weather being still perfect, though we had now and then to splash through or go round numerous pools on the ice. We found and shot deer as we wanted them, but at times they were not plentiful, and now and then, several consecutive days had to be spent in hunting and hauling in and dressing the meat. About this time geese, ducks, ptarmigan, hawks, loons, gulls, and other birds began to appear. As we ascended the Inlet, the ice got worse, and at one place it was so rough that the dogs' feet were cut almost to pieces. We retraced our steps for a long distance and then, getting near the shore, managed to travel along the rafted ice, so as to avoid the hummocky places. Towards the head of the Inlet the ice was smooth and from three to four feet thick, but for several days we had to travel through water from one to two feet deep on its surface. Several times the smaller dogs were actually swimming and still trying to haul.

On June 21 we reached the head of the Inlet, where we met some starving Huskies, who had no nets for fishing, and had been unable to find deer. On June 23 we made a short portage to a Husky camp on Arkok, the deep-water bay at the south-east corner of Baker Lake, near the head of the southern outlet of the Lake. We had the canoe hauled over the bare ground by dogs, and we carried all the stuff over on our backs, with the cheerful help of the Huskies. On June 27 we reached another Husky camp at Arkok, where our nets kept us well supplied with fresh-run salmon from three to ten pounds in weight. After waiting for several days we were able to launch our canoe, and Milūk his kyak, and proceed along the narrow strip of water which had opened along the shore. Following the south shore of Baker Lake we reached the mouth of the Kazan River on July 12, but here a delay of five days was necessary, the ice ahead being still compact. Deer, although fairly plentiful, were very difficult to get near, owing to the plague of mosquitoes, which was now at its height, but I managed always to kill enough for our immediate use. The flesh of the deer at this time was hardly fit to eat, being discoloured all through. The marrow, usually a luxury, was now of the consistency of blood and water, owing to the "fly-time," the wretched beasts being kept on the run day and night.

On July 19 we reached the head of the lake, which is some sixty miles in length, east and west. Here we met

trusting to our rifles and nets to provide us with a living, and to the good fortune which, up till now, had attended us. But the journey turned out to be so absurdly easy, that I more than once regretted that I was deprived of the pleasure of meeting and surmounting difficulties. We explored the main Ark-i-linik for a distance of 182 miles, and its western branch for 117 miles. We crossed the divide between the waters of the Hudson Bay and Great Slave Lake on the one side, and the Mackenzie River on the other, at an altitude of 1394 feet, a short distance beyond which we reached Clinton-Colden Lake, and our journey of exploration was safely accomplished.

The Ark-i-linik is a fine large river about 300 yards wide, having an even, steady current of from four to five miles an hour. For the entire distance over which we followed the main river, there is not a sign of any rough water which could possibly be called a rapid, and the stream is navigable for a steamer of considerable draught nearly the whole way. About fifty miles from its mouth wood (spruce) of fair-size growth is to be found, and the woods then increase in size of timber and in extent until the river divides, the larger branch coming in from the south, the smaller—which we followed up—joining from the west. The western branch has numerous small and some large lakes on its upper waters. Although not free from rapids and rough water, it presented no difficulties worth mentioning; a few portages of a mile in length, one of two and a half miles, and several smaller ones. At its head is the large, peculiarly-shaped lake usually indicated on maps by dotted lines. Failing to ascertain the native name of this lake, I called it after my friend and old travelling companion in Central Asia, Dr. W. L. Abbott.

After ascending the main Ark-i-linik River for about thirty-five miles, musk-ox tracks commenced to get very numerous. The muddy shores in places were so ploughed up with them as to give the idea that a drove of cattle had passed along.

On August 9 our eyes were gladdened by the sight of a band of musk-oxen, numbering eighteen. They were lying on the low, sloping, grassy bank on the south side of the river, and were quite unconscious of danger. I had with me two Huskies from Baker Lake, and while laying plans for approaching the animals, I made them promise only to kill one apiece. When the three of us had managed to crawl unobserved to within 200 yards of the herd, the two Huskies suddenly and without a word left me. The musk oxen very soon appeared uneasy; they rose, sniffed at the air, and seemed ready for a start. Being within range, and not knowing the whereabouts or plans of my Huskies, I fired and killed the only three large bulls in the band. The rest of the herd I allowed to pass me at close range unmolested.

The two Huskies now came up with very long faces, and said that I had spoilt the whole show. They had laid plans to surround and slaughter the whole herd, in spite of the agreement that only three—one apiece—were to be killed.

I give the weights and measurements of the largest bull :—

Tip of nose to tip of tail (2-inch tail)   .   . $92\frac{1}{2}$ inches.
Girth   69   „
Height from heel to hump (hair pressed down)   52   „
Horns—right, $25\frac{1}{2}$ inches; left, 26 inches.

The height of a large bull which I killed in 1896 at a spot about fifty miles further north was 55 inches; horns, 27 inches.

As my weighing-machine only weighed up to 300 lbs., I was obliged to weigh the animal piecemeal.

The following were the weights of the different parts :—

	Lbs.
1 shoulder with fore-leg and hoof . . .	45
„ „ . . .	50
1 hind leg with shank and hoof . . .	43
„ „ . . .	43
Entrails	46
Paunch (full)	80
Liver	7
Head and neck	75
Brisket	13
Ribs	17
Ribs and part of back	52
Rump	35
Heart and lungs	13
Hide , ...	38
Off piece of belly flap	7
Blood (allowed)	10
Extras	5
	579

I have seen larger and heavier beasts, but this one was a fair average full-grown male.

On the main Ark-i-linik River there is a stretch of country about eighty miles in length into which no human being enters. The Eskimo do not hunt so far west, and Yellow Knives and Dog Ribs from Slave Lake do not go so far east. To penetrate this country in the dead of winter would be simply to court starvation. Then the deer have all departed, and to depend on finding musk-oxen at the end of the journey would be risky indeed. Thus there still remains one spot in this Great Barren North-land which is sacred to the musk-ox. Here the animals remain in their primeval state, exhibiting no fear, only curiosity. I approached several herds within thirty yards, photographed them at my leisure, moving them round as I wished, and then retired, leaving them still stupidly staring at me as if in wonder. When deer were not procurable, a musk-ox was killed. Fish were plentiful all along the Ark-i-linik; in fact, I never saw such a grand river for fish.

The nets were rarely set, however, when meat was procurable, as it caused considerable delay in the morning, and the nets had to be dried. Moose are to be found on the main Ark-i-linik, also black bears. On the western branch the woods decreased in extent and in size of timber as we ascended until at the height of land there were none, and we had to fall back on moss and heaths for fuel. Deer were then very scarce, and the musk-ox we had long since left behind; but something always turned up to keep the pot boiling. One day it would be a wolverine or glutton, another time a fat wolf. All animals appear to be good on the Barren Lands; or is it that one's appetite is good? An occasional goose was shot, or duck, or ptarmigan, or an arctic hare; we always had enough, being indifferent as to the exact kind of animal which satisfied our hunger.

We had the good luck to meet the Eskimo from the Arctic coast, who resort to this river to obtain wood for their sleighs. These natives had never set eyes on a white man before, and had no articles of civilisation whatever. They were all dressed in deerskins, and armed with long bows, arrows, and spears, beaten out of native copper. The use of tobacco was quite unknown to them, and firearms they had only heard about. They gave me a good deal of information about their country and the copper deposits along the Arctic coast, and I obtained from them several copper implements, such as dags, spear and arrow heads, needles, &c., all beaten out of native copper, giving them in exchange knives, files, and needles, which last appeared to have by far the most value in their eyes. They exhibited no signs of fear at our approach. They were a jovial lot, and camped with us that night. In the evening they sang together, rather nicely I thought, and next morning we separated, with many signs of friendship on their part.

On Clinton-Colden Lake, a very incorrect Dominion Government map in my possession was the cause of our going nearly a hundred miles out of our way. From

Clinton-Colden Lake to Fond-du-lac on Great Slave Lake, the geography of the country is well known, if not very accurately surveyed. On Artillery Lake we struck the green spruce again about half-way down, and there we bade fare-well to the Barren Northland, over which we had journeyed for well-nigh four months, and which had treated us so hos-pitably. Lockhart River flowing from the foot of Artillery Lake into Great Slave Lake is only navigable for canoes the first five miles or so, beyond which distance it flows torrent-wise through a deep precipitous chasm. In our progress down this troublesome stream we had made several portages, and it was getting on for camping time when an unlucky accident occurred. When the canoe was being let down a small side rapid by a bow-and-stern line, the stern line parted, and the tail of the canoe was quickly swung out into the current. In an instant it was caught by the rapids, and the bow-line wrenched from the grasp of the man who held it. We ran wildly down the river in the hope of the small craft being caught by some side eddy, and so brought close enough to the shore to be got hold of. It shot the first rapid broadside on and even survived through the second without capsizing. A faint gleam of hope sprang up in my breast, but only for a second. A glance down the river quickly dispelled any such hopes. The waters ahead, toward which the small canoe was being hurried, were all white, one broad expanse of seething foam, from which the tops of black rocks protruded in ominous fashion. The next time I lifted my eyes to look, the canoe was being tossed about, bottom up, amidst a sea of foam, and the stuff, such of it as floated, was being scattered and swept away down to the rapids. My heart sank, everything we possessed had disappeared—all gone! Rifles, guns, nets, axes, instru-ments, cameras, collections of geological and botanical specimens, note-books, and my precious photos, the result of a whole summer's work, irretrievably lost! Even the canoe itself was soon out of sight, and we were left with absolutely nothing but the clothes we stood in, staring as if spell-bound by the raging river. My first impulse was to feel in my pockets for matches, and to my joy I discovered nine dry wax lights, each one of which was good for a fire. This meant nine nights' fire, anyway. To cut a long story short, the canoe was eventually recovered, also a box, in which were my note-books and diaries containing the record of the journey, and a few other things. The loss of the geological and botanical collections, on which I had spent much time and trouble, I particularly regret; the loss of an exceptionally interesting collection of photos I deplore.

By the loss of the rifles, guns, and nets, we were now without the means of procuring food, and were in the middle of a very rough country. Deer were plentiful, and stood stupidly staring at us within easy range, fish were leaping in the pools on the river, but the means of killing deer or taking fish were gone. Not an enviable position in which to find one's self, and a very disastrous finish up to an otherwise successful and most enjoyable journey. For six days we lived on what cranberries and blueberries we could find. We then fell in with the Yellow Knives, many of whom I knew. From them I obtained some dried meat, sufficient to take us to Fort Resolution on Great Slave Lake, where we safely landed on September 25. At Resolution we heard all about the Great Slave Lake Mining bubble, which had finally burst, leaving many richer in experience if not in pocket. There still being a chance of reaching Athabasca Landing by open water, I availed myself of it, only remaining at Resolution a couple of days to get some very necessary clothes and footgear. A fresh start for the south was made on September 28, but we only reached as far as Red River post, thirty-five miles north from Fort McMurray, when the ice stopped us on October 17. The rest of the journey was accomplished with dogs.

CHAPTER II

PROJECTED EXPLORATION—JOURNEY FROM EDMONTON TO GREAT SLAVE LAKE

THE purpose of exploring the barren Northland, which has a wonderful fascination for those who have once penetrated its solitude, was not interrupted but rather confirmed by the vexatious canoe accident. There remained vast tracts still unknown, and it was my desire to traverse these as far as the Arctic coast, where I would find a welcome among the natives, favourable specimens of whom I had met on the Ark-i-līnik River. These men, intelligent, able-bodied, contented, and friendly, had given me much information concerning their country and their mode of life, and they had promised to assist and accompany me if I visited their coast. Their equipment of implements and arms of native copper beaten into shape by their own hands, was of much interest, and they had offered to guide me to the localities where copper was to be found. Copper deposits on that coast would probably be of no commercial value, but I might at least see the beginnings of the metal industry among a primitive people. Thus the outline of a new journey was formed, and I decided to reach Hudson Bay near the mouth of Chesterfield Inlet in autumn, spend the winter among the Huskies of that region, and set out in spring with dogs and sleighs due north for the Arctic coast. On reaching the ocean I should turn westwards and make my way to the Coppermine River, which I would ascend for some distance, and then strike westwards across the divide separating the waters of the Coppermine River from those of Great Bear Lake, whence I should return to civilisation by way of Fort Norman and the Mackenzie

River. On this journey I should .make a survey of my route, take meteorological observations, collect geological, botanical, and entomological specimens, and, of course, take photographs of the country and of the Huskies.

Various matters detained me in England, but, at length, in May 1901, I had reached Winnipeg, and was ready to set out for the north. Here details as to the precise route were arranged, but as these will appear in the course of the narrative they need not now be given. My outfit was made as light as possible. The scientific equipment was limited to a sextant prismatic compass, two aneroids, hypsometer, maximum and minimum thermometers, and a patent log for measuring distances travelled by canoe. A solar compass and a theodolite were purposely left behind as they were not likely to stand the long journey on a sleigh, which we should have to make, without getting hopelessly out of adjustment. For photographic work I took three cameras and a large supply of both glass plates and films. Everything that was likely to be damaged by water or damp I packed in two of Silver's watertight tin boxes. The films and glass plates were put up in separate tin cases, each containing one dozen, and hermetically sealed. I had determined, in the event of another canoe accident, to save some of my things if possible. My battery, which I considered complete, consisted of two Mannlicher carbines fitted with sporting sights, and a double-barrel breach-loading 28 bore shot-gun. About three thousand rounds were taken for the carbines. For catching fish we took six nets of different-sized mesh. As the larger part of the journey would have to be made through a country where we should have to depend absolutely on deer, musk-oxen, or fish, fire-arms, ammunition, and nets, formed the most important part of our outfit.

I had ordered two cedar canoes, 19 feet and 19½ feet in length respectively, to be specially built for the journey by the Peterborough Canoe Company of Ontario, and to be forwarded to Edmonton. As these canoes would only hold a limited amount of stuff, arrangements were made with Messrs. Thomas Luce & Co., New Bedford, Mass., to ship up the balance [1] of the outfit by their whaling schooner *Francis Allyn*, which was due to leave New Bedford for the Hudson Bay about July 1. The outfit I sent up, and which amounted to about 1½ tons, included food supplies for the coming winter, trade articles for the natives, such as guns, rifles, powder, lead, caps, knives, files, awls, beads, needles, thimbles, clothes, &c. A reserve of Mannlicher cartridges, photo plates and films, a spare set of canoe paddles, a "primus" cooking stove, and fifty gallons of kerosene oil, completed the list. Marble Island, which lies about 40 miles south from the mouth of Chesterfield Inlet, was the place mentioned as the probable winter quarters of the *Francis Allyn*. As the owners were not absolutely certain as to the winter quarters of their vessel, the captain being absent at the time, I informed them that it was a matter of indifference to me where the vessel wintered, for I should have no difficulty in finding her, a remark which I afterwards had cause to regret.

As I had frequently travelled between Winnipeg and Fort Churchill by Norway House and York Factory, that route could now present little in the way of novelty. I had discovered a new and easy route by the Ark-i-linik, with which I desired to become familiar, and I had no hesitation in deciding to travel by rail to Calgary and Edmonton, whence, after a short land journey, I should be able to proceed almost the whole way to Hudson Bay in a canoe voyage on rivers and lakes. There would be portages, but for these provision could easily be made. By leaving Edmonton about the middle of June I expected to reach the shore of the Bay early in August.

At Edmonton, which I reached early in June, I found the two canoes I had ordered, and, all other arrangements having been completed, I turned my attention to the

[1] See Appendix.

engaging of men for the journey ; and here a few general words on this subject may not be out of place.

I have learned from experience that an expedition to the north has the better chance of success the fewer white men are connected with it. In travelling over the " Barren Ground " one cannot have more suitable companions than the natives of the country. A white man there is in a strange land, and, however willing and able to stand cold, hunger, and fatigue, he is a novice in this experience. The conditions and work are unfamiliar to him, and if he were to meet with a bad accident, or to fall ill, or to lose himself in a fog, his misfortune would probably be the ruin of the expedition. Husky servants, on the other hand, are always at home, for their wives and children join your company along with them, so that they never leave off their customary life. If one of them falls ill and has to be left behind, his wife remains with him ; they build their snow-dwelling, and their household is at once complete. All the work which has to be done, such as hunting, cutting up meat, looking after dogs and sleighs in winter and boating in summer, is done better and more quickly by Huskies than by white men. The wives somewhat retard the journey, but they perform services which are indispensable, making and mending clothes and foot-gear, which soon get worn out. Huskies are hard-working, honest, good-natured, and cheerful companions. They are unwearying on behalf of one who treats them well, and the traveller, on his side, must learn to exercise a little patience with them.

However, white companions, or else half-breeds, are necessary in order to reach Husky-land and to return from it. I decided to take only two. One, Sandy Turner by name, a half-breed, I engaged at Edmonton, and trusted to find another suitable man at Fort Resolution. Not that there was any scarcity of applicants, for it seemed as if the whole of Edmonton wished to accompany me. The fascination of the north had seized even sober business men and farmers. A freighter who owned a fine team of horses and was earning good money, was eager to join me, and when I asked what would become of his team during his absence, he replied: "To h—— with the b——y horses if I can only get along with you." Another man, engaged to be married shortly, protested his willingness to " chuck it " if he could only get to the north.

Transport of merchandise from Edmonton to Athabasca Landing, a distance of about ninety miles, is by wagon. The canoes and heavy "stuff" I despatched under the charge of Sandy Turner, and, a few days later, I followed by the "stage," which covers the distance in two days when the road is not unusually bad. There is no made road, but only a natural track through the bush, which here consists of stunted cotton woods, with an occasional bluff of pine or spruce. A few short and indispensable bridges have been put up, but otherwise hardly a cent has been spent in improving the track, though the whole of the traffic for the north has to pass along this route. The road winds about through the dreary scrub; one mud-hole succeeds another, each apparently deeper than the former, and at length the buggy sinks in a creek where the mud is bottomless, till nothing is visible but the box, which seems to float. In such circumstances the driver is helpless till a friendly freighter comes along, and, with his heavy team, pulls the vehicle on to *terra firma*. Road-mending has advanced no further than the placing of a few skids on the mud to support the waggon wheels at such spots. There are stopping-places at intervals of about fifteen miles, but they provide neither hay nor oats for horses, nor even a decent meal for human beings, and, as they are too filthy to sleep in, one wonders what purpose they are intended to serve. Mosquitoes, flies, and bull-dogs (large carnivorous flies) swarmed thick, and a violent hail-storm stripped the leaves from the trees. Notwithstanding the terrible condition of the road, the rates for freight from Edmonton to Athabasca Landing were not high, varying between a dollar and a dollar and a half per 100 lbs.

At the Landing I found my men in camp; everything had got through safely, and the canoes were lying in water to soak. This post, at the head of the navigation of the Athabasca River, serves as the port of shipment for freight to the north. It has been in existence for many years, and, besides a saw-mill for cutting the timber required for building scows to carry supplies for the many trading-posts scattered over the country, it possesses three stores, a boarding-house, and a church. The maintenance of order seems entrusted to a member of the North-West Mounted Police, while a bishop upholds the dignity of the Church. The place had a busy appearance, for now large cargoes were being despatched.

There is an easy passage down the river for about 180 miles, but for the next 100 miles there are rapids. To make the passage of the Grand Rapids in safety it is advisable, though not absolutely necessary, to have a steersman, who is paid fifty dollars for his services, and has to return from Fort McMurray on foot. All the men capable of acting as steersmen had already gone down the river except one who had been engaged by an American trader. I hoped to have my canoes and "stuff" taken on board this trader's scows on payment of a reasonable sum, but he made such a favour of this service, and, while needlessly delaying to come to terms, seemed so fearful that he would not ask enough, that on June 22 I set out in my own canoes with only my own men, trusting to find a steersman before reaching the rapids. After descending the stream for two days, I fortunately met Mr. Spencer of the Hudson Bay Company coming up with five large scows under full sail, and from him I obtained for steersman a Cree Indian, named Philip Powder. That evening we reached the Grand Rapid, and Philip surprised me by stating that, if we attempted to run it with canoes so deeply loaded, we should probably be swamped.

Considering that each canoe carried 350 lbs. and two men only, and that the capacity of each was about four times that amount, I began to think that the rapids were even more dangerous than I had been told. An accident which might possibly result in the total loss of my outfit was not to be risked, so we delayed for a day, hoping that some scow would come along and take part of the "stuff." None appeared, however, so when we had abandoned surplus food and tacked waterproof sheets over the canoes, Powder intimated that the dreaded rapids might now with great care be run in safety, and we ventured out. Dropping the canoe down the first rough piece of water by a bow-and-stern line, and packing the stuff along the shore on our backs, we negotiated the worst rapid in safety. Next day we ran most of the rapids, and early the following day, June 28, we passed the last and arrived at Fort McMurray, an abandoned Hudson Bay post, at the junction of the Clearwater River with the Athabasca.

The ninety miles of dangerous rapids are, for the greater part, swift water only. There are some twelve or fourteen rapids, none of which presents any very great difficulty or danger, nor do they call for any special knowledge or experience on the part of the steersman, so far as I could judge. At very low water they may be dangerous (I do not know), but no one has ever been drowned there. From the rocks on either side, the proper passage can always be ascertained; there are no whirlpools, and only one small fall at the Cascade, which is spoken of with bated breath.

Just above the dreaded Cascade Rapid there is a small riffle, not worth the name of a rapid. At the time of the Klondike rush a number of inexperienced men, in descending the stream, mistook this for the place of danger of which they had heard. They landed, unloaded the canoe, and carried their "stuff" along the shore on their backs, letting the canoe drop down by bow-and-stern line till it had got below the riffle. Then they re-loaded and re-embarked, thankful for escape from danger. To their dismay they were soon swept over the real Cascade at its worst part, but beyond a wetting, suffered no damage.

From Fort McMurray we paddled to Fort Mackay, 35 miles in six hours, assisted by a moderate current. At Fort Mackay there was famine, for, through the mistake of some official, the usual supplies had not been sent; sickness had broken out among the Indians, who were consequently unable to hunt, and the water in the river was too high for successful fishing. Dogs as well as men were in a pitiable state. In fact, at most of the Hudson Bay Company's posts the dogs, though hard-worked in winter, are utterly neglected in summer. From Fort Simpson and a few other places they are sent to summer where fish are plentiful, but at most posts they are left to pick up a living or starve. If a society for the prevention of cruelty to dogs existed in Canada, its officers would find plenty of work, summer and winter. Leaving Fort Mackay on June 29, we reached Fort Chipewyan, at the north-west end of Lake Athabasca, on July 1. The distance was 150 miles, but for the greater part of the last day we had to lay by, as the lake was very rough. The wind on these great lakes generally rises and falls with the sun, so that, in travelling over them, it is necessary often to turn night into day. Fort Chipewyan is celebrated throughout the north as affording the best goose and duck shooting in these parts.

From Lake Athabasca we descended the Slave River 90 miles to Smith Landing, where, to avoid the rapids, we followed the waggon-road of 16 miles which has been cut through the bush by the Hudson Bay Company, and on reaching Fort Smith we again found smooth water on which to proceed. Travelling 180 miles further down the river we arrived at Fort Resolution on July 7.

There we found a large encampment of Indians—Dog Ribs, Yellow Knives, and Slave Indians. They assemble here annually at this season to await the arrival of the Indian Commissioner and receive their treaty money and allowances. The Yellow Knives and Dog Ribs have only recently "accepted treaty," *i.e.* have renounced all claim to exclusive ownership of the district, and placed themselves on the same footing as white men with respect to land and game, receiving in return five dollars per head and allowances of flour, bacon, tea, tobacco, and ammunition. What advantage the Government expects from this convention is not clear, for it is unlikely that white men will ever settle in this region.

I had to spend several days here to select and engage suitable men to go with me. I required one companion for the whole journey, and four Indians to help me towards the borders of the land of the Huskies. For the former purpose I engaged Hubert Darrell, a young Englishman of good family, and the owner of a ranch in Manitoba. Tiring of the monotony of life on a farm, this young man had turned his steps northwards at the time of the rush to Klondike, and like many others over whom the far north had thrown its spell, he had remained in the north. He had accompanied the Yellow Knives to the "Barren Ground" on their annual winter hunt after musk-oxen, and was thus well acquainted with the cold and hunger incident to the journey which he now undertook.

An Englishman generally knows his own mind, and does not waste time coming to an arrangement. It is otherwise, however, with the "poor Indian" who, when any sort of negotiation is in progress, has to keep his friends fully informed, and deliberate with them at great length. Consultations are held with brothers, uncles, aunts, and cousins, and, after much tea-drinking and tobacco-smoking, a promise or bargain of some sort is made. But a bargain does not bind an Indian, if, next morning, he thinks he has not asked enough. He then comes to announce that his wife is ill and he must therefore remain at home, but he hints that, if he were to receive a few dollars more, he might contrive to leave her. When this difficulty is apparently disposed of, he solicits money to pay for some one to look after his wife in his absence, and for some one else to look after his dogs. He wants more money to provide moccasins, pipe and tobacco, and a blanket. In fact, his demands extend to the provision of a complete outfit, and if this were granted he would still be dissatisfied. With the assistance kindly bestowed by Mr. Gaudette, the Hudson Bay Company's officer at Fort Resolution, and by his interpreter, Michel Mandeville, I was able to arrange for the services of three Indians and one half-breed, on the understanding that they were not to be taken near the region frequented by the dreaded Eskimo. We were to set out on July 13, and on the 12th I gave orders for the start at four o'clock next morning. The three Indians, however, came with long faces and told me that they wished to attend the sacrament next day. I gave them permission to attend the early celebration which was to take place at six o'clock in the morning, and ordered them to start with me at seven o'clock.

I had thus three hours in the morning to muse on the ways of the Indians. They may be good Christians; I do not know; but notwithstanding the labours of missionaries, they are Indians still, and the return for the time, trouble, and money expended on them seemed to me very inadequate.

At this season there were, I was told, about eight hundred Indians encamped at Fort Resolution, many of them having brought "furs" (chiefly musk-ox robes, and musk-rat skins, though I saw also two silver-fox and a few good marten skins) to trade with the Hudson Bay agent and others. A trader dealing with them has need of a good temper. Prices for "fur" have been pushed higher and higher in recent years, owing to competition between the Company and the free-traders, but still the Indians are not satisfied. They require a whole day to settle one bargain, and then think they should receive more, even demanding a gratuity, which is given more and more freely with the arrival of each new trader. The Indians (those who come to Fort Resolution, at least) are now masters of the situation, and can afford to be lazy and extravagant. Among the "furs" I noticed a number of skins of unborn musk-ox-calves. I understand that there was and is a legal close-time for the protection of the musk-ox, but it is disregarded, as it would be almost impossible to enforce it among the Indians, few of whom are aware of its existence. The sale of these unborn calf-skins might, however, be stopped. The demand for them is increasing, but, if the possessor or the purchaser of every such skin were laid under a heavy penalty, the trade in them would soon cease, and there would be no temptation to the Indians to provide them.

Big game requires protection from other than human enemies. The wood buffalo which roams over the country north of the Peace River has been protected against the hunter for several years, and the protection has been extended to the year 1907. The Indians respect this law, for they know that in this case protection can be enforced, and they have a wholesome dread of the consequences of violating it. But the buffaloes are in danger of extinction from the ravages of wolves which have rapidly increased in numbers within the last few years. If the Government were to give help in the war against wolves; if they would grant a bounty of at least twenty dollars per head, so that it might be worth while for a white man or an Indian to prosecute the war, and if they would grant permits for the careful use of poison, the threatened extinction of this race of buffaloes might still be averted.

CHAPTER III

FROM GREAT SLAVE LAKE EASTWARDS TO THE
MAIN ARK-I-LĬNIK RIVER

On the morning of July 13 we bade farewell to Fort
Resolution, and started on the canoe voyage up to the
east end of Great Slave Lake, or Fond-du-lac, as it is
called.

The party consisted of Darrell, Sandy Turner, and
myself, with the three Indians and half-breed interpreter.
In addition to the two Peterborough canoes, we had a
birch bark canoe for the Indians to return in. For the
first fifteen miles we followed narrow channels, or "snyes,"
as they are called, to the mouth of Slave River. We thus
had a shorter route than if we had followed the shore, and
we could proceed along the "snyes" though the weather
might be stormy on the lake. We reached the big lake
the same evening, and camped on Stony Island, where
we were wind-bound till after eight o'clock next evening.
Then we proceeded, and, paddling steadily, we made the
traverse of about twenty miles to a long, continuous group
of small islands.

This distance can be shortened by about eight miles by
continuing to follow the south shore of the lake some distance eastwards before striking across.

Our route wound in and out among the small islands,
which are chiefly of red granite, sparsely timbered with a
stunted and scattered growth of spruce and white birch,
presenting a very pretty view, especially in the fall of the
year. Round them the water is icy cold and beautifully

clear, so that on looking down we could see large trout lazily swimming or playing about in the depths.

The land on the south of the lake is flat and low-lying, productive only of beds of red willow and alder growing along the muddy shores. The shore on the north side is rocky, the land high, and spruce, of somewhat reduced size, is abundant.

I know of no accurate map or chart of Great Slave Lake. Dr. Bell, of the Canadian Geological Survey, was on the lake in the summer of 1900. I hope that, besides geological work, something was done towards the fixing of a number of prominent points by accurate astronomical observation.

Three years ago Great Slave Lake attracted much attention owing to the reported discovery of gold there in large quantities. Several companies were formed, and miners and prospectors flocked in; but the boom lasted only a short time, for iron pyrites had been taken for the precious metal. The bubble burst, and many were left richer in experience but poorer in pocket. In passing along the north shore we saw evidences of the boom in many places; old claims staked out with posts and piles of stones, and a broken skiff here and there. Close to the shore we saw in the shoal water the veins of quartz in which are embedded small and large chunks of glistening metal, very pretty, but worthless.

The weather was oppressively hot on the lake, and paddling for long hours proved tiring and monotonous work. Every evening at camp time the nets were set, and seldom failed to furnish a supply of trout and white-fish. Trout are very plentiful at the head of the lake, some of them very large, 25 or 30 lbs. being not uncommon. They take a spoon readily, but in canoeing the pace is usually too fast for successful trolling. As far as I can make out there are two distinct species of trout in the lake. Those caught near Fort Resolution are very large, generally white in flesh, with a huge, ugly head; whereas most of those we caught towards Fond-du-lac were of a smaller size, had a small head and flesh nearly always pink, and proved excellent eating.

There was no game of any kind, either on shore or on the lake.

We reached Fond-du-lac on July 20th, after paddling for a long day on perfectly calm water. Three tall lopped trees mark the first portage between Fond-du-lac and the foot of Artillery Lake. On landing we at once observed the trail which has been used by generations of Indians.

Here we left the birch bark canoe and a cache of food for the Indians on their return, and after making the nine portages, which are required between the small lakes which extend from Great Slave Lake to Artillery Lake, we reached the latter on July 23. The first portage, which is about two and a half miles in length, is the only long one. On one of them fresh caribou tracks were observed, which indicated that the annual migration from the north had already commenced.

Artillery Lake looked very picturesque in the bright sunlight; the water, which was of a beautiful blue, was fanned into ripples by the gentle summer breeze. The " Barren Ground " lay on either side beautifully green, and decked gay with a variety of wild flowers. Its charm, and the sense of freedom which it gives, are very impressive, but cannot be described.

There were no human beings within 200 miles of us, and, in fishing and shooting over the lakes and the surrounding country, there was no fear of intrusion on the part of outsiders.

I have always maintained that "Barren Ground" is a misnomer for the Northland of Canada. No land can be called "barren" which bears wild flowers in profusion, numerous heaths, luxuriant grass in places up to the knee, and a variety of moss and lichens. It is barren only in the sense that it is destitute of trees; hence the name " De-chin-u-le " (no trees), which is the Indian name for it.

On Artillery Lake we expected to meet caribou, or deer, as I shall now call them, and we kept a keen lookout over the hilly ground on either side as we paddled along, for we were getting hungry for fresh meat.

On July 25, while ascending the river flowing into the head of Artillery Lake, we shot our first deer, which occasioned great excitement among the Indians. After examining the hoofs and inside, they were positive that the animal had just come from the main bands, which they asserted we were sure to meet the following day. In this opinion, however, they were completely wrong. This small bull was one of many which had separated from the main bands on their migration northwards, and had then remained in the south by themselves during the summer.

Next day a bull musk-ox was spied and shot. Not very many years ago musk-oxen were plentiful round and to the north of Artillery Lake, but they were killed off by the Indians and are now extinct in these parts. Where this old bull had wandered from it would be hard to say, but he must have come a long way. The Indians are now obliged to travel a long distance to the musk-ox ground. When I accompanied them in 1896, we travelled for twelve nights out from the edge of the wood before we fell in with them. Every year they have to travel further, and so it will be till the game is not worth the candle. The Indians will find that it pays better to remain at home and trap "fur" than to make their annual musk-ox hunts, which entail much discomfort, hunger, and thirst, and are not altogether without risk to their dogs, if not to themselves. Distance will ensure effectual protection for the musk-oxen.

On July 26 we camped on the waters of the Mackenzie River basin, and on July 27 on Campbell Lake on the headwaters of the Ark-i-linik River, and our journey would be then down stream all the way to Hudson Bay. The divide is only a low moss swale, about 300 yards across. It is just possible to observe the water trinkling here to the west, there to the east. Next day we reached Abbott Lake.

The last woods had been behind on Artillery Lake. The spruce got more stunted and scattered as we proceeded north to the lake-head, until they finally disappeared, and tall willows took their place. These also disappeared before we reached the divide, where we had to fall back on heaths and moss for fuel to "boil our kettle." It is always possible to make a fire on the "Barren Ground" except after a very heavy rain. In winter the moss from underneath the snow, having been perfectly dried by the frost, provides a better fire than in summer, a fact of which the Indian is ignorant.

On Abbott Lake we saw a good many bull caribou. They could be seen in every direction racing at full gallop over the moss, driven half crazy by the warble or bot-fly, which in appearance resembles a yellow-striped humble-bee. This fly has a sting about $1\frac{1}{2}$ inch in length, which penetrates the hide of the deer, in depositing the eggs. These develop into large maggots, which form a bed or layer underneath the hide, more especially over the loins, and eating through the hide renders it worthless. The flesh of the animal is not affected by them. In the fall when the deer get into condition the maggots disappear and the holes in the hide close up. Though flies and mosquitoes annoy the deer during the summer, it is the warble fly which drives them into a frenzy, and in their endeavours to get clear of this tormentor they keep on the dead run day and night, or plunge into lakes and rivers ; in fact, they do not appear to know what they are doing. One swam right up to our canoe and never saw us until within a few feet.

For some days the three Indians had been dilatory and dawdling, and they had put forward excuses with respect to working on the Sabbath. Now, July 28, they intimated through the interpreter that they were about to return home, having accompanied me as far as they had agreed to come. This I knew was only a threat in order to extort more pay and presents, but their help was not indispensable. They had acted as guides at the portages to the foot of Artillery Lake, but now, on Abbott Lake, they were in a strange country and I was the sole guide of the party. A few portages remained, but my "stuff" was not very heavy, and Darrell, Sandy, and I were well able to handle it and the canoes. I never yet was accompanied by an Indian who did not threaten to leave me. Any excuse is good enough for him, anxiety about his wife and children, ignorance of the country, the danger of being lost, the dilapidation of his foot-gear, or, finally, the state of his health. Only the threat to withhold his pay will induce him to complete his contract, and, if he has been paid in advance, he is master of the situation The representatives of the Hudson Bay Company have introduced the system of making advances to Indians. This system may suit them, but its general effect is bad, and every Indian now expects to be paid beforehand for his services. It is usually necessary to make some advance where a wife and children are to be left behind, but to pay a man for a journey of 500 miles before he has travelled a yard is demoralising. A few years ago, when descending the Liard River in British Columbia, I paid an Indian $100 to accompany me as guide, and see me over the long and steep portage called the Devil's Portage. I was new to the country ; the Indian had received his $100 in advance, and he took wing the night before we commenced the portage. On the present occasion I had only made small advances, and the Indians were by no means masters of the situation. I told them that I was tired of their laziness and of their attempts to delay me, and I bade them go right away. I added that ammunition and tobacco would be given out in the morning, but that I would certainly not give them a letter to Mr. Gaudette asking him to pay them. Next morning, July 29, they were in a repentant mood and professed there had only been a misunderstanding as to the distance they were to come. But such a misunderstanding was impossible, for, in anticipation of such troubles, I had engaged them by time as well as by distance, two moons

C

being the period agreed on.   However, no evil came of the incident, and, as we proceeded on our journey down the western branch of our Ark-i-linik River, it was amusing to see with what eagerness they did their portaging, rustling to push forward and evidently accepting the altered condition of affairs.

The western branch of the Ark-i-linik River flows through many small and large lakes in its course.   These lakes are most irregular in shape, bays and inlets running from them in every direction.

In 1899, when exploring this river, I had the greatest difficulty in finding my way out of some of the larger lakes, and owing to the thick, misty weather which at that time prevailed, I was unable to fix the positions of the inlets and outlets with any accuracy.   On that occasion I found the gulls of some assistance, for their presence generally indicated the outlet.   It was here, a short distance east of Abbott Lake, that, on my former trip, I discovered that my compasses refused to work.   On the present occasion I found them equally unreliable.   However, the weather was clear now, and after a little exploring and making some bad shots up blind inlets, we managed to make fair progress.

We met large bands of deer on their migration to the south.   Some of these bands were composed of bulls only, others of cows and calves by themselves, others again were mixed.

The deer when gathered together in these huge bands paid little or no attention to our presence.   We passed through them freely without occasioning alarm.   A bull was shot whenever we required meat for the pot, but they were all in wretched condition, owing] to the incessant attacks of winged pests, notably the warble fly.

The first spruce, very stunted, were seen on July 29.

On August 2 we reached the only lengthy portage on the western branch.   The river cuts its way through the rock, forming a deepish gorge.   The rock is of felspathic granite, and is massive, the beds dipping south at an angle of 60 degrees. It varies in character, quartz being very much in the ascendant in some places, biotite in others. The portage is about 2¼ miles in length, but the going is excellent, hard and dry. At the end of the portage a change in the formation is at once apparent. The older plutonic rock is replaced by white sandstone, which latter formation is then continuous, with occasional breaks, to the mouth of the main river.

At this time of the year the shores of the river are thickly covered with the hair of the deer, which they shed as they swim across.

A little above the junction with the main river there is a fine fall about thirty feet in height.

The general character of the western branch of the Ark-i-līnik is very similar to that of many rivers in Scotland. The water is swift and heavy in some places; in others swift and shoal, with a few stretches of quiet water. The lakes very much resemble Scotch lochs. The water looks black, the bottom rocky or sandy, and the shores boulder-strewn. The surrounding land, near the height of land especially, is very flat or gently undulating, and mostly rocky.

At the junction the main river widens considerably. In some places the banks are precipitous, the river having cut its way through thick horizontal beds of red and white sandstone; but for the most part the banks are low and sloping, with gravel and sandy shores.

August 5 being Sunday, we made it a day of rest. We had now passed all the portages, and were but a short distance from the junction with the main river. Beyond flowed the main Ark-i-līnik, wide and deep, with a steady current, and with no rough water which could possibly be described as a rapid. A smooth waterway would now take us right to the Hudson Bay, with the exception of one portage at the foot of Schultz Lake.

The Indians were now allowed to return, armed with

my letter to Mr. Gaudette, which would ensure the promised payment. They had behaved very well in the latter part of the journey. I heard afterwards that they reached Fond-du-lac in seven days.

A few words concerning the name of the fine river we were about to descend may not be out of place. As I was the first white man to explore this river, I considered that, in virtue of this priority, I had some right to name it. On old maps it is called the Thelewdezzeth, but this Indian name seems dropping out of use, and the Indians now call it the Thelon. The main part of the river is not visited by Indians, and only Yellow Knives from Great Slave Lake occasionally visit the upper waters of its western branch. The Eskimo, on the other hand, frequent and always have frequented the lower waters of the main river, and among them it is known as the Ark-i-linik, which in their language means the Wooded River. Considering the great advantage of using local names which are not merely known to the natives but are descriptive of natural features of the country, I have no hesitation in adhering to the existing name of Ark-i-linik. The Canadian Geographical Board, however, have thought fit to take exception to the Eskimo name, and I do not know at present what name they have decided to adopt. Mr. Tyrrell, who visited the river in the summer of 1900, informs me that he has named its western branch after me—an honour for which I thank him, but for which I was not at all anxious. Wherever I have been in unexplored regions I have invariably made it a strict rule to ascertain and adhere to local and native names, whether of lakes, mountains, rivers, or other physical features of the country, and I wish to lay particular stress upon the importance of following this plan, for it is of the greatest service to the traveller who finds himself in the country for the first time. If he has a map in his possession, and on this map finds the native name for every place, he will have no difficulty in making the natives understand the route he wishes to follow.

CHAPTER IV

DOWN THE ARK-I-LĪNIK MAIN RIVER AND DOOBAUNT RIVER TO FOOT OF BAKER LAKE

THE summer was now nearly over. Already there was a suspicion of frost at night, and there was a feeling of autumn weather in the air. Mosquitoes had almost disappeared, but black flies were still very troublesome, more especially in the early mornings and evenings.

On August 6 we commenced the descent of the Ark-i-līnik proper. The southern and main branch of the river rises, as I am informed by the Indians, not far from the north-east end of Lake Athabasca, and it would be interesting to start from the Athabasca Fond-du-lac and follow the river from its source.

Mr. J. M. Tyrrell, of the Canadian Survey Department, and his party descended the main river in the summer of 1900, the purpose in view being, as I was told, the construction of a railway through this region to the Hudson Bay. This is the pet scheme of a gentleman whom I happen to know in Ottawa. In fact, the railway company has already been incorporated, and at this stage I fancy the concern will remain.

Talking on this subject my Ottawa friend said : " You have no idea of the vast resources of the north, or of the importance of this railway, by which in summer wealthy Americans will flock to the Hudson Bay to reach the summer residences, which will quickly spring into existence on the shores of the Bay." But talk of this sort only amuses those who are familiar with the Hudson Bay coast and its climate, though it would be foolish to deny the vast resources of the north, not yet discovered.

It is surprising that, in the early days, the Hudson Bay Company never explored this route to the Mackenzie River, the only route then available being by York Factory, Lake Winnipeg, and up the Saskatchewan to Edmonton. The head of the Chesterfield Inlet is as quickly and safely reached by vessel as York Factory. From the head of Chesterfield Inlet to Great Slave Lake the distance is not greater than from Edmonton to Great Slave Lake. The long journey from York Factory to Edmonton would thus be saved. Railways have now altered conditions, and the Ark-i-lïnik River route to the Mackenzie River basin is, of course, out of the question, except to the traveller, who will find the country interesting and easy to traverse.

The peculiarity of the Ark-i-lïnik is that, though so far north, it is wooded on either bank, and in places one might even say heavily timbered, spruce trees, with butts measuring $1\frac{1}{2}$ to 2 feet across, being by no means uncommon. It is a long way north of the limit of trees marked on the maps, and there is a large extent of country to the south of it, destitute of trees. I can find no explanation of this peculiarity from the geological formation, for the same red and white sandstone which prevails nearly the whole length of the river also occurs at places which are without trees.

The heavy growth is confined to occasional bluffs, the largest and heaviest of which occur, not along the main river itself, but a short distance back. Mr. Tyrrell, I find, on his way out, gave his interviewers an exaggerated estimate of the timber of the river. His description was, however, probably amplified by the over-fertile imaginations of those who questioned him, and I am sure that he will not mind these remarks. The woods as a whole amount only to a rather deep fringe, the trees for the most part being scattered and not continuous. Here and there along the banks are spots and short stretches quite bare of timber. After a short walk away from the river on either side one reaches the outer edge of the woodland fringe beyond which the land is typical prairie. Along the creeks and affluents, however, the growth extends to a considerable distance, in places as far as the eye can reach, the trees diminishing in size until the spruce is mere scrub.

Should gold or other precious metal ever be discovered in these regions—and who can tell ?—this timber would be of economic value.

Paddling down the river, we came on signs of musk-oxen, and shortly afterwards saw an old bull lazily wandering through the thick willows on the bank. As we were getting tired of living on deer's flesh, which was wretchedly poor, I landed with a carbine. There was no necessity for caution, as the musk-oxen are absurdly tame here. I soon rolled him over, and he proved to be in excellent condition. The flesh of the musk-ox, in spite of the strong smell of musk, which at this time of the year is particularly noticeable, is excellent eating, but it is generally pretty hard and requires much cooking. When the animal is in prime condition and rolling in fat, the meat is as tender as English beef. But he is not often found in this condition.

The skinning and cutting up of the animal occupied some little time, black flies swarming about us in clouds. We took enough meat to last us several days and proceeded down the river, meeting the same day several more musk-oxen. One remained close to us while we were pitching the tent in the evening. As he did not appear disposed to move off, I took my camera and approached within about thirty yards, when I snapshotted him. He remained feeding on the willows, so I went still nearer. He showed no sign of fear, but I did, for I carried no arms. I ascended a small knoll below which he was feeding, and thus got within a few yards of him and snapshotted him again. I then wished for another shot in a different position, so I threw a piece of rock at him, which only produced an angry shake of the head. I threw several other missiles, but he only stood, angrily shaking his head, pawing the ground, and making a low, guttural grunt. I took one more photo and then retreated, leaving him to finish his evening meal in peace. He remained near our camp all night.

I was surprised to notice how little difference there was between the summer and winter coats of the musk-ox. At this date, August 12, one would naturally expect the robes to be worthless, but they were quite handsome. The fact is that the long black hair, which often reaches nearly to the ground, is never shed. Once the undercoat of wool has been rubbed and scraped off, the robes are good and certainly worth preserving. The trees and bushes along the river were loaded with this wool, which is very fine in texture, much resembling the pashmina of Kashmir. Bags of this wool could be collected from the bushes. It would be a novelty to have a shawl made of it.

Of other game found on the Ark-i-linik River I may mention moose. I have not come across the animals themselves, but I have seen numerous fresh tracks, and the places where they have browsed on the willows. On my last trip I picked up the jawbone of a moose. Black bears are also found, their tracks and other signs being fairly plentiful. Geese (Canada) nest along the main river and on the " Barren Ground " along its western branch. Ptarmigan are very numerous in the willow beds all along the river. Excellent sport might be had by any one with time and ammunition to spare. On a journey small game is not interfered with unless other meat and fish give out. The ptarmigan were very handsome at this time of year. But for a few white feathers in the wings, they might easily have been mistaken for grouse, the colour, flight, and call (both in the early morning and when flushed) exactly resembling that of the red grouse. The young birds were strong on the wing, fully as forward as grouse in the north of Scotland about the middle of August.

Trout, white-fish, and toolabies (very similar to white-

fish) abound, and large numbers can be taken with nets
of from 3 to 4½ inch mesh. There are few rivers equal
to the Ark-i-līnik for food fishes. Salmon do not run
so far west. Pike and suckers do not exist here, I believe, for I have never succeeded in taking any on the
main river, though setting nets regularly. The only
suckers I caught were found nearly at the head of the
western branch.

The spruce, which had been diminishing as we proceeded down the river, now (August 13) appeared in the
form of scrub only. About twenty miles west from the
point where the Ark-i-līnik discharges into Ti-bi-elik Lake
the woods ceased, and we were on the "Barren Ground"
once more.

On August 15, near Ti-bi-elik Lake, we met a small
party of Huskies from the Doobaunt River country. They
were passing the summer on the river fishing, and waiting
for the arrival of the bands of migrating deer from the
north. Their camp was at a spot where the deer in crossing are easily speared by men in kyaks.

I was delighted to be once more among the Huskies,
whose disposition presented a striking contrast to that of
the "poor Indians" we had recently left. The Indian is
morose, even sullen, rarely smiles, and of late years has
acquired a slovenly, swaggering way of going about. When
one arrives at his camp and proceeds to pitch his tent,
the Indian never offers a helping hand. Pipe in mouth,
he stands sullenly looking on, his hands thrust deep in
his trousers' pockets. The contempt which he nourishes
in his heart for the white man is expressed on his
countenance.

The Huskies, on the other hand, when the strangers'
canoe is sighted in the distance, put out at once in their
kyaks to meet them and conduct them to the camp. They
appear delighted, overwhelmed with joy, to see and welcome "kablūnak," or white people. Women and children
rush down to the canoes, seize hold of the "stuff" and

carry it up to the camping ground, never stopping to ask whether one is to camp or to go further on. They bring large stones, which in these parts serve for tent-pegs, and all lend a hand to pitch the tent. Amid much laughter, screams, and yells of joy, the tent is erected, and then they rush off to their own tents to bring what they have in the way of food. It is often not much; the meat and fish may be, and very often are, stinking and putrid, but it is the best they have.

The Huskies are like happy and contented children, always laughing and merry, good-natured and hospitable. Everything that they possess, food, clothes, footgear, and services are at the disposal of the white strangers. Their wives even they freely offer, shocking as this may sound to respectable people at home. This subject need not be discussed here, but I must add that to accuse the Huskies of immorality on the ground of such practices would be grossly unjust.

Ti-bi-elik Lake, which lies about north-east and south-west, is thirteen miles in length, has a breadth of five or six miles at the widest part, and is the only lake on the main river. Its name implies the existence of driftwood, "ti-bi-ŭk" being the Husky name for driftwood.

A short distance east from the foot of Ti-bi-elik Lake the Ark-i-līnik joins the Doobaunt, and the united river discharges into the head of Aberdeen Lake. At the junction the Ark-i-līnik appears to be the larger of the two rivers.

When the Indians left us there were only the three of us to manage two canoes, and we had therefore taken one of them in tow. However, when we reached the Husky camp I got two men to accompany us as far as Ŭdi-ek-tellig, another Husky camp at the head of Schultz Lake, where I expected to meet Amer-or-yuak, an old Husky friend, whom I intended to engage for the whole journey. Husky camps inland, and there are many, are usually at places where the deer cross on their migration south.

The natives were now laying in their supply of meat for the fall and winter, and most of the camps were occupied.

On Aberdeen Lake we met with some bad weather, which obliged us to lay by, and we did not reach Ūdi-ek-tellig till August 20. Here I found my old Husky friend and four tents. He appeared delighted to see me, and had much to say. I found that I had almost completely forgotten what Husky language I had picked up on my former trip, but it soon came back to me, and I was able to make myself understood.

These Huskies, like the others we had met, were looking for the arrival of the deer from the north, but as yet only a few had come. The deer arrive in bands of from about a dozen to as many as two hundred. Trotting quickly down to the edge of the river they take the water without a moment's hesitation. They swim with marvellous speed, almost appear to be trotting, and they keep up a peculiar grunting noise while in the water. The Huskies wait till they are fairly in midstream, then shoot out in their kyaks and surround the band. The spearing then commences. The deer are rounded up first in one way and then in another until each has received its death-thrust, when after a short spasmodic struggle, it floats down with the current, now red with blood.

These deer are mostly cows returning from near the Arctic coast with their young. On their way to the south they have many rivers to cross, and they naturally choose the narrowest parts. A place such as Ūdi-ek-tellig, with large lakes to the east and west, and a river connecting them, constitutes an ideal crossing-place. The slaughter is sometimes great, and, if deer are very plentiful, unnecessary spearing may take place; but this is exceptional. A Husky cannot be expected to be imbued with the same notions of game preservation as sportsmen. Their fathers and fore-fathers always slaughtered deer in this fashion, so they think it all right. The deer show no signs of diminution at present, nor will they so long as the population of the

north remains as it is. They exist in hundreds of thousands ;
it is safe to say millions ; and the few hundreds, perhaps
thousands, killed by the Huskies are insignificant.

The meat is stored, the carcases being piled in a heap
and stones placed over them. The horns of a bull are left
sticking up to indicate the spot after the snow has fallen.
The weather is often warm at this season, but the blue-bottle
flies are dead, and though the meat turns rather putrid, it
does not get fly-blown and walk off. The hides are wanted
to make clothes for the approaching winter, and the tongues
are generally taken to trade on board the whalers wintering
in the Hudson Bay.

The Husky is not wasteful by nature, but the reverse.
The Indian, on the other hand, will waste meat or ammunition in the most reckless fashion. Those who have read
Warburton Pike's book, "The Barren Ground of Northern
Canada," will call to mind some of the episodes of his trip,
three hundred carcases of deer having been counted at one
place, where they had been ruthlessly slaughtered and left
to rot in the water. I am told that this recklessness is now
restrained, and that the chiefs of the Yellow Knives and
Dog Rib Indians limit the number of deer to be killed,
allowing each man only what he requires. I have never
witnessed the spearing of deer in the vicinity of Great Slave
Lake.

The Huskies at Ŭdi-ek-tellig were poorly off, and had
run out of both ammunition and tobacco. Few of them
had ever been to Fort Churchill. What little "fur" they
had caught had been traded to the whalers many months
before. The arrival of white people was very welcome to
them, and I was glad to be able to provide them with a
few of the necessaries of life, such as ammunition, tobacco,
knives, files, needles, matches, &c. They made no complaint of their hard life, for they are happy and content in
the struggle for existence. It is a pleasure to give to them,
for they never beg, and are grateful for so little.

When trading with them, it is customary to take what

you require, and in return to give them just what you like. They trust you, and are always satisfied. There is no word for "Thank you" in their language, but they express their gratitude with their eyes.

To be generous towards them it is not necessary to give much. They might easily be spoilt and led to expect too much for the services they can render, or the supplies of meat and clothes they may be able to furnish, if overloaded with presents which appear to be of trifling value to white men. This would be unfair to the natives themselves, as well as to other travellers who might happen to be less abundantly provided with articles of trade. But, to my knowledge, Huskies are sometimes unfairly dealt with. It raises one's indignation to find that a white man has given nothing more than a single needle for a good pair of long sealskin boots, or than a thimbleful of beads for a suit of deerskin clothes; for sealskin boots and deerskin clothes are of value to the Huskies, and represent much time and labour. That white men can make such bargains and afterwards boast of them passes comprehension.

The nets we set at Ûdi-ek-tellig took many white-fish, toolabies, trout, and one salmon. Salmon do not run much further west. The one caught showed signs of having been some time in the fresh water. I shall have something to say about these salmon later. I am not sure if they are true salmon. They average in weight from 3 to 10 pounds. In colour they are greenish along the back, with silver bellies; the sides are speckled with small, circular, pink spots. All the rivers flowing into the north part of Hudson Bay, as well as all the rivers flowing into the Arctic Sea, abound with these salmon or salmon trout.

I was on the lookout to purchase dogs and sleighs for the projected journey to the Arctic coast, but dogs were scarce, and of sleighs there were none. Amer-or-yuak, however, informed me that I would find both at Mawren-ik-yuak, a Husky camp at the foot of Baker Lake.

At Ŭdi-ek-tellig I found a man, Sahk-pi by name, whom I had known at Churchill. Sahk-pi was the cold-blooded murderer of no less than six of his fellow-beings on the Hudson Bay coast. The Huskies told me that they were going to shoot him the following winter, but here he was strong and well. For a long time he had carried his loaded rifle wherever he went, but had now apparently recovered from his alarm, for he had discarded his weapon, and the murders seemed to lie lightly on his conscience. His quarrel and its murderous results had been about a woman.

I formally engaged Amer-or-yuak, his wife, and an adopted son, a lad of about eighteen, to accompany me as far as Marble Island, where I expected to find the whaling schooner *Francis Allyn*.

We were delayed several days at Ŭdi-ek-tellig by wind and rain, common in the fall of the year in these parts. All the bad weather appears to come from the north-north-east and north-west. When the wind gets into that quarter it remains there for days and brings up heavy rain or snow storms. Delay from this cause is the most objectionable and patience-trying feature of travel in the north at this time of year. One is kept in his tent day and night; the moss being soaking wet, a fire is impossible, and not even the comfort of a cup of hot tea can be obtained. We had nothing in the way of literature, and the hours passed slowly by.

The Huskies did not mind; they remained in their tents, smoking and sleeping alternately, and were perfectly happy; but to the more active temperament of the white men this enforced idleness was almost insupportable. Yet the temperament of the Huskies is by no means sluggish. I found them wonderfully quick in learning, and they never needed a second lesson. They could understand a chart the first time they ever saw one, and could use a pencil to supply details respecting distances and the features of the country. Their manual dexterity made them serviceable in many ways, in pitching a tent, fixing an instrument on a stand, or in cleaning and taking a rifle to pieces. They are far ahead of Indians in intelligence.

On August 25 we made a start from Üdi-ek-tellig. Besides Amer-or-yuak, his wife, and son, I had arranged for two other Huskies to accompany us and lend a hand in packing our stuff over the portage at Ulek-sek-tuk, the rapid at the foot of Schultz Lake. The murderer Sahk-pi was one of them. I had always found him a very good and willing worker and a keen hunter.

It is very convenient, almost necessary, to have a woman in the party. Husky women are excellent workers. In camp they collect moss for fuel, do the cooking, and keep one's clothes and footgear in decent repair. They are good walkers, and across a portage take a fair share of the packing.

We had fair weather on Schultz Lake, and made good way. Hunting did not delay us, for we killed deer on the portage at the foot of the lake, and our own stock of provisions, taken from Fort Resolution, still held out, though it was getting very low. The river connecting Schultz with Baker Lake is wide, deep, and swift, confined by steeply-sloping banks. The country, more especially on the north side of the river, is hilly and rocky. We got about half-way down Baker Lake before we were again stopped by rain and wind.

There were no black flies now, August 30, and mosquitoes had long ceased to trouble us. The Huskies say that black flies are unknown on and near the coast of the Hudson Bay.

The bull caribou were now commencing to get into good condition, but the tips of the horns were not yet set hard.

All along Baker Lake and also down Chesterfield Inlet small willows and dwarf birch grow in sufficient quantity to ensure a fire even in the rainiest weather. In dry weather, of course, there is abundance of fuel from the moss and heaths with which the ground and rocks are covered.

When the weather became moderate we, on September 3, put out early in the morning. A dense fog lay on the lake, so that we could not see a canoe-length ahead. However, I knew the course, and we steered by compass. We paddled steadily for eleven hours, taking our midday meal on board, and reached Mawr-en-ik-yuak, at the foot of the lake, in the evening. Here we found six tents. All the Huskies in camp were old friends whom I had met on my journey in 1899. They were not having a very good time; deer had been very scarce, and being without nets, they were unable to catch salmon. In the spring and early summer these salmon take a bait and hook readily, but they refuse to be caught in this fashion in the fall. However, our nets took a 5-lb. fish next morning.

A few deer cross Mawr-en-ik-yuak, but this is not a favourite crossing. Those that had been speared were made good use of, and not an ounce of meat was wasted. The hides, now in good order and getting thick, were being stored to make the winter clothing.

These Huskies supplied our party with long boots, meat, fat, and deerskin robes and clothes, for the weather was already turning cold. The tide from the Hudson Bay rises about six or eight feet at the foot of Baker Lake.

CHAPTER V

FROM BAKER LAKE TO MARBLE ISLAND, AND THE WHALER AT DEPOT ISLAND

ON September 5 we left Mawr-en-ik-yuak, and proceeded on our way to Chesterfield Inlet. There are two outlets from Baker Lake. That to the south is about twenty miles in length, and the water is deep and rapid. This is the last portion of the Doobaunt River, discharging into the head of Chesterfield Inlet.

We ran down the inlet in three days, being favoured with a fair wind from the west, and on September 8 we were south of Fairway Island, which lies opposite the mouth of the inlet. Three large bull caribou were shot in the afternoon, and we had therefore to camp early. All the bulls were very fat now and the horns commencing to clean, but the Huskies say that the deer on the coast are always exceptionally fat at this season. I should have guessed the weight of any one of these bulls to have been something over 400 pounds, live weight. On Great Slave Lake I remember weighing a very large bull. This was at the end of October, and the animal was completely "run." It weighed 295 lbs., live weight. In prime condition 100 lbs. would not be too much to add to the weight. The back fat alone I have seen weigh nearly 50 lbs.

The Huskies are wonderfully expert at cutting up a carcase. They are well up in the anatomy of a deer, and every part of the animal, each sinew, muscle, joint, bone, or portion of the meat, has its name. One stroke of the knife suffices to separate any two parts. The process of cutting up is invariably done in the same regular order, and is never reversed.

We were now camped on the main coast. Fairway Island lay to the north and east of Baker's Foreland, a few miles to the south. We were detained here for several days by a regular hurricane which I have rarely seen equalled. The wind blew with terrific force for two whole days. In the small shoal lakes the water was piled up in a heap at one end, leaving the bottom bare at the other, so that one could almost walk across dry-foot. Ducks were killed by the score, and the ground was strewn with the bodies of small birds.

The land a short distance back from the coast is undulating, stony and rocky, dotted with small lakes. Moss swamps occur between the lakes and in depressions of the land. Taking a walk one afternoon I came on two Husky graves. The customary pile of stones marked the place, on or near which were piled the tent-poles, sleigh runners, and musket of the deceased one. I have seen many Husky graves, but very rarely have I found the skeleton, only the old deerskin robes in which the corpse had been wrapped remain.

I questioned Amer-or-yuak, whose name I must really shorten to Amer, about this. He replied that bears and wolves remove the stones, devour the bodies, and pack away the bones. He also stated that it is not uncommon in times of starvation for the Huskies to have recourse to eating a dead body. He said that he had seen it done, but that he had never participated in the feast. Huskies, however, in mentioning objectionable practices, never acknowledge that they themselves are guilty of them.

On September 14 we put out, but rough weather compelled us to land when we had travelled only about eight miles. Next morning we made a start at 4.30, when it was just dawning, the wind being off shore and the sea smooth. We camped in the afternoon on the point of land just opposite Marble Island, which appeared to be about ten miles beyond Rabbit Island, a small island near the main shore.

We were delayed on September 16 by too much wind and too heavy a sea. Almost any wind from the north-east, east, or south-east soon brings in a lop of the sea, which is too much for a Peterborough canoe, splendid little sea-craft though it be. It is surprising what one of these small canoes will stand in the way of wind and sea when light and properly handled.

Deer were plentiful around us, so that there was no fear of starvation, or even of running short, but all our supplies from Fort Resolution, hard tack and tea, had been finished some days before. There were large numbers of duck along the coast, and a few flocks of swans passed over our camp. I stalked and shot one of these birds with my Mannlicher carbine one afternoon, and I was rather proud of the feat. I had often attempted it before, but had found it difficult to raise myself sufficiently to get a shot at the bird's body without being seen. The head is always the first part that comes to view. That is a very small mark to shoot at, but if you attempt to get a sight of the body] the bird will be off. This bird, which proved to be 'a full grown male, weighed 14 lbs., and measured 6 feet 10 inches from tip to tip of wings, and 4 feet 1 inch from beak to tail.

We had up to this date no snow and only sufficient frost to put a thin coating of ice on the small pools.

The morning of September 17 was perfectly calm, so we lost no time in getting under way for the passage to Marble Island. Large numbers of walrus played round our canoes as we paddled across. Many of them would raise their ugly heads and half of their huge bodies right out of the water within a few feet of our small craft. "It would have gone hard with us if one of these animals had put his tusks over the gunwale.

The hopes of meeting the whaling schooner *Francis Allyn*, in which was the whole of my outfit for the coming winter, were doomed to disappointment, for, on rounding the south-west point of Marble Island and entering the narrow gut, which leads to the inner and almost land-locked harbour, there was no sign of a living creature, and I read bitter disappointment on every face, white and Husky alike. We were out of tea, sugar, flour, &c., but these were details. What we most wanted was warm clothing and foot-gear for the now fast approaching cold weather. On the *Francis Allyn* were all my food supplies, the "primus" stove, a good tent, and also a four months' mail, which I had been eagerly looking forward to receiving. I was so used to disappointments, however, that I accepted this one in the spirit of resignation and patience. We had plenty of meat and fat anyway, and sufficient ammunition for our return to Mawr-en-ik-yuak at the foot of Baker Lake. There was no immediate or even remote prospect of starving. Nevertheless, I regretted the remark I had made to the owners at New Bedford, that it was a matter of indifference to me where the vessel wintered, since I could easily find out her winter quarters from the Huskies.

One of two things might have happened. (1) The vessel might have gone to other winter quarters, in which case I was bound to find her, or (2) she might have been wrecked on her way up, in which case the sooner we made our way to Fort Churchill and thence to Winnipeg and civilisation the better for us. Deciding to accept the former alternative we returned to the mainland without delay, while the weather was still fine and the sea smooth. We had provided ourselves with a large supply of meat lest we should not find the whaler and be storm-stayed on the island, but fortunately the weather had remained good.

Marble Island has been fully described by Dr. Bell of the Canadian Geological Survey Department. It is about 25 miles long, lying east and west. The coast, except for the harbour near the south-western corner, is straight, rock-bound, and forbidding. The peculiar quartzite of which it is composed has a very white and dazzling appearance when seen in the distance in the bright sunlight, hence the name "Marble Island." When seen nearer the rock presents a rusty or yellow appearance. Its surface has been smoothed and flattened by ice action, being in this respect similar to the rock surfaces on the coast and throughout the "Barren Ground."

The inner harbour, a circular basin, is completely land-locked but for the narrow gut already mentioned. The anchorage outside does not appear to be of the best, for my Husky informed me that two vessels had dragged their anchors, gone ashore, and broken up some years before.

We found some old wood, not very much, barrel hoops, broken stoves, and other rubbish left by whalers. A well-marked track led to a small lake a short distance up the rocks, which was evidently the source of their fresh water supply. But the water was believed to be the cause of all the scurvy on board the vessels that wintered there, and since 1891 the place had been deserted. That many had died there the number of graves testified. The island is regarded with superstition by the Huskies, who say that long ago it did not exist, that its appearance was sudden, and that at first it was solid ice with one huge cavity, which is now filled by the sea and forms the harbour, believed to be bottomless.

The western coast of Hudson Bay, with its many deep inlets and islands, was a long and difficult coast on which to search for a small whaling schooner of about 100 tons register. I knew that between Churchill and Marble Island, with the exception of Term Point, there were no suitable winter quarters for a vessel. No vessel, to my knowledge, had ever wintered at Term Point, and I determined to go north and search. The Huskies, who are generally informed the year before as to the winter quarters of a vessel, had been surprised when I told them that I was going to join a whaler at Marble Island. They said they had not expected a vessel there, but did expect one at {Piki-ular (Depot Island), just off Whitney and Winchester Inlets.

Repulse Bay, to the north, the favourite winter quarters of a good many whalers, was, I knew, regarded as too far north by the owners of the *Francis Allyn*. Cape Fullerton, a short distance to the north of Depot Island, was a likely place. Wager Inlet, to the north of Cape Fullerton, was a possible but not probable place at which to find the vessel. The final decision was to return without delay to the mouth of Chesterfield Inlet, and thence to take a run north to Depot Island if weather and time permitted. If not, then to return up the Inlet to Mawr-en-ik-yuak at the foot of Baker Lake, remain with the Huskies till the "freeze up," and then make the journey overland to Depot Island with dogs and sleighs. Failing to find the vessel at Depot Island I would go on to Cape Fullerton, and, if *still* unsuccessful, send a party of Huskies to search Wager Inlet and bring back word. If nothing could be seen or heard of the vessel, I should be obliged to abandon the projected journey and get the Huskies to take me down to Fort Churchill, the nearest post of the Hudson Bay Company.

In any case, I wished to place my canoes in cache at the foot of Baker Lake, ready for a start thence to the Arctic coast in the early spring. If the vessel were found, all would be well and the canoes would be so far on the way. If nothing could be heard of the vessel, then the retreat would have to be sounded and our steps would be turned south toward Fort Churchill, with Winnipeg as our ultimate goal, and one more failure would have to be debited to my wanderings in the Great Barren Northland.

But I am going too fast. In the event of failing to find the *Francis Allyn*, I still had another vessel to depend on, the whaling schooner *Era* belonging to the same owners. The captain of the *Era* had been instructed, I knew, by the owners, to treat my party "white" should we put in an appearance. This vessel probably would be able to supply immediate wants, and might even furnish us with enough provisions, ammunition, and other necessaries to prevent the abandonment of the expedition, but she certainly could not replace the carefully selected outfit which I had sent up in the *Francis Allyn*. However, enough to proceed on and carry through the journey to the Arctic coast would be thankfully accepted.

We had left Fort Resolution on July 13, and the journey so far had taken two months and four days. Had we left two or three weeks earlier it might have been done in six weeks, for in the earlier part of the season the weather on the lakes is more settled.

On September 18 we started on the return journey to the foot of Baker Lake. About two inches of snow had fallen during the night, and ice had formed on the small lakes. The long dark winter was fast approaching. There is but a short spell between the disappearance of ice in the spring and its re-appearance in the fall. On my journey in 1899 we travelled on the ice with dogs the last days of June, and were beset by ice on Schultz Lake on July 31. Now in the middle of September we had ice again, and it looked as if it had come to stay. We had not gone far when we were obliged, by the state of the weather, to put ashore and camp. The rest of the day was spent in repairing our tent, which had suffered considerably during the recent storm.

In the evening I took the opportunity to acquaint Amer-or-yuak with the fact that, if we failed to find the vessel, I had nothing to give him. He, with his wife and son, had been with me since leaving Ŭdi-ek-tellig. Amer was good about it, and if he experienced disappointment he certainly did not show it. He said that it was not my fault, that any small present or nothing at all would satisfy him, but that he was sorry for the white men, who were now without provisions. He said that it was right to return to Mawr-en-ik-yuak, where he and the other Huskies would look after us, and keep us supplied with deer's meat. The Huskies, he said, would certainly be willing to take us with dogs and sleighs overland to search for the vessel, and that if we failed to find her, they would take the white men down to Fort Churchill in the winter.

Next morning, September 19, the wind having moderated, we put out and resumed the journey. We were now dependent on the rifles and guns to keep the party alive. Deer's meat would be our only article of diet until we found the *Francis Allyn* or some other vessel. The Barren Northland has its drawbacks, but there, while rifles and ammunition last, one is pretty sure of a subsistence. The life is wild and rough, but so remarkably healthy that one can undergo hardship for which, in his own country, he would be quite unfit, and eat food which at home would be condemned as little better than poison. The commonest diet is deer's meat, often in a condition inadequately described as "high," and of this the hungry traveller not seldom bolts enormous quantities at a meal. Yet beyond the slight temporary inconvenience which is expected, there are no evil consequences. Fever is altogether unknown.

But to continue. The recent fall of snow had rendered our supply of fuel somewhat precarious, for heaths and moss will only burn when dry, and of willows and dwarf birch there were none along the coast of the Bay. I happened to know of a Husky grave not far off, on which were piled the defunct one's worldly effects, consisting of the usual tent poles and the runners of his sleigh. I suggested to Amer that we should appropriate this wood; for the man himself, or rather his body and bones, were gone, having been long since devoured by wolves and bears, if not by the Huskies themselves. Amer shook his head, saying, "Dead Husky wood very bad."

I was rather surprised at this, for, on my former journey on this coast, Milūk, who then accompanied me, when once out of his own part of the country, distinguished himself as a rustler of wood, and would spy for signs of a grave as keenly as he did for deer.

One cannot regard this respect for a dead man's worldly possessions as superstitious any more than the respect for head-stones in our own churchyards, and I well remember with what a look of horror a proposal to cut scythe stones from a neglected head-stone at one of the Hudson Bay Company's posts in the north was received.

Proceeding up the coast to the mouth of Chesterfield Inlet we reached Baker's Foreland and camped. This part of the coast is characterised by long stony points projecting into the sea. Shoal bars extend a long distance out from these points, so that even a canoe, with its light draught, has to keep well out to sea. At high tide it is possible to come closer in. On camping we observed that all small and some of the larger lakes were coated with ice, which already had attained a thickness of two inches. This was on September 19. It froze sharp in our tent at night, but we still slept comfortably enough without deerskin robes.

We were here delayed by wind for a couple of days. Paddling against a head-wind, be it ever so light, is slow work ; against a steady breeze no headway at all can be made, and it is a waste of energy to attempt it.

We resumed our journey on the 21st. Putting ashore about noon to eat, under the lee of some rocks, we found two skulls and a number of human bones. Amer informed me that a few years ago a great many Huskies had died at this place. Being stricken by some kind of sickness they were unable to go out and hunt, and so perished from starvation.

On my journey in 1899 I was much struck by the number of sites of old Husky camps along both the north and south shore of Chesterfield Inlet, and also inland wherever the hunting of deer used to take me. They were indicated by the circles of stones which had been used as weights to keep the deerskin tents down, and seemed to show either that the Huskies in former times were much more numerous than at present, or that they must have been great travellers. I am well aware that the process of decay is very slow in these parts, and that a circle of stones may remain in evidence indefinitely, but still this would not account for the number of old camping grounds which one comes across.

I now questioned Amer on the subject, and he replied that long ago ("itchuk" was the Husky word he used, which exactly expresses our "long ago") the Baker Lake and coast Huskies had been a very large tribe, but that they had been decreasing since then. It would be interesting to trace the beginning and cause of this decrease. It can scarcely be attributed to contact with white men, which is usually attended with disastrous results to the aboriginal races. The Huskies have never changed their mode of life. They live in deerskin tents and snow-houses as formerly. They wear the same kind of clothes now as of yore. The same animals, caribou and musk-oxen, roam the country, seals and fish are found in the sea and rivers to-day as in former times. The conditions seem not to have changed at all, and yet the Huskies have decreased until the families on Baker Lake cannot show more than a score of tents.

Ducks, especially the eider, were very numerous along the coast and in Chesterfield Inlet. Deer were leaving the coast and travelling inland. Nearly all small birds had departed for the south, but snowbirds (buntings) still remained.

Canoeing was cold work, and our hands suffered considerably from being continually wet by the paddles.

On the evening of September 23 we ran into a small bay which offered good shelter, and camped for the night. Next morning, the tide being dead low, we discovered that we could not get out again, and were obliged to lay by till half-tide. We were now close to the mouth of Chesterfield Inlet, and I decided to return direct to Mawr-en-ik-yuak.

The cold weather was fast approaching, and the ice already three or four inches thick on the lakes. We might easily have run up to Depot Island or Cape Fullerton, but in the event of not finding the vessel the return journey might have presented difficulties in the shape of floating ice. It does not do to take chances at this time of year. A very small amount of drift ice is sufficient to stop a canoe.

When the tide rose and released us from our rocky prison we had smooth water, and, rounding Spurrell Head, we made about twenty miles up the Inlet. The Huskies killed a white fox as it was swimming from a small island to the main shore. It only measured 36 inches from tip of nose to tail.

A few white whales showed their backs, and numerous seals kept popping up their heads in all directions as we paddled along. The sea being dead calm I stopped, and we shot several of the seals, but only secured three. They sink directly the air leaves the body, so no time must be lost in securing one that is shot. These were the small bay seals, and a fair specimen scaled 155 lbs. The Huskies were delighted, and said that the blubber meant three months' oil for their lamps, and the skins would be useful, of course, for boots.

There is a much larger seal found in the Hudson Bay, on which the natives set great prize. I do not know its scientific name, the Husky name is "ūgyūk." The skin, which is very thick and tough, is used for the soles of boots, or is cut into lines for dog harness, traces, and other purposes. These lines are almost unbreakable.

We were favoured with glorious weather on our return up Chesterfield Inlet. One would have been inclined to laugh at any person who suggested that the winter was close upon us, and that we should soon be unable to navigate these waters. But here the weather changes with surprising rapidity. The wind chops round towards the north, threatening clouds roll up, the thermometer drops, and the change from summer to winter is complete.

I measured the rise and fall of the tide about half-way up the inlet. It was 12 feet between ordinary high and low tides, but it decreases as the inlet is ascended.

Numerous large flocks of ptarmigan were seen flighting across the inlet. They pack, like grouse in Scotland, before taking their flight to the woods in the south.

Nell-yŭk-yuak, a Husky camp about half-way up the southern outlet from Baker Lake, was reached on September 28. Here I was met by Uttungerlah, an old Husky friend of mine, and a great musk-ox hunter. He had just returned from Repulse Bay, whither he had gone in his whale-boat to find out the winter quarters of any whalers remaining in Hudson Bay. As I hoped and expected, he proudly handed me two letters, adding that he had been instructed by the captains of two vessels to cruise along the coast and search for a party of white men, with whom he was to return in his whale-boat. One of the letters was from Captain Santos, master of the *Francis Allyn*, informing me that he was in winter quarters at Depot Island, giving his reasons for not carrying out his owner's instructions and wintering at Marble Island, and expressing the hope that I had not been put to much inconvenience by the change of plans. The second envelope contained a courteous note from Captain Comer, of the *Era*, who promised that if I came up to Repulse Bay, he would do his utmost to further the ends I had in view.

These two letters raised my spirits considerably. I should not now be compelled to beat a retreat on Fort Churchill, and I thought with satisfaction of my provisions for a whole winter, and of ammunition, tobacco, and trade articles which would last for two winters with judicious economy.

The season was already far advanced, and I had some doubts about the wisdom of undertaking the trip to Depot Island and back again. I had never intended to winter on board the whaler, but had decided to live with the Huskies and hunt musk-oxen. Uttungerlah, however, felt confident

Chesterfield Inlet would be open for another ten days yet; so I decided to go to Depot Island in his whale-boat, obtain such provisions, ammunition, and Husky "trade" as were necessary, and return without delay to Mawr-en-ik-yuak, if the ice permitted us to get so far.

The next morning, with a fair wind and ebbing tide, we set sail for Depot Island. Westerly winds prevail at this time of year, and these are fair for the run down Chester-field Inlet. With a free sheet we reached the mouth of the Inlet in two days. On rounding the north-east point at the mouth of the Inlet we were very close-hauled. The wind was strong, and although it blew fairly off shore a consider-able sea got up, and we shipped a lot of water. A whale-boat sails capitally off a wind, but when close-hauled does not make much headway, and if there is any lop of a sea on it takes in water.

Depot Island is a small, low, rocky island lying off the west coast of Hudson Bay, about forty miles north from the mouth of Chesterfield Inlet.

We reached the *Francis Allyn* on the evening of October 2, and Captain Santos, a Portuguese by birth, welcomed me heartily on board. He stated that he had felt uneasy in his mind, as he suspected that we had no provisions left. Neither had we, but the Barren North-land luckily furnishes a meat supply when provisions give out.

Captain Santos gave his reasons for not wintering at Marble Island. He maintained that the water there pro-duced scurvy, and said that there was always danger and difficulty in crossing on the ice between Marble Island and the main shore. Depot Island had many advantages, ne informed me, as the winter quarters of a vessel. At low tide it was almost land-locked by outlying reefs, and it was easy to get out of when the ice broke up in summer.

We found that the crew had already been busily en-gaged in preparations for the winter. The quarter-deck had been boarded in and covered with old canvas, and made quite a comfortable house. I don't think any of us were sorry to step on board into comparative civilisation, to see and hear white men, and to sit down to a square meal of bread and butter and hot coffee with sugar, to which we had been strangers for over a month.

The whole of my outfit was safe on board; nothing had been forgotten.

The next day was spent in opening the different casks and boxes in which my outfit had been securely packed. The "stuff" was then divided. Part of it was to remain on board until we returned, but I took the opportunity to remove as much as possible to the foot of Baker Lake in the whale-boat. It was easier to take it by water now than overland by dog-sleigh in the winter.

The crew of the *Francis Allyn* was a large one for a vessel of 105 tons. There were twenty-four hands all told. They were of various nationalities (Portuguese, Negroes, English lads, Americans, Canadians), and they were from different paths of life. The captain, mates, and boat-steerers (harpooners) were all old hands at the whaling business, but the rest of the crew were novices. They had shipped in response to an advertisement inserted in a Boston paper, some from a spirit of adventure, others because they were "broke," while a few thought that there was big money to be made out of it. They were all youngsters, and the experience would doubtless be of benefit to them, if it only taught them to remain at home and stick to regular work. A long cruise on board a small whaler and the experience of an Arctic winter in confined quarters are convincing arguments, and do no one any harm.

With so many men in so small a vessel it surprised me that more precautions were not taken against the dreaded scurvy, from which the crews of vessels wintering in Hudson Bay invariably suffer. On the *Francis Allyn* there were but five gallons of lime juice, though the ship was to remain nine months in winter quarters. But plenty of fresh air and outdoor exercise would go far towards the maintenance of the general health. The diet, failing a supply of fresh deer's meat, could not be changed. Salt beef and pork figured prominently at every meal. Such things as dried or evaporated fruits, pickles, vinegar, desiccated potatoes were not included in the ship's stores, or, if they were, the quantities were so small as to be worthless.

I allowed myself two days on board. The fast approaching cold weather made it imperative for us to return up the Inlet with as little delay as possible. Ice was already forming round the vessel and along the shores.

I made arrangements to leave Sandy on board. I had seen that he found the travelling life somewhat tough. The absence of fire and the diet of meat "straight" were not to his taste, and, being a new-comer, he could not make up his mind to disregard hardships. Darrell was to return with me to hunt musk-oxen.

CHAPTER VI

LIFE IN AN ESKIMO CAMP ON BAKER LAKE

ON October 5 I bade farewell to the captain and officers of the *Francis Allyn*, and we were soon under way in a fully-laden whale-boat for the south and west.

The return journey was not very easily accomplished. Westerly winds prevailed, and we were obliged to lay by several days, the weather getting colder every day. The north-east point of land at the mouth of Chesterfield Inlet is a peninsula, only a low, narrow neck of stones about twenty yards wide connecting it with the mainland. The Huskies have cut a small canal, if one can so call it, across this miniature isthmus, by removing the stones and opening a narrow passage through which a whale-boat can be hauled at ordinary high tides. At spring tides there is plenty of water, and it is possible to run through all right.

This passage saves a considerable distance, about twenty miles I should judge. The charts do not mark the point as a peninsula.

A phenomenon of these parts is the mirage, which is much more marked on some days than on others. It is observed on the larger lakes and along the coast particularly. Land which is only a short distance away appears suspended in mid-air, and great distortion takes place. Captain Santos informed me that owing to this peculiarity it is impossible to get good sights at sea.

The voyage up Chesterfield Inlet was slow and far from pleasant; the cold was severe, for although the thermometer never dropped even to zero, it was our first touch of winter cold, and was keenly felt. We had to sit still for twelve hours at a stretch, everything on board coated with ice

and with a cutting wind in our teeth. The whale-boat
leaked so badly that every night it had to be unloaded and
in the morning loaded afresh. This necessitated wading.
We all had long sealskin boots luckily, but these would
freeze stiff directly we left the water.

Our one comfort was the "primus" oil-stove, which,
after the first few trials, worked admirably, and we were
always able to have hot coffee or cocoa when we wanted it.

On the morning of October 12 the Husky tents at
Mawr-en-ik-yuak were sighted, and shortly afterwards we
effected a landing through the heavy slob ice, which had
already formed at the foot of Baker Lake. We were back
just in time, for next day the river was frozen solid. The
Huskies, now all assembled at this place, soon emerged
from their tents and lent willing hands to land and carry
up all the stuff. When I suggested to Uttungerlah that
one of the Husky deerskin tents would be more comfortable for us than our own canvas ones, he immediately
acted on the suggestion, striking his own tent and pitching it on fresh ground.

Darrell and I were now fairly installed within the Husky
camp, and became familiar with the every-day life of the
Huskies. With the exception of four families inhabiting
as many tents at Ŭdi-ek-tellig, all the Baker Lake Huskies
were now here, and we had altogether sixteen tents. The
conditions of life were severe, as they always are here in
the late fall. There was, as yet, no snow to speak of, and
therefore snow-houses could not be built, while the tents
afforded little shelter from the weather. The wind blew
cold through rents and slits in the deerskin tents, and
falling or drifting snow found easy entrance. The temperature rarely rose above 10° Fahr. New deerskin clothes
were not yet made, for Husky superstition forbade the
commencement of work on these till snow-houses had
been built, and, besides, it was too cold for the women
to sew in the tents. I had difficulty in writing up the few
notes I kept.

E

There were no deer within walking distance, and it was too early in the season to travel with dogs and sleighs to hunt. The supply of meat was not plentiful, and the Huskies had nothing better to live on than the meat which had been killed in summer and was now putrid. Discomfort and privation, however, did not suppress their cheerfulness. On the first evening a deputation, headed by Uttungerlah and Amer, visited me for the purpose of ascertaining whether I had been satisfied with the journey to and from the whaler, and was now satisfied with the camping-ground and the tent. They regretted they had no deer's meat fit to give me, but they expected to be able to travel with dogs in a few days, and would then keep me well supplied. I replied in set terms that I was well satisfied with everything, and appreciated the attention they had shown me; that I was pleased to come and live among them, and hoped they would all have a successful musk-ox hunt before long. These words delighted them, and they rushed off to hold a great dance in honour of the occasion.

Here I may set down a few remarks about Husky fashions and Husky legends, jotted down at different times. Most of the grown-up Hudson Bay women are tattooed on the face, a thick paste of charcoal and water being rubbed in after the application of a needle. The most popular ornament among them is a brass band, about half or three-quarters of an inch in width, placed across the forehead and extending behind the ears. The material for these is no doubt obtained from empty cartridge-cases and other pieces of metal given by the whaling crews. Other ornamental appendages are cylindrical pieces of wood, about sixteen inches in length, which, covered with beaded cloth, hang from the ends of their tresses, and end in a tassel or tuft of false hair. The men are almost as fond of beads as the women, and a long-tailed deerskin coat covered with beads excites admiration and envy. White beads were in fashion at the time of my visit, but possibly Husky fashions change as ours do.

The deerskins for their fancy garments are first cleared of the hair and then made soft, pliable, and beautifully white by being scraped with a blunt instrument. I have never seen Huskies rub skins with brain or liver as the Indians do, and they never put them through the process of smoking. This process, the Indians assert, keeps the hide from becoming hard after being wet, but I could never detect any difference between an unsmoked skin and one that had gone through the orthodox process.

A few finger-rings are worn, but as these have been supplied direct by the whalers, they are of no interest. The principal toys of the children are models of men and women, and of dogs, kyaks, pipes, lamps, kettles, &c.

In smoking, the Huskies are very careful of their tobacco, mixing it with the leaf of the cranberry vine. The mixture makes rather pleasant smoking, but is no saving on tobacco. The bowls of their pipes are of stone; the stems consist of two pieces of wood hollowed out and then fitted together. When the stem gets saturated with tobacco juice, a new stem is made and the old one carefully laid by till the sad times when the tobacco supply is exhausted; then the old stems are cut up and smoked instead of tobacco.

The chief musical instrument, if musical it may be called, is the drum, which is indispensable at their dances. They have also small flutes, like penny whistles, made of wood. Drums and flutes are their own instruments, but they receive Jews'-harps from the traders, and, if a Husky is rich enough to purchase an accordion, his happiness is complete. They are really very fond of music. On my journey in 1899 I had with me two graphophones, which afforded endless amusement. For the Huskies on the coast the one attraction which the church provides is the harmonium.

Among them there is no knowledge and no idea of a Supreme Being or of a future state, so far as I could discover. One whom I questioned said, " Husky die, no more

Husky." They have no account of the creation of the world, and their story of the origin of the human race is incoherent. They told me (through George Oman, the interpreter at Churchill) that long ago, in an island far to the north, there was a woman, the only woman in existence. This woman had a father, and he gave her to be the wife of a dog, so that she became the mother of a litter of pups. When her father went in a kyak with food for them, the woman told the pups to lick the blood off the kyak and then capsize it. They did so, and the father was drowned. Then the woman, dividing her progeny into three groups, told them that from them three races would spring, two of which would be at enmity and war with one another for ever, while the third would be at peace with all. The first group she sent inland to the west, and from them sprang the Indians; the second sailed away to the east in a boat, and of them came the white men; while the third were sent north and became Eskimo. I was told also of another woman who was said to have made the caribou, the large seal (ūgyūk), and the common seal. This woman was one day chopping wood when the wind was high, and the chips which were blown into the water became fish. There was also some belief that bears, foxes, and other animals had been at one time human beings.

One superstition with respect to deerskin clothing has been already mentioned; but further, they affirmed that blindness would befall any one doing needlework in spring on the skins of newly-killed deer, though repairs to old garments then are permitted. The marrow bones of deer must not be broken with anything but a stone.

When a woman has given birth to a child she is not allowed to leave the place where she is lying for a whole moon. If the tribe happens to be travelling at the time, she must get along as best she can, but must on no account follow in the track of the party. She must keep at a safe distance on one side. If one woman gives birth to a boy at the time when another gives birth to a girl, the boy must become the husband of the girl. Relations nearer than cousins never marry.

It is customary for the men to have only one wife, but some have two, and Sahk-pi, whom I have already mentioned, had three. When a second wife is desired, the reason is generally to be found in the domestic arrangements of the Husky. When he goes in winter to hunt the musk-ox he takes his wife with him. She helps to build the iglu or snow-house, prepares the food, collects moss for fuel, and keeps his clothes and foot-gear in repair. She is almost indispensable on such expeditions. But naturally her services are not always available, and hence arises the wish for a second wife. A double matrimonial arrangement does not disturb the domestic harmony. The two wives show no jealousy; they smoke the same pipe, rub noses (their form of kissing), eat together, and sleep together in tranquillity. There are no marriage rites among the Huskies. Their notions of conjugal fidelity are different from ours, free love is universal, but there are no divorces. It is very rarely that a husband sends his wife away. I was not acquainted with a single case, but was told that on one or two occasions a wife had been turned away for gross neglect of her children. The husbands are fond of their wives and children, and treat them well. Girls are given in marriage very young, matters being arranged by their parents. A girl seven years of age, belonging to my party, was already bestowed on a man of thirty.

Baker Lake was now (October 15) covered with ice, which along the shore was thick, so that the travelling was good. Having had a couple of days' rest, all the Husky men went off to hunt deer. During their absence we amused ourselves and passed the time as best we could. We used to go and fish through the ice on a lake about three miles distant. The fish (trout) did not appear to be hungry, and the result was generally nil; but the old women, by exercising a wonderful degree of patience, were more successful.

The men returned after a few days. Some of them had gone as far as the Kazan River, more than half-way up Baker Lake. Most of them had killed deer, and the bulk of the meat had been left in cache under rocks till such time as the snow fell, when it could be hauled by dogs. They each brought back a small load, which they at once offered to us, evidently thinking that the white men who were their guests must not want for meat.

The dogs, which had found a scanty living by gnawing the old hoofs and bones of deer, had now got their winter coats, and looked well.

The days passed slowly. We spent an enormous time in sleep. The English newspapers and some old magazines which I had received on board the *Francis Allyn* helped to pass away many a weary hour. It is astonishing what rubbish a man will read when he is hard put to it. The most stupid and puerile story is eagerly devoured. All the advertisements are scanned through again and again, till patent medicines, soaps, and permanent youth blooms disturb one's dreams at night.

We were one and all longing for the snow, but the wind persistently remained in the north-west quarter, and the prospect of snow appeared remote. At length, on October 22, there came a change; the wind chopped round, the temperature rapidly rose, and a small amount of snow fell, which, in places, formed deep drifts. Next morning the Huskies were all busy tramping down snow in order to pack it. It would then freeze into a compact mass, from which could be cut the blocks required for the construction of a snow-house.

Still there was not sufficient snow for our purposes, and we had to wait. The Huskies spent the evenings in dancing, which was their favourite amusement. They assembled in one of the large tents, and the performance began with the pounding of the drum, a piece of deerskin stretched over a wooden hoop. The women broke out into a shrill, monotonous chant, which they kept up incessantly. A man then advanced into the middle of the tent, holding the drum in one hand and pounding it with the other. Slowly turning round, he kept time with his feet to the beating of the drum, every now and again emitting a most diabolical yell.

This he kept up until he got tired, his efforts on the drum became feebler, his yells lost their frequency and force, and he finally sank exhausted to the ground. His place was taken by a fresh dancer, and the performance was repeated, the dance being sometimes kept up the whole night.

I had expressed a desire to witness the great "antikūt," or conjuring performance, of the wise men. The favourite trick is the production of a small pair of walrus tusks in a man's mouth. The man's head was covered with a deer-skin robe. After some delay the robe was partly withdrawn, so as to show his face, and then from his mouth there protruded two small walrus tusks, which he was plainly holding there with his hand. There was apparently little or no attempt at deception, and I could not think that the older and more sensible men believed in it, but the women implicitly believed it all. The men nevertheless assured me that the tusks had grown in the man's mouth. They said that there were no walrus tusks in the camp, so they must have grown, for this man was a great medicine man.

The camp was out of meat. Half the Huskies were starving and the other half were living on putrid carrion, yet still they were all content to wait. I resolved to set them a good example, and, on October 26, set out with two young men, Ilartnark and Pitzeolah, the adopted sons of Uttungerlah and Amer respectively, on a hunting expedition up Baker Lake. We took one small sleigh and six dogs, and we intended to go westwards for about twenty miles.

The going was bad, as the recent snow had not packed hard, so our progress was slow, the two Huskies being without snow-shoes.

We arrived after dark at a couple of miniature snow-houses, which had been built by the deer-hunters the week before. Into these we crawled, and spent the first night with scarcely room enough to move hand or foot.

Next morning, leaving Pitzeolah to build me a larger snow-house and feed the dogs from a meat cache close by, I set out accompanied by Ilartnark. There was more snow here than at Mawr-en-ik-yuak, and the going was heavy. I was wearing snow-shoes, and Ilartnark had difficulty in keeping up with me.

Deer were sighted in the afternoon, and two were shot by the Husky, who nearly exhausted his supply of cartridges. In the evening I found that Pitzeolah had erected a new snow-house, in which I had plenty of room. Shortly after dark the wind changed to the east, and snow commenced to fall and drift. I felt comfortable enough in my snow-house, and listened with pleasure to the howling blizzard which was by this time raging outside, as I lay snugly rolled in my " Jaeger " blankets.

In the middle of the night I was awakened by a small snow-storm inside the house. I had been told that a snow-house would stand any wind, but the snow which had been used in the construction of this one was freshly fallen and loose, and it was being gradually blown away. My blankets and everything inside the house were, in a moment, covered deep with the snow-drift.

An attempt to plug the hole with a deerskin only resulted in the collapse of half the wall. When I turned out I could not see a yard for the flying scud.

The snow-house in which the two Huskies slept almost adjoined mine, and after much shouting I managed to arouse them. They turned out, and eventually contrived to rebuild the broken side. They then retired with the consoling remark that it would probably break again, as the snow was not yet fit for building houses. I crawled back, and rolling myself in snow and blankets, lay down to wait for morning. The heat of my body melted the snow on the blankets, and when morning broke I was soaking wet. However, the weather had moderated, and the air was quite warm. The thermometer registered 36°.

On looking out I could see deer in thousands away to the west. They seemed like small black stones in the distance, but with the glass their movements could be distinctly seen.

It was now the height of the rutting season, and many fierce combats were taking place between the old bulls.

I despatched Pitzeolah (whom I shall henceforth call "Pitz") at once back to Mawr-en-ik-yuak to tell the other Huskies. Ilartnark and I started off in the meanwhile to shoot a few of them. Such an array of deer was unexpected, and only a small number of cartridges had been brought. The Husky had but three remaining. With these he did good execution, and killed three. Getting in amongst them I shot eight. The deer kept so much on the move that most shots had to be taken walking or trotting, and although they did not move from the ground and go right off, they would not permit an approach within 100 yards. Our supply of cartridges being exhausted, we returned to our camp to pass another anxious night in the snow-houses, which, owing to the high temperature, threatened to collapse at any moment.

Our supply of oil for the "primus" stove was exhausted, and, as we had not time to collect dwarf birch, which was abundant enough, we had no fire, and had to eat the meat raw. I have never yet got accustomed to eating meat raw, and I have to be very hungry to do it. The Huskies eat it raw and frozen, and may possibly appreciate it, but I know very well that they do not prefer raw meat to cooked. To me it is almost tasteless, or rather, when fresh, has a kind of flabby taste, though that way of expressing it may not be very intelligible. When frozen it is too cold on the teeth.

The snow-houses held up well during the night, but they settled a good deal, and in the morning I could just sit in mine.

The mild weather continued and made travelling most disagreeable. Everything we had was wet. Footgear became soggy at once, for the snow was almost in a state of slush.

I shot a large bull in the morning. We were not shooting bulls, for they were not fit to eat, but this one happened to be close to camp and would make a good feed for the dogs. This animal had evidently been engaged in combat and had received a most terrible wound, several inches deep, right behind the shoulder, so that we could see the ribs. Caribou are impervious to cold I know, and they appear to be almost insensible to pain. This beast did not even walk lame from the wound.

Early in the afternoon the Huskies from the main camp were descried coming along the lake. The enormous bands of deer had moved, and were now right in their way. When the party got close, the men ran ahead of the dogs and sleighs, and the shooting continued till darkness afforded the animals protection. Some of the Huskies came to our camp; others remained out to cut up and cache the deer they had killed, and to prosecute the hunt on the following morning.

During the night the weather took a decided change. The wind veered round to north-west, and the thermometer fell to twenty degrees. Then the wind rose and the snow commenced to drift. We were in for a blizzard.

Next morning I decided to return to the main camp at Mawr-en-ik-yuak. I had no deerskin clothes, and the Huskies did not wish me to start, as the blizzard was in full force. However, we had got to face it, so I started. The going was good, the pace fast, and we arrived at the main camp early in the afternoon of November 1.

Some of the Huskies had built snow-houses during my absence, but most of these had collapsed, and tents had been erected again. Amer had built the walls only of his house, or "iglu," as I shall now call the snow-hut, deer-skin being used for the roof. The walls had bulged considerably, but still stood.

This is a common experience. The Huskies are naturally anxious to change from the tents into iglus, so these are built at the first opportunity, only to be demolished by the spell of mild weather which is almost certain to come before the winter cold settles down in earnest.

The weather being good and cold, Amer, who was my host, commenced the reconstruction of our iglu. The walls were strengthened, and it was then roofed in.

In the construction of an iglu the Husky shows much ingenuity. The bricks of snow are cut about 2½ feet in length, 1 to 2 feet in height, and 6 to 10 inches thick. Either long-bladed knives, similar to butchers' knives, or else snow-dags are used for this purpose. A dag (so called by whaling crews) is a flat, double-edged, and pointed piece of steel, about 8 inches in length and 3 inches wide. It is attached to a handle about 1½ feet in length.

The long-bladed knives are in favour with some. The snow-dags with others. Both are in great demand.

All the snow-bricks for the construction of the iglu are cut from the snow on the ground on which the iglu is to be built, or from what may be called the floor of the house. Two Huskies work together, one cutting the bricks of snow, the other placing them in position. The bricks are laid in an endless coil, which, as it increases in height, decreases in breadth. The walls are thus gradually drawn in towards each other, until finally only a small hole remains at the top in the centre of the roof. Into this a circular or square plug of snow is inserted, and the edifice is complete. The iglu is circular in shape, and the roof, when built by experts, forms a perfect dome. All the work is done from the inside, and when the iglu is finished the two workmen are still within.

They cut a hole, crawl to the outside, and then close up this hole with a snow-brick. Next, snow-bricks are cut for a distance of some 10 feet outwards from the snow-house, and are laid close against each other in two lines so as to form a passage, the bricks being piled higher on the windward side. Through the side of the iglu a square hole for a permanent doorway is then cut on a level with the floor of the passage. The two builders now re-enter and inspect the result of their labour. Some of the bricks are seen not to fit closely, light appears in the inter-stices. These are carefully gone over and plastered with loose snow. There still remain a considerable number of bricks in the interior, for the area of the floor has furnished more bricks than were required for building up the walls and roof. These spare bricks are now used to form benches, one on either side. On these snow benches the inmates sleep and sit. Only a narrow passage is left between them. While the Husky men complete the iglu, the women shovel snow against its sides and on the roof to ensure perfect freedom from draughts of cold air.

When the house is completed, inside and out, the women enter with the deerskin robes and the rest of their "stuff." Mats made of dwarf birch are laid on the snow benches on either side. The deerskins are laid on these, and the iglu is ready for occupation.

At Churchill I had been told a good deal about life in an iglu. The heat inside had been described as intense, a large hole in the roof had to be kept open day and night to prevent the house from melting away. The Huskies had been represented as panting with heat, tearing off their skin clothes, and calling loudly for long draughts of ice water. In many books about the Arctic Regions one reads about the filth, squalor, vermin, and stench with which life in an iglu is associated. I have lived for eight months with Huskies in their iglus, and have visited some hundreds of other iglus inhabited by the different parties we met, and it seems to me that the authors of such statements have been singularly unfortunate in their experiences. I have found no such condition of things.

I took the temperatures of different iglus all through the winter. For the first day of its occupation a newly-built iglu remains cold. When the thermometer outside registers any temperature from −20° to −50° Fahr., the temperature inside is only about 10° higher; sometimes not so much. Next day, however, when the iglu has settled somewhat, and more snow has been thrown on the roof, the temperature is brought to about 24° or 26° (*i.e.* 6° or 8° of frost), and here it remains, the temperature outside having little or no effect on that inside. To a person sitting still in a newly-erected iglu with the ther-mometer at 10° (or from 20° to 25° of frost), the temperature appears to be cool, rather too cool for perfect comfort, but not cold. When the thermometer registers 24° to 26° (or about 7° of frost) the temperature seems perfect, and any kind of work with the hands and fingers can be done. Deerskin clothes need not be, but usually are, worn. The temperature is quite right, and corresponds to our 60°.

If the temperature is raised higher than 27°, either by the presence of a crowd or the use of a seal-oil lamp, the difference is at once perceptible. When it rises to 28° (or 4° of frost) it is decidedly unpleasant, and should it rise to 30°, ventilation must be provided. This is easily done by shoving a pole through the roof, and the holes are filled up again when the temperature has fallen. If seal-oil lamps are in use, as they are everywhere along the coast, the temperature varies with the size of the lamp used. My remarks as to temperature apply only to iglus inland, where lamps are not in use.

As to the filthy condition of the iglus and their occu-pants, I have seen nothing of it. When seal-oil lamps are used, there is, of course, the smell of seal-oil. This is not more unpleasant than the smell of cod-liver oil. The principal objection to the use of seal-oil is that it makes everything greasy to a certain extent, and the smoke from the lamp blackens the sides and roof of the iglu, but I fail to perceive filth in this.

Of vermin on the persons or garments of the Huskies there is almost none. They do not wear underclothing at all corresponding with ours. Their deerskin garments are reversible, being put on sometimes with the hair next the skin, sometimes with the hair outside, and this reversing process in these latitudes leaves no hope for small parasites. The statement as to foul air and stench in the iglus are grossly exaggerated. There is no more smell in an ordinary iglu than in a public room in a large building. When a number of men, women, children, and babies crowd into one iglu, all clad in deerskin clothes, then the smell is one of overheated humanity plus deerskin.

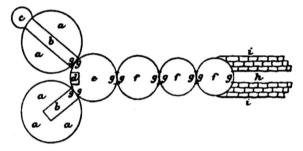

GROUND PLAN OF TWO ESKIMO SNOW-HOUSES AND CONNECTING KITCHEN AND OUTHOUSES.

a, raised benches of snow on which Huskies live and sleep; b, passages down middle; c, meat-safe or cellar; d, fireplace in kitchen—flat stones laid on raised snow-bench; e, kitchen; f, outhouses for storing stuff, shelter for the dogs, &c.; g, doorways, about 2½ feet high; h, passage to outside; i, walls of snow for protection from wind and drift.

When the iglu has been completed, it is customary to build a kitchen adjoining. This is only another small snow-house, a hole in the roof answering the purpose of a chimney. Flat stones are used for the fireplace. In permanent camps a line of very small snow-houses is very often built, connecting one with the other to the kitchen, and the kitchen connects with the main iglu, so that when you crawl through the doorway you find yourself in the kitchen, the exit from which is by another hole to the first out-house, and from that to the next, and so on. It is necessary to crawl on the hands and knees. The out-houses afford shelter for the dogs, and are also used to store such things as the dogs will not devour.

I often wondered that the Indians, Yellow Knives and Dog Ribs, who make two trips annually after musk-oxen on the "Barren Ground," have never learnt to build snow-houses. In the small tepee which they take they nearly freeze to death. The dogs tear holes in it, and at the end of the trip it affords little or no protection from the storms. They are without fire, for they have not yet discovered that the moss underneath the snow is quite dry and furnishes an excellent fuel. They carry no ice-chisel for making holes through the ice to procure water. When the small stock of wood which they carry comes to an end, they are without fire, and cannot even melt snow and ice for drink-ing-water. They have then to eat snow or suck ice the whole day long, in order temporarily to satisfy the un-assuageable thirst with which one is consumed when travelling fast in very cold weather. I had this experience when I accompanied them in 1896, and found it the worst feature of the whole journey.

It is possible to travel with perfect comfort the whole of the winter over any part of the barren Northland, if accompanied by Huskies.

CHAPTER VII

ESKIMO AMUSEMENTS—A HUNTING EXPEDITION

THE time was now approaching for a start to the musk-ox ground. On November 10 a council of war was held, and it was decided to start on the 13th. The party was to consist of four—Darrell and myself, Amer and Uttungerlah. One sleigh, 25 feet in length, was to be taken.

The sleighs used by the Huskies are usually long and narrow, 36 feet being no unusual length. The runners are shod with hard wood, or whalebone (the ribs), or mud. This last is by far the best. It slides over the crushed snow in intensely cold weather more smoothly than anything else. It is easily knocked off, however, if it happens to come in contact with rocks, and cannot be used in the spring and early summer when the weather gets mild. Metal in any form under the runners is quite useless in cold weather.

The mudding of the runners of a sleigh entails considerable trouble. The mud or peat bog has to be dug out of the frozen ground, brought to the iglu, and thawed out.

It is mixed with sufficient water to bring it to a stiff paste, and then plastered on the runners to a thickness of about two inches. It takes but a short time to freeze it hard as rock. It is then planed quite smooth, and water is poured on it, which forms a thin sheet of ice on the bottom. It is not the frozen mud which slides so easily over the crushed snow, but this thin layer of ice. On a journey the ice layer is renewed every morning.

We had glorious weather at this time. The skies were

clear, and there was little or no wind. The days were pleasant and the nights cold. We lived in our iglu in perfect comfort.

The Huskies informed me one evening that an important "antikūt," or conjuring performance, was to take place that night, and the presence of the white men was requested. The summons came about nine o'clock, and we were conducted to one of the larger iglus, in which were assembled all the Baker Lake Huskies then living at Mawr-en-ik-yuak. The atmosphere in the interior was somewhat thick. After a couple of songs, with the usual drum accompaniment, and the shrill "hah-yah-yah's" of the chorus sung by the women, a move was made, and several Huskies went outside. Then there was a short delay, and I was requested to go outside and listen. The night was clear and the stars bright; everything was still, no sound could be heard. The arrangements were evidently not complete; there was a hitch somewhere, so back we returned to the iglu. After a short interval I was requested to crawl out of the door a second time. I listened intently. A single shot broke the stillness of the night, and I was hustled back into the iglu to wait events.

Presently a line was pushed through the doorway, and was immediately laid hold of by some half-dozen Huskies, who commenced pulling vigorously. Then the stiff body of a Husky, dragged by the neck, was brought into view. A long knife was produced, and handled so as to suggest that it was plunged to the hilt several times in the man's body; but the performance was so clumsy that a child could see that the blade was buried each time in the snow beneath the man's body. After a great many groans and simulated efforts to rise, the man appeared to come to life again, and, walking slowly round, shook hands with every one.

The explanation of all this was that the man, being under a spell, was invulnerable. He had been shot by

F

the rifle of which I had heard the report when I was sum-
moned outside; he had been stabbed after being hauled
into the iglu; nothing could harm him. We were not
sorry when the performance was over.

November 12 was spent in getting everything ready for
a start next day. Winter clothes were tried on and altered
where necessary; a good supply of extra foot-gear was
packed up; and our blankets, with a young deerskin robe
sewn on the inside, were made into sleeping-bags, sewn
up half-way only.

The ordinary winter dress of the Husky is an inner
deerskin coat (u-u-pak), worn hair inside, and a thicker
deerskin coat (kūl-ik-tak) over this, with the hair outside.
His nether garments are a pair of loose, short pants, open
below the knee, worn with the hair inside, and an outer
pair with the hair outside. These garments, however, as
has been already stated, are often reversed. On the feet
are young deerskin socks, hair inside, and, over these, long
leggings with feet attached, also of young deerskin, with
hair worn outside. Moccasins, or short deerskin shoes, are
pulled over the feet. Mits, made of deerskin from the legs,
protect the hands.

A butcher's knife suspended round the neck hangs
down inside the u-u-pak. A small telescope, a rifle, a
small bag (for ammunition, pipe, tobacco, and matches)
slung over the shoulder, and the long snow-knife, without which the Husky never travels, complete the outfit.
Head-gear the Huskies do not wear, but both the inner
and outer deerskin coats are provided with hoods, which
are pulled up in bad weather.

The Husky mits and footgear cannot be excelled.
White men who go north would do well to copy them.

On November 13 we set out, but as the interest of this
expedition did not lie in successful hunting, I shall now
pass rapidly over the ground.

We went up Baker Lake for a short distance, and then
struck in a north-westerly direction. It was the intention

of the Huskies to hunt the country between Baker Lake and Pelly Lake on Back's River. No white man had ever been over this country. Following up a small river which flows into Baker Lake, we made our first camp on a small lake. "Rugged" is the word which best describes this kind of country. The rock was of the granitic formation, with which every one who has travelled much in the Northland of Canada is familiar. In travelling there in winter, when snow is on the ground, the geological formation can always be studied. Nearly every exposure of rock is drifted clear of snow.

Our two Huskies, Amer and Uttungerlah, proved themselves experts in the quick construction of an iglu. It used to take them about an hour to build our temporary shelters. Darrell used to shovel snow on the top, and my job was to cut a water-hole through the ice with the icechisel.

We delayed next morning to fish through the ice in the small lake on which we had camped. We caught two salmon and several large trout.

The weather continued perfect, clear and cold. Deer were plentiful, and appeared in small scattered bands. The required amount of meat for ourselves and the dogs was generally procured without much trouble as we travelled along. We made a few caches of meat to be ready in the event of our returning the same way.

About noon on November 21 we struck a large lake, and, after travelling on it for seven miles, we camped.

This was Ti-her-yuak-lūg-yuak Lake. It is twenty-eight miles in length, and lies about north-north-west and south-south-east. Like all other lakes in these parts, it is irregular in shape.

The water from it flows east, and unites with the Quoich River, which discharges into the head of Chesterfield Inlet.

The going on the lake was splendid, and we made over five miles an hour. But we did not travel every day, for deer at times were scarce, and we had to halt for hunting. On these occasions the Huskies would start off long before daylight without any breakfast. They would take nothing with them in the shape of food, trusting to procure that with their rifles. Snow-knives, of course, were not forgotten. When unsuccessful, one or both of them would remain out the whole night and continue the hunt the following morning, and if still unsuccessful, would not return till the middle of the night. "Nawk," uttered in a lugubrious voice as they crawled into the iglu, announced that no deer had been killed. They would go without food of any kind for forty or forty-eight hours, and think nothing of it.

When they went long distances to hunt I followed the chase in the vicinity of the camp, where Darrell remained to look after our stuff, and see that the dogs did not destroy things.

Every evening when we camped, as soon as the iglu was completed, the Huskies cut large slabs or bricks of snow, and arranged them in two piles four or five feet high. On these supports the sleigh was placed, and our surplus "stuff" deposited on the top. It was fairly safe there from the curiosity of the dogs, which as a rule did not give trouble by eating skin lines, harness, &c., but could not quite be trusted.

Deer appeared to be more plentiful towards the head of Ti-her-yuak-lūg-yuak, but the country was very open and flat, and close approaches to them could not be made. I kept the party supplied with meat by long-range shooting with the Mannlicher carbines. To be of use here rifles should be sighted, and shoot accurately, up to 800 yards. Not many deer are killed at this extreme range, but a large number have to be shot at distances of from 300 to 500 yards. At such distances deer were beyond the range of the Winchesters 44 to 40, or 38 Remingtons carried by the Huskies, but I was able to do good execution with my Mannlicher. Shooting at ranges of 700 to 800 yards is only practised should the party be starving and the deer unapproachable.

Occasionally, in fact very often, deer in the Northland behave like mad animals. Sometimes when travelling on large lakes, and on very open flat country, where an attempt to stalk an animal would be waste of time, a band of deer will approach as soon as they see the dogs and sleigh. They will come right up within easy range, and even after several have been killed, the others will continue to run round and round the sleigh, and keep the party company the whole afternoon. Very often it is wiser to continue travelling, on the off-chance of deer behaving in this manner, rather than to go after them and attempt an approach on hopelessly open ground.

On the "Barren Ground" the charge of cruelty cannot be brought against the practice of long-range shooting. A wounded beast need never be lost, for he will at once leave the rest, and, after going a very short distance, will lie down. An approach can then be made and the animal despatched, or, if that is not possible, a couple of dogs can be loosed, and they will soon account for a deer with a broken hind leg. Should the foreleg only be injured the dogs will have a chase, but they will get him.

The nights were cold about this time, $-32°$, $-38°$, and $-40°$ were registered as minima.

On November 23 I remained in camp. The temperature in the iglu did not rise above 8° all day.

On November 24 we crossed a divide and arrived at another largish lake, Ti-her-yuak-rar-yu. We had now left the waters of Lake Ti-her-yuak-lūg-yuak, which flow east into the Quoich River.

We saw a few ptarmigan as we travelled along. Only a very few of these birds remain through the winter on the "Barren Ground." They nearly all migrate south to the woods at the first approach of the very cold weather.

Wolves and their tracks became more numerous, a certain sign that we were on or near musk-ox ground.

Though unable to kill the full-grown animals, they are always on the look-out for small stray ones.

In the evening when we camped the Huskies warned us not to make any noise. They would not even permit the beating of the deerskins. Snow and ice accumulate on the deerskins, which are used as mattresses in the iglu, and they are beaten at night with a short stick carried for this purpose.

November 25 was spent in scouting the country ahead, for we did not wish to run unexpectedly on musk-oxen. However, all was clear before us, and next day we continued our journey north-north-west.

On November 27 the wind, which had been west-north-west for many days, changed to the south-east. The weather became quite mild, and snow commenced to fall. It was no sort of day on which to look for musk-oxen or their signs, for one could not see any distance through the snow-storm. However, the Huskies said they would just go a short distance and then return. Darrell and I remained in camp, and were busy fixing one of the rifles, when the snow door was burst in, and Amer's head and shoulders appeared. Sweat was pouring down his face and neck. He had evidently returned in great haste. "Quick, quick, the dogs," he said; adding, " I am afraid the musk-oxen have already smelt the iglu."

We were out and away in a moment, each leading two dogs. A run of about three miles without snow-shoes, over broken and rocky ground, brought us, badly winded and bathed in perspiration, to the spot where Uttungerlah awaited us.

The musk-oxen (eight of them) had gone, of course. They had not got wind of the snow-house, but they had smelt and seen the wretched Huskies, who had deliberately hunted down wind. This might have been excusable in flat and open country on a clear day, but it was a mad act of folly to commit when the weather was thick and the ground much broken.

The Huskies stood solemnly staring at the tracks and dung, all that now remained of the small band of musk-oxen. I returned to camp at once, and they followed at a short distance very shamefaced.

Musk-oxen when disturbed leave for another part of the country. It is hopeless to follow them.

That evening I remarked: "The next time we hunt musk-oxen we will go up, not down, wind;" and the subject was not again referred to, for I knew the Huskies were feeling very sore about it. Thermometer, −35° at night.

We were now but a short distance from Pelly Lake on Back's River, which could be seen from a highish hill to the north of the camp. There is a large exposure of white or grey quartzite at this spot, very similar to that found on Marble Island. Fragmentary rocks were granitic. The quartzite, I believe, is classified as Huronian.

November 28 and 29 were spent in cruising the country far and wide in quest of musk-ox tracks, but none were seen. The weather was glorious, clear blue skies and cold. It was a pleasure to be out and travelling. Sometimes one would walk the whole day without seeing a living thing, or hearing a sound of any kind.

This silence was very impressive, but I never found it in the least degree oppressive. In the climate of the north the feelings never become depressed. This is the only reason that I have been able to find to account for the wonderful spirits, the happy and cheerful dispositions of the Huskies.

On November 30 a council of war was held in the early morning. The Huskies were anxious to return to Mawren-ik-yuak, fearing that their wives and families might be running short of meat.

Uttungerlah proposed that Amer, Darrell, and myself should return with the dogs, and that he should take a small hand-sleigh and prosecute the hunt after musk-oxen.

He said that he would not return without my "bones." I was anxious to secure a complete skeleton of a musk-ox, but I did not wish him to go off alone on a hunt and haul the bones the whole way back to Mawr-en-ik-yuak. He would have had a terribly tough time of it; so this was rejected, and I proposed that one more day should be devoted to looking for tracks, and if we failed to find any, we should then bear up for home. This was finally carried. Next day, December 1, we were unsuccessful, so it was decided to set out for the main camp at the foot of Baker Lake on the day following.

Uttungerlah, who had been the guide of the party, was now out of his country. Since leaving Ti-her-yuak-lūg-yuak Lake we had travelled over unknown ground. He proposed to travel about south-east and strike the east end of Ti-her-yuak-lūg-yuak Lake, where we would find the outlet forming the head of the river, which would bring us to the Quoich River.

On December 2 the return journey commenced. It was impossible to hold a very straight course, as the country was very rugged, but by following dips, hollows, and small lakes we were able to avoid most of the rocky ridges. The dogs were starving, for we had failed to get near any of the few deer seen.

We struck the big Lake Ti-her-yuak-lūg-yuak at 3 in the afternoon of December 4, and camped shortly afterwards. Our hours of daylight were very short. The sun rose at 10, and set at 2.30.

Travelling across the east end of the lake we sighted the vapour rising from the open water at the outlet. The river takes a bend, so we kept on a straight course, intending to strike it further down.

We were in a bad way for meat now. We had none left, and the dogs had starved three nights already. Deer had been seen almost every day, but, in the calm weather, owing to the crusted condition of the snow, it was useless to attempt to approach them. In hunting, the man ahead having sighted deer, at once signals to the others by raising his arms. I have invariably found that deer are more easily frightened by the sound than the sight of a strange object, and we were hoping for a high wind. On December 7 it was blowing and drifting. No deer were seen until the afternoon, when one of the Huskies killed a female and calf. This was a godsend for the wretched dogs, which had not been fed for five days, and we camped at once. The Huskies appeared to think nothing of the dogs having wanted food so long. They said that they might be unfed for ten days and still be able to haul, and that they would not die of starvation for a long time.

The river from Ti-her-yuak-lūg-yuak, on which we were travelling, varied in breadth from forty to sixty yards in some places to between a quarter and half-a-mile at others. It appeared to be navigable for canoes, but one cannot judge of a river in the winter time.

On December 8 the thermometer dropped to $-40°$. Two wolves came close to camp, but were off before the rifles could be got out.

It had often been a puzzle to me to account for the number of wolves which died of starvation during the winter, in a country where deer were so plentiful. I questioned the Huskies about this, and they replied that wolves had great difficulty in running down a deer. The safety of the deer, no doubt, lies in their number. If one is singled out and pursued, it does not go far before it joins another band, and the wolf, or pack of wolves, change their quarry a great many times. The deer seem to possess considerable staying power, as well as speed, and when once a wolf becomes weak his career is at an end.

December 11 broke calm and cold. The minimum thermometer registered $-48°$; in the afternoon, when we camped, the mercury in the maximum thermometer still remained a solid ball in the bulb.

As long as there is no wind it is delightful to travel when the temperature is low. It is possible to travel fast without getting sweated, and when going slowly one does not get cold. When the wind begins to stir the change is at once noticeable.

The Ti-her-yuak-lūg-yuak River, on which we were travelling, was very crooked, and we must have gone fifteen miles to make seven in a straight line. On December 13 we reached the spot where it joined the Quoich in its southerly course. The Quoich River appeared to be very much the smaller of the two, this being evidently one of its main tributaries.

The following day we went east-south-east for eight miles down the Quoich River, and then struck due south overland, on a direct course for Mawr-en-ik-yuak.

The weather continued cold. The maximum readings gave $-33°$ and $-35°$; the minimum $-38°$ and $-42°$.

The country, after we left the Quoich River, became flat and prairie-like, with small scattered lakes. A few deer were killed, for we wished to take along a supply of meat in case the Huskies at the main camp had run short.

The country remained flat and open, and the going was excellent until within a few miles of the shores of Baker Lake. It then became very rough and broken, almost mountainous, but the mountains were not high. We were obliged to pick and choose our way between the rocky ridges as best we could. Being compelled to leave our direct course, we struck Baker Lake too far west on December 16 at two in the afternoon.

The going on Baker Lake was splendid, and as the Huskies said we should be able to reach the main camp that day we continued travelling. It was after six o'clock in the evening when the steam from the open water at the outlet loomed up like a column of smoke through the semi-darkness. It can never be called dark in the north, even in the dead of winter.

Shortly afterwards the lights from the iglus blinked through the mist, the dogs set up their customary howl, and men, women, and children rushed out to welcome us. Thus ended the musk-ox hunt. Though unsuccessful in killing musk-oxen, we had enlivened the long winter by a pleasant expedition, and had kept ourselves in perfect condition.

We found the Huskies at Mawr-en-ik-yuak hard put to it for meat as usual. Deer had been killed and promptly eaten. No stock or store had been laid up. Nevertheless, of all the stuff which I had left in Amer's iglu, including biscuit, sugar, pork, and tobacco, nothing had been touched. Even two hind-quarters of meat, which I had told Amer's wife to eat if supplies ran short, had not been touched, although she had starved. She said that she had been afraid that if the white men failed to kill deer, they would be hungry when they arrived.

CHAPTER VIII

WINTER JOURNEYS BETWEEN BAKER LAKE AND DEPOT ISLAND

THE next day, a day of rest, was spent in talking about the musk-ox hunt, and in much smoking.

I had now been both with Indians and with Huskies on a musk-ox hunt, and could compare notes. I had been successful with the former and unsuccessful with the latter, but that was the chance of war. With the Huskies we did not have a repetition of the hardships I had endured among the Indians. There was no suffering from thirst, from cold, or from sleeping cramped up under a heap of fighting dogs. With the Huskies we travelled with ease and slept in our iglus with perfect comfort. We did not suffer from hunger, and we were free from the annoyance of swarms of lice.

I intended to return to Depot Island, and spend a few weeks in preparing to set out in the early part of February for the Arctic Coast.

Four Huskies had already left Mawr-en-ik-yuak for the vessel, and as none of the others knew the way we were left without a guide. However, we hoped to be able to follow their sleigh tracks, for, on the packed and crusted snow, tracks do not become obliterated for a long time. In journeying over the Northland in the winter the services of a guide are not strictly necessary, but a man who is well acquainted with the country can be helpful to the traveller. He can take him along streams and small lakes so as to avoid the stony and rocky ground, which knocks the mud off the sleigh-runners, and causes much delay.

I decided to take Amer and Uttungerlah to the *Francis*

Allyn. The latter's son, Ilartnark, was told off to follow later with a sleigh, and as many dogs as he could rustle up.

Both Amer and Uttungerlah had agreed to accompany me to the end of my long journey, or until I did not require their services any longer, but, as they had not the faintest idea where I was going, some explanation was necessary. They had easily learnt to read a chart. They could always point out our position and the different places in their own part of the country, which were laid down.

I now laid out the chart and showed the proposed line of travel. I indicated Cape Barrow on the west side of Bathurst Inlet as the spot from which they could return. At the same time I gave them some sort of an idea of the distance, and a fairly correct estimate of the time it would take. I pointed out that we could either follow the route on which we had travelled out to the musk-ox ground, and so strike Pelly Lake on Back's River, or could go up Baker, Schultz, and Aberdeen Lakes, and then strike north from Ti-bi-elik Lake. I did not know if we would find deer in sufficient numbers along the latter route, and I wished them to give me information on this head. According to this information I would decide as to the route. For the success of every long journey over the Northland, either in winter or summer, depends on the presence of deer in sufficient numbers along the route. Uttungerlah had already spent a winter on Ti-bi-elik Lake, and he said that in that neighbourhood there were fair numbers of deer, but none further west. He had heard that bull caribou remained all winter along Back's River. I knew that in March and April, when we should be travelling north, deer also would be going north, so I anticipated no scarcity, and decided to go up the lakes and strike north from Ti-bi-elik Lake.

I had strongly objected to the women and children accompanying the party, for the journey would be long, the weather cold, and there would probably be times of scarcity, but on this point the Huskies remained obdurate, replying that they could not accompany me without their families, who would starve during their absence. But they promised to leave the women and children at Pelly Lake, under the care of Ilartnark, and with this arrangement I had to be content.

I settled some details as to dogs, sleighs, and outfit, and arranged everything for an early start. There were many risks to be considered, one of them being that of an early spring. There is never much snow on the "Barren Ground," and a few warm days suffice to lay the country bare. If spring overtook us far inland on rough ground, we should have an almost impossible march over bare ground to the Arctic Coast. I therefore decided to begin that long journey not later than February 15.

Before setting out for the whaler we had to put the two canoes in cache to be ready for our return.

We carried them to an open sandy spot, which had drifted clear of snow, placed them bottom upwards, and laid beneath them the surplus stuff which was to be left behind. Loose, dry sand was then piled on them and round the gunwales, and on this were thrown buckets of water, so that the canoes were frozen firmly to the ground, and the stuff was safe from the depredations of wolverines, the greatest robbers of the north.

The weather continued perfect, cloudless skies and gentle breezes. Minimum readings for December 23, 24, and 25 were $-39°$, $-41°$, and $-40°$, with maxima of $-36°$, $-37°$, and $-35°$. The cold was not felt, for there was little or no wind.

On December 26 we set out for the *Francis Allyn* along the southern outlet from Baker Lake, and we camped for the night at the head of Chesterfield Inlet.

The next day was quite mild. The dogs kept up a smart trot, and running proved hot work. Darrell and I first stripped off our deerskin coats, then our coats, and then mits and headgear were discarded. Bare-headed and bare-handed, and with coats off, we jogged along behind the sleigh.   In the afternoon Amer shot a large bull, which had already dropped his horns.   We then left the Inlet and struck north-east overland.   The distance from the head of Chesterfield Inlet overland, in a direct line to Depot Island, is about 140 miles, but it is not possible to travel straight owing to the nature of the country.   We eventually covered more than 180 miles before reaching the vessel, but we went a great deal too far north.   As we travelled, typical rugged country changed to undulating and flat prairie-like stretches.   In places small lakes and streams were so numerous as to remind us of the Irishman's remark "that all the land is water."   Deer were numerous till within sixty miles of the coast; there were none beyond.   Very often they behaved in the foolish manner already described, and we could have shot them down by the dozen.   At other times they appeared to be wary, and were difficult to approach.   All the large bulls had by this time dropped their horns.   We met with a few wolves, and occasionally shot one; we killed also a white fox, but foxes appeared to be scarce.

On January 5 we reached a moderate-sized lake called Ti-hĭt-yuak.   The river from this lake flows into Chesterfield Inlet near Lake Harbour.   Both river and lake were resorted to by the Huskies in days gone by.   Leaving Ti-hĭt-yuak Lake we crossed a small divide, and struck a river which flowed east.   Here we found the sleigh tracks of the Huskies who had left Mawr-en-ik-yuak some days before us.   We continued to follow this river, which was taking us direct to the coast, the land becoming lower, and the small lakes very numerous.

We sighted the vessel soon after starting on the morning of January 10, 1902, and about two o'clock in the afternoon we drove up at a smart trot.   Dogs, which have hardly been able to keep up a slow walk, on approaching a vessel or a camp forget all about the heavy load and put on their best trot.   We had spent sixteen days in travelling 180 miles, an average of under twelve miles a day, and this may be taken as an ordinary rate. Huskies do not travel fast; they take numerous and long "spells" for smoking; they have often to spend a day or more in hunting, and sometimes are delayed by having to renew the mud on the runners of the sleigh.

We found the crew of the whaler in good health and free from scurvy; but an English lad had died from a night's exposure. He and a companion had been caught by a blizzard at some distance from the ship, and being unable to find the way back he had at once given in, while the other had kept his courage up. The companion had carried him as far as he could, and, when obliged to leave him, had continued walking about till found by a search-party in the morning. The English lad was found alive, but too far gone for recovery, and he died on board ship. His companion was none the worse for his night's experience.

The crew were out of fresh meat, though deer were plentiful only sixty miles from the vessel.

Several iglus had been built close by; in these lived the Huskies who formed the crews of one of the whale-boats. It speaks well for their smartness and daring that they are trusted for this work.

When the whaling schooners bear up for home, it is customary to leave one or more of the whale-boats, together with the whaling-gear, such as darting-guns, harpoons, and lances, in charge of the natives, who prosecute the whaling until the same vessel, or another belonging to the same owners, returns.

Life on board ship, though somewhat slow, passed pleasantly enough. Every day, weather permitting, I used to accompany the Huskies to the "flaw" to shoot seals. The "flaw" is the place where the open water commences. For a certain distance out from the shore the ice remains solid all winter, being kept in its place by the rocks and shallows. Beyond this is the open water or "flaw." When the wind, however, is from the east or south-east, large pieces of ice are brought in from the bay, and, if the weather is calm and cold, these become frozen to the shore ice, so as to form one compact sheet. There is then no open water for several miles.

We used to drive to the "flaw" with dogs and sleigh, hauling a small skiff.

We took up our position along the edge, and waited for seals to put up their heads. When one was shot, the skiff was instantly launched, and the seal brought on the ice. Clad in deerskins as we were, this was not the cold opera-tion that might be imagined. If the wind was not excessive we could remain for hours at this watching game, but it was very monotonous and not very productive.

Eider-duck and one or two species of small divers were numerous, and some of the forecastle lads occasionally did fair execution among them with the scatter-gun. The captain was always willing to lend either rifles or guns to any of the crew. In this he was wise, for it induced them to remain out for air and exercise.

When the main body of ice from the bay was penned in against the shore ice, the "flaw" was miles away and too far to reach.

The Huskies used then to search along the ice for the blow-holes of seals and ūgyūk (the large seal). When a blow-hole was found, the native would take up his position over it, and there await with poised harpoon the advent of the seal. In this they showed the greatest patience, and would remain for hours on the watch. A fair number of ūgyūk were killed in this manner.

When an ūgyūk is harpooned several men unite in hauling it on the ice. All the Huskies who are out on the ice then gather round, and each touches the animal on the nose, implying that he has-been in at the death. He may have been a spectator only; but he is supposed to have assisted, and comes in for his share or strip of the skin. Walrus were sometimes hunted, but they were only to be found far out on the floe-ice. I only saw one at

G

the "flaw." An eider-duck had been shot, and had fallen into the water about thirty yards from the spot where I stood. A walrus instantly appeared, and tried for several minutes to get its tusks over the duck, and so take it down. Whether this was in play, or whether it intended to eat the duck, I cannot say. A Husky eventually got a rifle, and shot but did not kill the animal.

A few tracks of polar bear were seen occasionally, and one day, when we were on our way to the "flaw," a large bear was sighted. He was making his way across the ice at a great pace. The dogs were instantly loosed, and we all gave chase; but the bear was too smart, and gained the open water before the dogs came up.

The weather remained cold, but the skies were cloudless, and we had sunshine every day. Although the days were short, we were blessed with a larger number of hours of sunshine during the month of January than I have ever seen in January in England.

We lived in comfort on board. The deck-house, which was provided with a stove, was comfortable both day and night, and I used to sleep there in my sleeping-bag. The fare was good enough, but I missed the fresh deer-meat to which I had been accustomed. The captain said it was useless to send his Huskies out for deer, for they invariably returned empty-handed, having fired away all their ammunition and eaten all the deer they killed. I therefore determined to send Amer and Uttungerlah. The captain furnished a bag of biscuits and a can of molasses, and on January 19 they made a start for Ti-hīt-yuak Lake, the nearest point to the coast, where we knew that deer were in fair numbers. Two of the captain's Huskies decided at the last moment to accompany them.

The deck-house over the quarter-deck was used as a general workshop, and on days when the weather was bad, and all hands were obliged to remain on board, it presented a busy appearance. Harpoons and lances were ground and sharpened; darting-guns were fixed; in fact, all the whaling gear was overhauled and got ready for the spring, or early summer, whaling, which is carried on in the whale-boats for the first two months, or until such time as the vessel gets free from the ice. Some of the forecastle lads found occupation in making models of ships or small ornaments out of walrus tusks or whales' teeth.

Literature was scarce on board, for the usual supply provided by the owners had been forgotten.

However, there was endless entertainment in listening to the tales of adventures encountered in pursuit of the monsters of the deep, related by the captain and his officers. We had whales at breakfast, lunch, and supper, and all the hours between. If the subject of "whaling it" commenced, it continued the whole day. The captain would get fast to a whale long before breakfast, and would not kill it until that meal was finished. Then the mate would start in with a sperm and fighting whale, which, after killing all the men and smashing all the boats, was at length despatched, and ultimately gave the record number of barrels of oil. Now it was the second mate's turn. One could see that he had been holding himself in readiness. His experience had been with a bow-head which, after getting itself and the boats hopelessly tangled up in icebergs, was finally slain by the intrepidity of one of the men, who died shortly afterwards, as the wonderful men usually did. The third mate, who had been with difficulty restrained from breaking in with his experience, now got a show, but he had hardly got his boat clear of the vessel when some one else was fast to another whale, which yielded the record amount of bone. And so it continued, yarn after yarn, the stock of whales being inexhaustible.

January 25 was our coldest day on board (or, in fact, the whole winter), a minimum of $-57°$ and maximum of $-37°$ being recorded. It was blizzarding at the time, and the weather not fit for travelling. Amer and Uttungerlah told me about this day on their return from the deer-hunt. In the morning they had managed to kill deer close to their iglu, but were obliged to remain inside the rest of the day. With the exception of a few days such as this, travelling in the Northland can be kept up the whole winter through, and with perfect comfort, if Huskies are included in the party.

The deer-hunters returned on January 27 with a welcome supply of fresh meat. Uttungerlah had accounted for five deer, Amer for three, and the two Huskies from the ship had slain one apiece.

I was getting a few things made by the Husky women, such as sealskin boots, deerskin moccasins, &c. Some of the women had their iglus close to the vessel on the ice; others on the main shore. According to their tradition it is not lawful to sew and cut sealskin on land, or to perform any work on deerskins on the ice. If this un-written law be transgressed, a failure of the deer or seal hunt will inevitably be the result. This custom proved a great nuisance sometimes when we were travelling. The Huskies near the vessel overcame the difficulty by keeping some of the women on the shore busy on deerskins all winter, while others had iglus on the ice and worked on sealskins. In this manner the law was observed.

On February 2, Amer and Uttungerlah, who had gone to the "flaw" in the morning, did not return, and I felt considerable anxiety about them. The main body of ice from the bay was right in, and the "flaw" was con-sequently a long way off. The ice was hummocky, the wind rose, and the snow drifted so that the men could not see to travel. They, however, made an iglu in which they spent the night, and next day they returned in safety. At such times, however, accidents may happen. While the men are a long distance out on the ice the wind may change and blow strong off shore. The main body of ice then breaks off, and is carried out to sea with the un-fortunate men on it who have not had time to return.

Some years ago this happened. A party of Huskies, with their dogs and sleighs, and two whale-boats which had been hauled down fully equipped ready for the spring whaling, were all swept out to sea. They were given up for lost, and their wives went nearly frantic. Several days afterwards a weary and forlorn-looking Husky made his way on board. He spoke a little English. "My God, captain," he broke out, "both whale-boats and all the gear gone." The captain naturally was delighted to see a survivor, and replied: "Never mind the whale-boats; where are the others?" But this poor fellow could only think about the boats. "Huskies all right coming; but the whale-boats and all the gear—my God, captain—all gone; not our fault." The rest of the party dropped in one by one. They had been carried out on the ice, and drifted about for several days. They had built snow or ice-houses, and lived on their dogs. On the wind changing, the main body of drift ice was penned in against the shore ice, and they were enabled to reach land. This was near Marble Island, and they had walked for five days without eating and without resting.

February 7 was a red-letter day, two large ūgyūk and three seals having been harpooned at their blow-holes. One of the ūgyūks was an enormous beast, almost as large as a walrus. Within it I found a large quantity of small smelts, besides prawns, shrimps, and a few small crabs. There must be splendid food in this bay, for all the seals and eider-duck (which are bottom feeders) are wonderfully fat.

The weather got slightly warmer about this time. The minimum and maximum readings taken for the days and nights gave a mean of -30.5 for the month of January.

There was already a marked difference in the hours of daylight, especially noticeable in the morning.

On February 14, a positive reading of two degrees was registered as a maximum. One felt inclined to rejoice that the backbone of the winter was broken at last, but

I knew the cold weather is never over until the geese arrive. When one is properly clad, and living in an iglu, he can afford to laugh at the cold; but, when travelling with dogs and sleighs, it is otherwise.

The snow then becomes so powdery that it acts like sand on the runners, and makes hauling terribly heavy. I generally found the hauling heavy for the dogs when the thermometer stood below ten degrees.

Uttungerlah's son, Ilartnark, had arrived with a sleigh, a wife, and four dogs. I was now informed that, in addition to Amer's wife and Pitzeolah, and Uttungerlah's two wives and family, I had to receive Ilartnark's two wives into my party. My Husky family was increasing by leaps and bounds. However, all the women and children, with Ilartnark in charge, were to be left at Back's River. They could fish and hunt during the summer, and the others would pick them up on their return. This was their own arrangement. They had evidently discussed the matter among themselves.

The party was now in number sixteen human beings; it included one of Uttungerlah's wives, who had a baby at the breast. "It" was to come along to help explore part of the bleak Northland.

CHAPTER IX

A TRAVELLING CAMP FROM BAKER LAKE TO BACK'S RIVER

ON Sunday, February 16, 1902, we bade farewell to the captain and crew of the *Francis Allyn*, and were soon under way for the shore. The ice was smooth and the pace fair, considering the loads that were piled high on the two sleighs.

I had managed to secure a few more dogs at the last moment, bringing the number up to eighteen, nine to each sleigh. We took along about 400 lbs. hard tack, 160 lbs. sugar, 40 lbs. coffee, 150 lbs. fat pork, 25 lbs. gunpowder, 60 lbs. lead, about 80 lbs. plug tobacco, 3 cans (15 gallons) kerosene oil for the "primus" stove, and a general assortment of trade articles for the Eskimo, whom we expected to meet along the Arctic Coast. This list of supplies seems a fairly large one, but we would be a large party before finally leaving Ti-bi-elik Lake, which was to be our starting-point for the north.

At this time our company consisted of Amer-or-yuak and his wife Nanou, Ilartnark and his two young wives, and Uttungerlah, besides Darrell, Sandy, and myself.

Uttungerlah's two wives and families we were to pick up at the head of Chesterfield Inlet. Pitzeolah, Amer's adopted son, we would pick up at Iglor-yu-ŭllig, where he had been sent to fish, and if possible to lay down a cache of fish for our dogs. He had been supplied with nets for this purpose.

We could not have had a more favourable day for a start. The weather was bright, clear, and frosty, with a gentle north-west breeze. The going over the land was good, for the snow was packed hard. The dogs went a good three and a half miles an hour.

We followed nearly the route by which we had come to the ship, and made fifteen miles by camp time. I was particularly anxious to reach Ti-hĭt-yuak Lake in order to kill deer for the dogs. The only food supply we had for our dogs was a sealskinful of oil and blubber. Eskimo dogs will not eat biscuit unless they have been trained to do so.

The next morning, after travelling for an hour, we struck Armit-or-yuak Lake. On this lake we travelled west about eleven miles. It is long, narrow, and irregularly shaped, with arms, bays, and inlets running in every direction. In the evening we came on a few fresh deer-tracks, a welcome and unexpected sight, apparently showing that some of the deer were already working their way towards the coast, and there was a chance of our falling in with a band at any moment. We made twenty miles by account before we camped.

The next day, in beautiful weather, we knocked off another twenty miles, and camped within two miles of Ti-hĭt-yuak Lake, which we reached next morning.

On February 19 we had to face a strong north-west wind, and our faces suffered severely. The minimum thermometer in the night had registered $-42°$, and the maximum during the day was $-30°$.

It is always cold travelling against any wind, however light, when the thermometer stands at or below $-20°$. I did not happen to be wearing deerskin pants, and my legs became almost benumbed by the cold. Deerskins are the only clothes that afford protection against the Arctic cold. Woollen garments, no matter how thick they may be, are not suitable. As everybody knows, it is the layer of air within one's garments that keeps the warmth necessary for comfort. Skin clothes retain this layer of warm air better than anything else, and on that account form the most suitable clothing.

Many people who ought to know better think that the Huskies do not suffer from cold. The only foundation for this supposition lies in the fact that the sufferers do not complain. Strong men and women are alike susceptible to frost, and their hands, feet, cheeks, neck, nose, and ears get frozen if not properly protected. On the other hand, they do not render themselves unnaturally sensitive to cold by indulging in fireside comforts, for they show no desire for a fire.

The following day, February 20, we did not travel, as the sleighs required fresh mud on the runners. Amer went to hunt deer, but failed to sight any. He met a Husky, however, who was on his way from the head of Chesterfield Inlet, and reported plenty of deer within two days' journey. I was surprised to find no deer where they had been numerous just six weeks before. But the deer of the Northland of Canada are for ever on the move, and about their habits, distribution, and migration it is very difficult to speak with certainty. I shall have something to say on this head later.

On February 21, in going thirteen miles, we saw deer in four different places, and were able to give a square meal to the dogs, the first they had got since leaving the vessel.

The weather continued cold at this time, the maximum reading during the day being always about −30°, and we always had the prevailing west wind more or less in our faces. Next day was spent in hunting, but only one animal was killed, and that a small one. On February 23, at the usual hour, 8 A.M., we were once more moving slowly westwards. After travelling seven miles, which took us three hours, we struck a largish lake called Pung-ak-hi-or-wik, which means "The place where many large bull caribou were seen," "pung-ak" being the Husky name for a full-grown bull. We were now to the south of the route by which we had travelled to the ship. Next day the minimum thermometer registered −42°, and the maximum

—35°, and with a strong north-west wind the snow was drifting thick. This was one of the few days on which it was too cold to travel against the wind.

Uttungerlah went out to hunt, and shot three deer. All the tracks pointed to the west, so I was wrong when I wrote on February 17 that the deer appeared to be working their way back towards the coast.

On February 25 it was still blizzarding, but not so cold. Ilartnark started off with dogs and sleigh to haul the three deer killed by Uttungerlah, but he failed to find the cache owing to the thick drifting snow. On his way back, however, he killed a deer, which he brought with him, so the dogs were fed.

Next day, after travelling ten miles, we struck a smallish lake "Kummen-au-wet-yuak." Since leaving Ti-hĭt-yuak Lake we had travelled over a flat or rolling prairie-like expanse, with no rocks and but few stones; but, as we approached the coast of the Inlet, the country became broken and rocky. In travelling eighteen miles to the Inlet, on February 27, Amer was successful in killing four out of a band of six deer. The Huskies are good shots up to a distance of about 120 yards, and they take infinite pains in stalking a beast, invariably getting as close to it as possible, but they often spoil the whole show by attempting to get too close. Next day Amer went to haul his deer, and shot a wolf on the way. When a Husky has killed and skinned a wolf he cuts off the forelegs, so that, if the animal should come to life again, he may not be able to run away.

Here Uttungerlah went off to fetch his two wives and families, who were camped at a place called "Tiki-rar-yuak," on the south shore of the Inlet. He had intended to join us at Mawr-en-ik-yuak, but next day, March 1, he sent a party on sleighs to request me to visit his camp. When we met his messengers we were near the south shore, and had only to cross a point of land to reach Tiki-rar-yuak, where we found several Huskies in camp besides Uttungerlah's wives and families. There had been no scarcity amongst them, for deer had been and still were plentiful in the vicinity.

March 2 was a busy day at this place. Uttungerlah had to collect his own possessions, and the miscellaneous goods and chattels belonging to his two wives had to be looked through. He had a large box in which was stored a collection of rubbish, including a pair of old leather boots, old silk neckties, railway maps, and scraps of coloured cloth and paper, ornamented in various childish fashions. It goes to a Husky's heart to part with anything that has once belonged to a white man. I endeavoured to impress on Uttungerlah the uselessness of encumbering himself with anything not absolutely necessary for the journey. I explained that I wished to travel as light as possible, and that whatever he carried now would have to be brought back from the Arctic Coast.

He replied that I was quite right, that he would take along nothing, but that it was very hard to leave things behind. With great difficulty did I prevail on him to leave behind the fashionable old pair of English boots which he had brought back after a visit to Winnipeg. He insisted that they would be good to wear in the summer time when the moss was wet, though knowing well that he would never wear them for fear of spoiling them. The desire on the part of attendants to collect and keep useless odds and ends is not peculiar to Huskies, but causes inconvenience to the traveller almost anywhere. I suggested that a cache of everything which was to be left behind should be made at Mawr-en-ik-yuak, but was told that this would not do, for the Kazan River Huskies, who often visited the place, would soon discover the cache and annex everything.

Although the Huskies preserve a sacred respect for a white man's belongings left in their charge, they do not appear scrupulous with regard to the possessions of their own people. Taking things from one another is not reckoned stealing. A Husky girl on board the schooner *Francis Allyn*, when I remarked that she was in possession of a certain article which I knew to belong to another of her tribe, replied, "I did not steal it, I just took it."

Our projected journey was discussed again, but the original programme was adhered to. We were to travel up Baker, Schultz, and Aberdeen Lakes to Ti-bi-elik Lake, whence we would take a northerly course for Back's River and the Arctic Coast. All the women and children, with the exception of Nanau (Amer's wife), were to be left on Back's River for the summer, in charge of Ilartnark, who would be supplied by me with ammunition, lead, nets, and a few articles of trade. Nanau was to accompany us farther in order to keep our clothes and footgear in repair.

We still had about a week's supplies of biscuit, sugar, pork, &c. These were to be held in reserve in case of emergency, and we were to depend henceforth on caribou or musk-oxen over the long stretch of country which lay between us and Fort Norman, the Hudson Bay post on the Mackenzie River, which was our ultimate goal.

I confess that I had considerable anxiety about our probable food-supply as far as Ti-bi-elik Lake; but about the first week in April, when we should turn due north, the female deer would have started on their migration towards the Arctic Coast, near which they drop their young.

In undertaking a journey without carrying sufficient supplies to keep the party alive, one assumes a great risk, especially if the journey is in winter. In summer one's nets usually provide an abundant supply of salmon, white-fish, and trout. There is then also a good deal of small game in the country, and the dogs require but little food during the warm weather. Nevertheless, it is exceedingly difficult to travel over the barren ground in summer if deer are scarce; and in winter, or rather, during the cold months, it is impossible.

On March 4 we left Tiki-rar-yuak, and next day reached

Mawr-en-ik-yuak, our old camp at the foot of Baker Lake.

The weather was cold, minimum readings for March 4, 5, and 6 being −41°, −43°, and −52°, and for March 5 the maximum −40°.

The two sleighs with which we had travelled from the vessel were already loaded high, and could carry no more. However, I had arranged for another sleigh and a few more dogs, and I had also brought two planks from the *Francis Allyn,* for a cradle on the sleigh, on which it was proposed to fit the two canoes. Amer-or-yuak proved himself a skilful carpenter, and we had no difficulty in making the cradle, placing the canoes "nested" upon it, and fitting the whole upon the spare sleigh. There were few things that Amer could not make. With his primitive tools he could fashion a tobacco pipe, or build a sleigh, or fix up a broken rifle.

We had a great quantity of stuff to find room for. Besides the indispensable articles, there were women's belongings, things which they said they would require next winter. These were contained in innumerable boxes and bags, and, if we could have carried more, still more would have been produced.

In order to reduce the weight and bulk of the loads, I decided to give Uttungerlah and Amer, before starting, all the presents I intended to give them for past and future services.

If I had not had complete confidence in these two men, I could not have done this. They could not possibly run away, Indian fashion, for their wives and children would be with us; but, besides, I knew they would not plead sickness as an excuse for wishing to return.

On March 8 the presents were equally divided between Amer and Uttungerlah, who subdivided them with others, when Ilartnark and Pitzeolah came in for a share. I had about 18 lbs. of beads still remaining, and these I gave to the women. The sight of so many beads sent the fair ones nearly crazy with delight. The division, and a good deal of swapping which went on afterwards, was most amicably conducted. I now had only sufficient trade articles to pay our way among the natives along the Arctic Coast.

A few more dogs were obtained, but a wolf took one of the best I had. The wolf was shot early next morning, and the remains of the dog, hair and all, were found inside.

On March 9, at half-past eight in the morning, we set out along Baker Lake with twenty dogs for the three sleighs, seven for one sleigh, eight for another, and five for the canoe sleigh. When travelling with dogs and sleighs it is customary with the Huskies to assist the dogs by hauling on a line. This is all very well when the loads are excessive, or the snow very stiff, or the way up-hill, but it is a bad practice to keep up continually. The dogs very soon understand the matter, and then the more you help the less they haul.

The women and children all walked, and walked well.

Cuckoo, Uttungerlah's wife, had an infant at the breast, but did not seem to mind this load. The youngster was carried naked in the hood of her deerskin coat. When the mother wished to feed the baby, she reached back over her shoulder and jerked the youngster out, sometimes setting it on the snow, which, though the thermometer was anywhere between −30° and −50°, it did not appear to mind.

There was a great difference in the length of the days now, and we could have travelled fast had we not been accompanied by the women and children. The going on the lake was excellent.

On March 12 we passed the mouth of the Kazan River and camped on an island called Ok-pi-tu-yok, which means "The island where deer's horns, seen in the distance, were mistaken for willows." There are four islands close together at this place, two of which are considered to be unlucky islands, and the Huskies give them a wide berth. To camp, or even to set foot on any one of them, would be followed by misfortune and death, according to Eskimo tradition. One may laugh at these childish superstitions, but do not superstitions as absurd linger among our own countrymen?

Deer were fairly plentiful along the south shore of Baker Lake, and our dogs were well fed.

On March 13 we camped near the head of Baker Lake, about eight miles to the east of an Eskimo summer camp called King-ak, which means simply "Hill."

The southern shores of the lake are very low. A range or ridge of hills runs parallel with the coast at a distance of about two miles. This range, commencing close to the Kazan River, extends almost to the head of the lake. A hill called No-a-shak stands about half-way between the Kazan River and the lake head, and eight or ten miles south from the shore of the lake. Circumstances did not permit me to visit it, but it is such a conspicuous landmark that I have marked its approximate position on the map.

We were delayed on March 14 by a blizzard, when the thermometer stood at about −30°. It was too cold for the children to face the icy blast from the northwest.

Some of the Huskies went to fish through the ice, and caught eight trout, scaling about 7 or 8 lbs. apiece. It must have been cold work; but they built shelters with blocks of snow, and did not appear to mind the wind and drift.

On March 15 we had a minimum reading of −51°, and maximum −36°. However, the wind had moderated and we set out; but it was too cold for the mother and baby to travel, and they remained behind. We camped close to King-ak, at the head of the small bay which lies to the south of the inlet from Schultz Lake. I have not seen this bay marked on any map yet published.

On my journey in 1899 we ran into this bay by mistake. For once by going wrong we had gone right, for we met the Huskies at their summer camp, at King-ak; they at once informed us that this was their route, and that they always made the portage from the head of this bay to the main river connecting Schultz and Baker Lakes.

A very small creek comes in at the head of this bay, which is certainly not navigable even for canoes.

It is probable that this is the stream to which Captain Christopher makes reference in his remarks on his chart: . "A small river, full of falls and shoals, not water for a boat." Captain Christopher, in 1761, was sent from Churchill, in the sloop *Churchill*, to examine Chesterfield Inlet and ascertain the possibility of a north-west passage in this direction. He ascended the inlet to a large fresh-water lake (Baker Lake), at the west end of which he saw the small river referred to. He then returned, and it would appear that he never saw the main river from the west.

From King-ak we struck straight overland for the south-east bay of Schultz Lake, a distance of about thirty miles. This was the usual Husky winter route. We passed three lakes, and the country was fairly flat. Our course would have been straighter and shorter if we had made for the south-east bay of Aberdeen Lake and avoided Schultz Lake altogether, but we were obliged to go to Iglor-yu-ŭllig, a Husky encampment between Schultz and Aberdeen Lakes, in order to pick up Pitzeolah.

We had now been just four weeks since leaving Depot Island, and we had travelled 230 miles by account. Delays had been frequent, caused by the necessity of hunting deer along the route, and also by the intensely cold weather and blizzards which we had experienced. With warmer weather, which would make easier hauling for the dogs, we expected to travel faster. We still had two months in which to cross the intervening country between Ti-bi-elik

Lake and the Arctic coast. There had been no sickness either amongst ourselves or the dogs.

On March 15, 16, and 17 we had minimum readings of $-51°$, $-51°$, and $-49°$, which seemed low for the middle of March.

We left King-ak on March 16 and reached Kunga-klwar-yu, as the south-east bay of Schultz Lake is called, on the 19th. Deer were seen in large numbers, and as many were killed as were required to keep the party in meat, but the country was very flat, and a close approach quite out of the question. The long-range rifles proved indispensable.

On March 22 and 23 we travelled slowly along the south shore of Schultz Lake. The weather was now much warmer. On these two nights minima were $-1°$ and $0°$ respectively.

The ice, which was six feet thick on the lake, presented a smooth and unbroken surface, and with the rise in temperature the sleighs slipped along easily.

We could have made long journeys every day, but so numerous were the "spells" for smoking and talking, that we rarely made more than twelve miles. There was no necessity to hurry, deer were plentiful, and the dogs were faring well. Every one appeared to be enjoying the trip.

One day I made the unwelcome discovery that our two remaining cans of kerosene oil for the "primus" stove were both leaking. Small cracks which could scarcely be detected by the naked eye, and which were too small to plug with anything, had opened, and through these our precious stock of fuel was leaking at a rate that promised to empty the cans in a couple of days or so. This was something new and unexpected. I had never before travelled with kerosene oil in tin cans in the very cold weather. The cracks were caused, I fancy, partly by the intense cold, and partly by the jolting of the sleigh.

On March 25 we arrived at Kunga-klŭk, near the foot

H

of Aberdeen Lake. We had passed Iglor-yu-ŭllig, which lay a short distance to the north of us, but I had sent a man to fetch Pitzeolah, and he arrived in the evening. Pitz had arranged to get married, but his girl had gone off with the Kazan River Huskies. He was not breaking his heart about this, however. He said any other woman would do as well, and he did not want any woman until his return from the Arctic coast.

For the last day or two we had walked without our deerskin coats, and sometimes the weather was so warm that life in a snow-house was decidedly unpleasant. The backbone of the winter had been broken.

On March 26 all the Huskies who had been in camp at Kunga-klŭk and Iglor-yu-ŭllig came to pay their respects. They brought what they had to give us, which was not very much; but one man supplied enough fish to give all our dogs a good feed, and another presented some deer-meat.

Of course they were out of tobacco, ammunition, and everything else. Primers (Winchester) for reloading their cartridges were always in demand.

To run short of ammunition is a very serious matter for the Hudson Bay Huskies, for, when they became accustomed to the use of the firearms supplied by the traders, they entirely discarded bows and arrows. In winter, however, they trapped caribou, and at this place I had an opportunity of inspecting their pitfalls, or "kud-gi-tak," as they call them.

In a deep snow-drift they dig an oblong pit about six feet deep, and then with blocks of snow build up walls about four feet high, so that for the deer there is a fall of about ten feet. An easy slope leads up to the very thin roof of snow, and the structure has a natural appearance. The deer are very fond of licking the snow on which dogs have deposited their urine, probably on account of the salt it contains, and of this queer taste the Huskies take advantage in laying down a bait, so that large numbers of deer are captured. Deer, however, must be numerous for a fair chance of success, and the pitfalls must be closely watched; for, as soon as a beast falls into a pit, he commences to fight and worry, and if he dies from exhaustion, as he soon does, the flesh is almost uneatable.

Iglor-yu-ŭllig has a wide reputation among the Huskies as a fishing place. There must be springs in the river here, for even during the most severe winters the ice never attains a thickness of more than two or three inches. I had given Pitzeolah nets, but he had not been successful, not knowing how to set them underneath the ice. White-fish and toolabies cannot be taken with a hook, but in winter they are speared in this manner: Through a longish hole cut in the ice the skin of a fish is passed down into the water, head up stream. This skin, being distended with water so as to have a natural appearance, acts as a decoy, and, when live fish approach, down comes the Husky's spear.

For two days the weather was so warm that it was not advisable to travel, lest we should have trouble with the mud on the sleigh runners; but on March 28 it was a little cooler, and we resumed our journey, accompanied by several Husky families from Kūnga-klŭk, who were bound for Ti-bi-elik Lake to get drift-wood for the construction of their kyaks the following summer. Among us we had over forty dogs, and I forget how many men, women, and children. Large numbers of deer stopped us soon after midday, when we had only travelled twelve miles, for it was necessary to procure meat. There was no cover either on the land or on the lake for making an approach. By running at the bands of deer, we managed to get within long range and killed three, but this sort of shooting runs away with ammunition.

Next day we camped half-way up Aberdeen Lake. Deer were very numerous, nearly all females; but our Husky friends were badly armed, and all we killed fell to the Mannlicher carbine, and to Amer's and Uttun-gerlah's Remingtons.

On March 30 we did not travel. This was the first day when it was possible to dry our socks and moccasins by the heat of the sun. All through the long winter they had had to be dried by the heat of our bodies every night, causing tedious and unpleasant but unavoidable work.

On March 31 we camped close to the head of Aberdeen Lake, where we found plenty of small drift-wood, which had, of course, come from the Ark-i-linik River, and next day reached Kek-ek-tellig, the name of which in the Husky language means "There is an Island." This is an important place for spearing deer in the summer time.

We had been starting at an early hour and camping late, and would by this time easily have reached Ti-bi-elik Lake but for the spells for smoking, which were frequent and lengthy. When I remarked to the Huskies on the amount of time this wasted, they exploded with laughter, and seemed to think it an excellent joke. Smoking appeared to be the most important affair in a day's journey.

Deer were numerous at the head of Aberdeen Lake, and now there were more bulls than cows. The horns of the bulls were just commencing to show in the shape of two small soft knobs about one inch in length. The growth of the deers' horns is carefully watched by the Huskies, for by it they think they know all about the coming weather. They now assured me that it would be a late spring, and that there would be plenty of snow and good hauling for another two months, or until the deer's horns were one foot high.

Next day, April 2, the Huskies requested me to camp early, as they were hungry for fish, and we were passing a good fishing place. One trout weighing 26 lbs. was hauled up through a hole in the ice by hook and line. I shot two large bulls in the evening, and as drift-wood along the shores was plentiful, meat was boiled for all hands.

The next day, April 3, saw us in camp on Ti-bi-elik Lake, whence our course was to be north instead of west. We remained at Ti-bi-elik Lake for a day in order to get tent-poles for Ilartnark, and for our own tent. I boiled three thermometers, and they all registered 211.4° Fahr. (as corrected). The altitude of Ti-bi-elik Lake was about 313 feet. The temperature at night continued low; minimum readings showed $-31°$, $-35°$, $-33°$, and $-31°$.

On April 5 we turned northwards towards the Arctic Coast. It was my intention to follow as nearly as I could by dead reckoning the meridian of 101° west long.

Ti-bi-elik Lake is about six miles across, as nearly as I could judge. I was carefully pacing the distance, when a sudden and unexpected north wind sprang up, and in a few minutes it was blowing a blizzard. We were compelled to make the north shore as best we could, and then all hands went to work at once to construct snow-houses. It was not very cold, but it was necessary to camp, for we could not see a yard ahead, and we were now on strange ground.

The building of snow-houses in a blizzard is not pleasant work, but the labour is fully paid for by the comfort and quiet enjoyed inside them.

Travelling northwards for nine miles next day, we passed over flat and undulating country, with a few low ridges and knolls here and there, these last being almost clear of snow. There were no rocks *in situ*, but red sandstone *débris* was in evidence wherever the ground was free from snow.

It was exceedingly difficult to keep accurate reckoning of distance travelled, and even of direction. The bare patches of ground obliged us to keep constantly winding in and out, and as hunting had to be carried on, I was often obliged to leave the sleighs, and not return till the evening. This was the driest part of the Northland of Canada that I had been over; we only found one small lake, and on this we camped.

Next day, April 7, we made fifteen miles, travelling in the forenoon over similar country, but in the afternoon the sandstone *débris* gave place to granite fragments and boulders. I boiled two thermometers, which registered 211° Fahr. The temperature of air was at 28°, and the altitude, therefore, about 515 feet above sea-level.

Hunting delayed us again, deer being numerous, mostly cows and small bulls. They did not appear to be going north, but were feeding, travelling in any direction. They were absurdly wild, and, as there was no wind and the land was flat, several attempts were unsuccessful, but Amer at length killed one, which provided the dogs with a scanty meal.

On April 8, after crossing two little lakes, we came to a small ridge, which I took to be the divide between the waters flowing south into Ti-bi-elik Lake and those flowing north into Back's River. The land was still flat for stretches, then rising into small, low ridges and sand hillocks.

Deer were numerous, bulls, cows, and calves (last year's, of course), but attempts to procure meat failed till Uttungerlah succeeded in killing a bull.

Stones on the tops of knolls, which we observed in the evening, had evidently been placed there by the Back's River Eskimo, and seemed to indicate that we were now over the divide.

Next day, after travelling about four miles, we struck a river flowing north. This I knew would lead us to Back's River, and might be either the McKinley or the Buchanan River, or possibly a tributary further west. It was decided to follow it, for although most rivers in the Northland are very crooked, still it is always easier hauling on the ice than over the land.

We could see deer in every direction, and shot four large bulls, one of which weighed 280 lbs. (live weight); the horns were still only 1-inch knobs. Four musk-ox tracks had been seen the day before, so that we had no cause for anxiety at present about our meat supply.

The river we followed turned out eventually to be the Buchanan River. In its upper course it was small, confined by banks generally low and sloping, but high in places. The land on either side consisted of small, sandy hills. The ice on the river was seven feet thick.

On April 10 we journeyed fifteen miles north, and reached a lake, on which we camped.

On the west side of this lake we saw a flat-topped gravel hill, about 120 feet high. It appeared to be almost an island, with steeply sloping banks on one side and cut banks on the other. It had no special interest, except as a very conspicuous landmark in a country where very few landmarks exist.

I regretted exceedingly at this time that I was without the means of ascertaining my longitude, especially as there is a large discrepancy, as to longitude, between the maps and the charts, which I might have been able to correct.

Hitherto I had failed to use my half chronometer watches with satisfactory results. This may have been due to my carelessness, but, in my opinion, the conditions of travel in the north are much too rough to permit one to carry Greenwich time.

I had with me a map by J. B. Tyrrell, of the Canadian Geological Survey Department, but as he had never visited Back's River, it is to be presumed that this part of his map was copied from one of the older maps, or possibly from Back's own survey. I also had with me the latest Admiralty charts. The discrepancies were : (1) On Tyrrell's map, the longitude of the west end of Baker Lake was given as 97° W., and on the charts as nearly 99° W.; (2) On Tyrrell's map the mouth of the Buchanan River was put at 102° 10′ W., and on the charts at 103° 10′ W.

There was splendid feeding for the deer, which were numerous all along the river, the ground being covered with moss and lichens.

There is a good deal of misconception respecting the migratory habits of the caribou. Thus, Mr. J. B. Tyrrell, in his Geological Report on the Doobaunt and Kazan Rivers, says with reference to the "Barren Ground" caribou : "A better knowledge of the habits and distribution of this animal would have saved us much suffering, but that knowledge was not then available." My experience convinces me that such knowledge respecting this animal is at no time available.

There is no doubt that caribou migrate. They go south in large herds in autumn, and north in spring. They cross the country east of Great Slave Lake, round Artillery Lake, and some distance east of it. They do not appear on the main Ark-i-linik River, but between Aberdeen and Schultz Lakes they pass with some regularity. The migration takes place on such a large scale, and over such a wide tract of country, that it has been assumed that all caribou migrate. The fact seems to be that the majority of the animals remain in the north throughout the year. I have myself shot caribou in winter along the west coast of Hudson Bay, and inland from the Bay ; along the north and south coasts of Chesterfield Inlet ; in the country north of the head of the Inlet as far as Garry Lake on Back's River, and along Back's River. I have also killed them to the north and south of Baker, Aberdeen, and Schultz Lakes in winter, and I know others who have killed them in winter in the country about Wager River and Repulse Bay. On the Arctic Coast, at White Bear Point, and on Kent Peninsula, and at other places which will be mentioned later, caribou are always to be found during the winter. Thus, I think it may be held as proved that very great numbers of caribou do not migrate. In fact, if deer left the north in winter, the Eskimo on Back's River and southwards would have to leave it also, for their food is mostly deer's meat, the little musk-ox meat, seal, and fish they eat being scarcely worth considering. It is quite true that the animals which remain in the north frequently change their ground. They wander about ; but their movements are not migratory.

The third point to be noticed is, that while many deer migrate, the course they will take cannot be predicted. The Yellow Knife and Dog Rib Indians and the Eskimo are careful observers of their movements, since their living mostly depends on the passing herds. They often state with confidence beforehand when and where deer will be found, but the information they give turns out wrong as frequently as right, and when they are shown to have been mistaken, they can only say that they have never known it so before. The fact that famine befalls both Indians and Eskimo through failure of deer shows that they do not know the habits of these animals. If the natives are intimately acquainted with the habits and movements of these animals, why are they in some years unable to hit off the migrating bands? Why do those who depend on deer's meat for a living periodically starve, when the woful cry of "et-then-ūlé" (a Chipewyan word, meaning "no-deer") comes floating into the nearest Hudson Bay fort, to be shortly followed by a ragged, broken-down and starving band of men and women, children and dogs, a truly deplorable sight?

Deer used to be abundant on the Mackenzie River, at Fort Simpson and Fort Providence, but for many years none have passed that way. The migrating herds one year may pass close to the east end of Great Slave Lake, and the next year so far to the east as to be inaccessible to the Yellow Knives and Dog Ribs. In the fall of 1896 the Indians with whom I was hunting musk-oxen told me, that on our return to Fond-du-lac we should find no deer, but when we reached Artillery Lake we found the country swarming with deer, a moving mass, and the bands extended westwards along Great Slave Lake to within a hundred miles of Fort Resolution. The Indians could only say that they had never seen it so before.

It would appear that information respecting the migratory habits of the caribou cannot be obtained, because, beyond the broad facts of the annual movements, the animals do not have settled habits. They have no definite routes, and seem not to remember the crossing-places. Though holding generally in a northerly or southerly direction, they appear to ˌwander aimlessly, for they will strike a large lake, like Aberdeen or Baker Lake, in the middle of the shore, and then follow it till they find a channel which they can swim. One day I saw a large bull speared while swimming across Chesterfield Inlet. Why was he swimming there if he knew of the crossing-places?

On April 11 we continued down the Buchanan River, which took us a very straight northerly course, though occasionally it would swing off north-north-east, or north-north-west. It maintained a varying breadth of from 300 to 600 yards, and flowed with a very slow current over a wide shoal sandy or gravel bed with occasional boulders. There were no rapids. The land on either side was flat or undulating and prairie-like; it was covered with moss or grass.

Towards camping-time the land became more broken and hilly, a sure indication, as I took it, that we were approaching Back's River.

We had trouble that evening in getting water, for nowhere could we find a greater depth than six feet, and to that depth the river was solid ice.

The next day, April 12, as we travelled, expecting soon to come on Back's River, Darrell spied a Husky in the distance. Sending two of our men to intercept his retreat and bring him to me, we continued down the river until we met. This native's name was Ĭt-ke-lek, and he belonged to Back's River. He was armed with bow and arrow, and carried the copper snow-knife, which is never left behind. His iglu was but a short distance away, and, at his invitation, we steered for it and camped alongside. The language or dialect he spoke differed considerably from that spoken by my natives, but they appeared to have little difficulty in conversing freely together. He invited us into his snow-house, set before us a large hind-quarter of caribou, raw, and entertained us in the best way he could.

It-ke-lek was a typical Husky in build; sturdy, large-boned, and strong, with a very pronounced hook nose, which is by no means uncommon among the Huskies. His wife was a wonderfully active, strong woman about middle age. She had four children with her and three were away, the largest Husky family that I have come across, but probably three or four of them were adopted children.

Their iglu was clean and tidy. They possessed nothing made by white men except three short knife-blades fitted into bone handles, the three having evidently been made from one large blade. A present of a butcher's knife, a file, and some needles delighted them, and the man promised to accompany us a short distance on our journey north.

We only now discovered where we actually were, and that it was the Buchanan River we had been following. We were within a very short distance of its junction with Back's River (Henning-ei-yok), but, instead of following its curve to the west, we were to take a straight cut across country to the spot where Back's River flowed into Pelly Lake.

It-ke-lek stated that there were only nine families of Huskies on Back's River altogether, and that his was the only one in the vicinity. They lived a good deal by fishing. In the winter they depended mainly on their kud-gi-tak (the pitfalls for deer already referred to) to supply them with deer's meat. He had just found two deer in his traps when we met him. In summer they speared deer at the crossing-places.

Questioned about Back's journey, he said that his father had told him that, long ago, two large boats (Back had only one) and about twenty white men (Back had about half that number) had come down Back's River and returned again the same summer. He was a small boy at the time and did not remember it. Back descended and ascended the river in 1834. This man could not be more than forty years of age, and his statement could not possibly be correct. I asked him if he was sure it was not his father who was the small boy when Back passed, but he adhered to his original statement.

We were the first white men that he had seen.

He informed us that the Huskies along the Arctic coast were numerous, and that shortly they would be leaving the coast to come inland and hunt deer. Musk-oxen he reported scarce, both to the north and south of Back's River.

Red bears (*Ursus arctus richardsoni*) were also stated to be very scarce. It-ke-lek had never seen a live one himself. Salmon occasionally ascended as far as the Buchanan River. White - fish, toolabies, and trout abounded in the lakes and rivers. The Back's River Huskies seldom starved, for deer remained all winter in large numbers. No copper was to be found on Back's River.

CHAPTER X

FROM PELLY LAKE TO THE NORTH COAST

ON April 13 we were detained by a strong north-west wind which raised considerable drift, but next day we resumed our journey. After following the Buchanan River a short distance down we struck north-east for five miles across the land, and reached the south-west shore of Pelly Lake. A run of six miles in the same direction over the lake brought us to its north shore.

One of our dogs, "Pūka," became ill during the day, foaming and bleeding at the mouth, and shaking all over. The Huskies informed me that this dog would certainly die, and that all the others would probably take the sickness, which was common at this time of year, and die. In the evening, however, they said that sometimes only one or two of the dogs took the sickness and died. I should have shot the sick dog at once, but at their request waited. He died two days later. We were not yet half-way to the Arctic coast, and to be left without dogs was not pleasant to think of.

The following day, April 15, we did not travel, as Uttungerlah decided to leave the women and children at this spot, with Ilartnark in charge. I gave them powder, lead, primers, matches, tobacco, and a small stock of "trade," sufficient to last them until Amer and Uttungerlah returned.

During the afternoon Uttungerlah presented himself, and implored me to take along his wife Panning-ei-yak and her two children. This was strictly against the terms of our contract, and I told him so. He replied that he understood this, and that though he could not make up his mind to leave them behind, he would do whatever I told him. I pointed out that he would be very foolish to take them along; that they were already a long way from their own country, and that in the event of sickness or starvation they would be better off where they were. He replied, that of course I was right, that his mind was now made up, and that they would remain behind. He changed his mind twice after this. In the evening he said that unless I absolutely refused he would like to take them, as they wished very much to come. I told him that it was a matter of indifference to me, but that he was very foolish. He promised to think it over during the night. Eventually the woman and her two children came along. Such is Husky indecision.

The company of the women and children is at times a great nuisance, but the Husky himself is much better satisfied by having them, and there is no chance of his dreaming of a sick wife or child, and on that account wishing to turn back.

Our plans again came up for discussion. I laid out my charts, and explained to my Husky friends their best way back from the Arctic coast; how from Cape Barrow they could travel south to the head of Bathurst Inlet, whence the portage over to Back's River could be made; they could then descend the river in the canoe which I had promised to give them, or, if too late in the year for that, they could wait for the "freeze up," and travel down on the river ice to Pelly Lake, and meet those left behind.

Our own plans depended a good deal on the season, and on what we should hear from the Arctic Coast Huskies. The original programme would probably be adhered to, but alternative routes were discussed. We could return from the Arctic coast by portaging from the head of Bathurst Inlet to Back's River. We could then ascend Back's River and so reach Aylmer Lake, whence it is an easy canoe journey to Great Slave Lake; or we could make the portage to the Ark-i-linik River, and return the same way we had come. Either of these routes offered good prospects of reaching Fort Resolution on Great Slave Lake by September 1, and then Edmonton and civilisation could be reached before the "freeze up."

Here I boiled two thermometers and both read 211° 5', the temperature of the air being 30° Fahr. This gives the altitude of Pelly Lake as 260 feet above sea-level. The distance we had travelled since leaving the *Francis Allyn* two months before we roughly estimated at 560 miles.

The following day, April 16, we bade farewell to Ilartnark and his two wives, Cuckoo and her baby, and another little girl who had accompanied us, and proceeded on our journey. We searched for the mouth of a small river, which, according to information supplied by It-ke-lek, flows into the north-west part of Pelly Lake from the north, but when we had gone a short distance the weather became thick, and we were obliged to camp. Next day it was still thick, and we remained in camp, but in the afternoon the hunters shot three female deer, all being with calf.

I anxiously watched our dogs at this time, but all appeared lively enough, and if a readiness to fight was a sign of health, they were all right.

On April 18 we resumed our journey on Pelly Lake, following an arm or narrow bay running in a northerly direction.

Just before camping-time a large band of bull caribou came trotting up towards us in the foolish manner I have already described, and would not be driven away. I shot two, all we wanted. The Huskies luckily did not happen to have any cartridges handy, or there would have been slaughter. The bulls' horns were still only small knobs, and the Huskies prophesied much cold weather yet. They said that even when the horns had attained the length of a man's arm there would still be good hauling on the snow.

It would be interesting to ascertain whether prolonged cold weather in the spring of the year has the effect of retarding the growth of the deer's horns. This is the supposition on which the Huskies base their theory. A very sudden change from a late winter to an early summer, which is by no means uncommon, would upset this theory. Their answer would then be "that it had never happened before."

We had another day of rest on April 19 on account of thick weather.

In this form I used to keep track of our direction and distance travelled.

N.	2½ miles on arm of Pelly Lake.	
N.	2 miles on a winding course up small stream.	
N.W.	3 miles ,, ,, ,,	
N.N.W.	2½ miles travelled on small lakes and land.	
N.N.W.	3½ miles ,, ,, ,,	
N.	1½ miles ,, ,, ,,	

Total,   15 miles.

On April 20, after travelling about 2½ miles, we came to a place where the Arctic coast Huskies had made caches of meat the preceding fall, so we knew that we were on the right track, but we still failed to strike the small river described by Ĩt-ke-lek.

The Huskies, when out of their own country, complain incessantly that they are lost. They are greatly afraid of taking their white masters wrong, and being blamed for it. On my former journey Milŭk, the Husky who then accompanied me, flatly refused to go ahead of the dogs when we got north of Marble Island, and he was out of his own country. We did not now find the proper track, but this was not a bad country to get lost in; it contained plenty of deer, and plenty of moss and heaths to cook the meat with; an abundant supply of good water, and any amount of snow for house-building purposes. The land was low and undulating with occasional gravel knolls and ridges, but became very rugged where granite rocks appeared.

The weather was now getting considerably warmer, and for two days we had maximum readings well above 32°.

On April 21 an observation of meridian altitude of the sun placed us in latitude 66° 25′ 26″ N.

In camp I boiled two thermometers and they both read 211.2°. The temperature of the air being 29°, the altitude was about 414 feet above sea-level.

The country was now very flat, one vast expanse of snow as far as the eye could reach, broken only by an occasional granite boulder. I was expecting to reach a largish lake called Ti-her-yuak, the existence of which had been reported to us by Ít-ke-lek. From this lake a river flowed direct to the Arctic Ocean, and this was the route usually followed by the Arctic Huskies when they journeyed to the Ark-i-linik River to procure wood for their sleighs.

The name Ti-her-yuak appears to be a common or general name for a lake. Kummenik is used in much the same way for a large lake, such as Pelly Lake.

Deer were seen in large bands in the evening. They now appeared to be moving north, for all the tracks were heading in that direction.

I was much surprised at the absence of all signs of musk-oxen in country which I thought was the very centre of the musk-ox land. This was afterwards accounted for by the Arctic Huskies, who explained that on their route to the Ark-i-linik River all the musk-oxen had been either killed or driven off; but that if we had travelled for a day, either due east or due west, we would have come on them.

In spite of the warm weather the mud on the runners of the sleighs still stuck on, but the Huskies took great precautions. Every time we "spelled" snow was immediately shovelled over the runners to keep off the heat of the sun.

These "spells," or intervals for rest, originated with the idea of giving the dogs a few moments to regain their wind. They had now been turned into long intervals, during

I

which all the dogs fell sound asleep stretched out full
length on the snow, and the Huskies, after they had smoked
tobacco, slept and snored. The children very often played
at a game of baseball, which they had picked up from the
American whalers.

On April 22, after travelling only two miles, we struck
Ti-her-yuak Lake. We had not followed the precise route
taken by the Arctic Huskies, for we struck the lake, not at
its head, but about half-way down. According to It-ke-lek
this lake is of considerable size; he had said we would
travel on it for a whole day, thus indicating a distance of
about fifteen or sixteen miles. We reached its foot after
travelling only eight and a half miles. The lake extended
away to the south as far as we could see.

Like other lakes in the Northland it is very irregular in
shape, full of rocky or stony islands, and confined by low
rocky shores. On arriving at the foot of the lake we had
difficulty in finding the outlet, so an early camp was made,
and several of the party went out in different directions
to search for it. Next day it was discovered a short distance to the west of our camp. As we expected, it was
well marked with stones "up-ended."

The out-flowing river is about forty yards broad, and
has moderately high and well-defined banks. We travelled
about two miles on it, and then, at a place where it must
have taken a sharp bend, we lost it; but, continuing on
our northerly course across the land, we found it again.
We had considerable difficulty in following this river, for
it spread out in places over a wide shoal bed, and at times
it was impossible to say with certainty whether we were
on small lakes, a moss swamp, or on a broad part of the
river. After travelling fourteen and a half miles we came
in the afternoon to a group of old snow-houses, where
Arctic Eskimo had evidently been a few months before.
Many deer had been killed at or near this place; large
numbers of horns were scattered about, and there were
piles of bones. An observation at noon gave our latitude

66° 42′ N. Ogden Bay, the nearest point on the Arctic coast, being in latitude 67° 36′ N., we were about fifty-four geographical miles (in an air-line) from the coast.

Deer were again very numerous, and behaved in their foolish manner. It was amusing to watch them, and the dogs got into a state of great excitement. At these times they forgot all about the weight of the loads they were hauling, and it was difficult to restrain them from running away with the sleigh.

With long swinging trot a band of deer would approach to within three hundred yards or so, and would then stand stupidly staring at us as we passed. Then with an impudent snort, toss of the head, and jump in the air, they would be off. But their curiosity had been aroused not satisfied, and with a dancing trot they would now advance to within a hundred yards of the sleighs, and then commence to cross our front, backwards and forwards, until their tongues lolled out, and they appeared to have had enough of the 'game. The Huskies showed a laudable amount of self-restraint on these occasions.

All the rocks were now granitic. Felspar being so much in the ascendant that it gave a pinkish appearance to the whole formation. The surface of the rock was smooth, but no striæ were observed.

On April 24 we did not travel, for having again lost the river we were obliged to search for it. Uttungerlah discovered it, and he also killed three bull caribou.

On the following night the minimum thermometer registered −29°, but at this time of year a low temperature like this lasted only for an hour or so.

The next day, April 25, we made fourteen miles, travelling chiefly on the river, and meeting with an occasional small lake. On one of these we camped. Although this lake was of no great size, it had a name, which we only ascertained after meeting with the Arctic coast Huskies. It was called In-ni-ŭk-tau-wik.

The river we were following was not very straight, but

it held a general northerly course, spreading out in places over a shoal sandy bed. At camp time we failed to strike water, the ice being solid right down to the sandy bottom. The coast Huskies informed us afterwards that we could have found water had we known where to look for it.

The country we were now in might well be termed "barren." It was the most barren part of the Northland that I had as yet come across. Even moss and lichens were conspicuous by their absence, the rocks being quite bare. Still when one thing played out something else generally turned up to take its place. We now fell back on a species of heather (*Cassiope tetragona*, L.) for fuel for purposes of cooking. This was plentiful in some places but very scarce in others, and it was not easy to loosen from the frozen ground. The collecting of enough to boil our evening pot of meat was laborious, and required patience and time. Our stock of kerosene oil had long since leaked away, so we were obliged either to gather this heather or eat our meat raw. The Husky name for it is I-klu-ti; in the summer time it bears a pretty white flower, not unlike our bell heather.

It looked ominous at this time that the deer were becoming scarcer as we proceeded north; we appeared to be running through them.

In the night we had a minimum reading of −41°, which seemed almost incredible at this season. The maximum reading of the following day was only −11°.

We camped on April 26 after travelling only eight miles, because we were running out of all sign of deer. There was not a single fresh track to be seen, though there had been large numbers here during the winter. The deer wander about and shift their ground in such a manner that it is quite impossible to gain a knowledge of their habits and distribution. Their habits and movements being quite uncertain, it is always possible that one might strike a stretch of country containing not a single hoof, but this would not necessarily imply that the deer had migrated from it to the south, but rather that they had shifted their ground, and would still be found in the north, perhaps one hundred miles east or west.

I believe it was with the migrating deer from the south that we had been travelling at this time, but it is difficult to say with any certainty. We now appeared to be in advance of them, for, on account of the prolonged cold weather, the deer were travelling very slowly. It was certainly neither my desire nor intention to reach the Arctic coast before them. We should get plenty of seals along the coast, I knew, if we fell in with the Arctic Eskimo, but, for my own part, I have no special hankering after seal's meat, though the flippers and tail parts of a young seal are not to be despised. My party was not equipped for hunting seals, for it was much too early in the year to expect to find them lying on the ice. We were about a month too soon, but this was decidedly better than a month too late.

Sandy made a remark in the evening to the effect that he found deer's meat most unpalatable and tasteless, and I hinted to him that possibly in a few days the taste of the meat would not trouble him, for there was no sign of deer to be found. He listened to my remark in silence.

Darrell, who had been for a long walk, returned late and announced that he had seen a band of over twenty deer, all females. This raised my spirits considerably, for now there seemed but a remote chance of our having to turn back to find deer. If there was one band in front of us, there were probably others.

On April 27 and 28 we were confined within our snow-houses by a blizzard.

On the morning of the twenty-ninth the blizzard moderated, and the evening turned out beautifully fine. As we were getting very short of meat, we lost no time in setting out to hunt deer. Amer and I killed four females, all with unborn calves. The majority of the cow caribou had by this date shed their horns. On my former trip

Milūk had informed me that the cows shed their horns at the time they drop their calves. He was not very far wrong.

On our return from hunting we came across the fresh tracks of three different bands, which were travelling north. Uttungerlah returned late, having slain three deer, so for the present there was no cause for anxiety about the food supply.

On April 30 the weather was again unsettled, and the day was devoted to hauling the deer shot the previous day. Darrell, while taking a walk in the afternoon, came on a pack of sixteen wolves. It is unusual for them to hunt in packs like this; they generally hunt singly, or in twos and threes.

On May 1 we resumed our journey, and travelled nineteen miles on the river and occasional small lakes. In the last mile we found several rapids still, of course, frozen solid. They had a considerable fall, and any one attempting the ascent or descent of this river by open water, in canoes, would most certainly have to portage at these places. Land in the forenoon was low and flat, but, about the rapids, it became very broken and rugged, and the river was confined by rocky and steep banks about twenty feet in height.

We again had difficulty in obtaining water. We tried at several places with the ice chisel, and it was no easy job. After cutting through seven or eight feet of ice, it was a great disappointment to strike the dry, sandy bottom. The fact is that these rivers carry off the whole of the water which results from the melting of the snow during the summer and fall. Then they dwindle down to small creeks, so that it is hopeless to expect water except in deep pools. These appeared to be scarce, but on this occasion we eventually struck water at a deep pool, after cutting through nine feet of solid ice. The nine feet of ice was not the result of repeated overflows, but had been formed on nearly still water.

On May 2 we halted, for I was afraid of getting ahead of the deer again. I sent Amer and Uttungerlah ahead to look for signs of them. Amer returned early and reported no fresh tracks and very few old ones. Uttungerlah turned up in the night, having killed and *cached* five cows, but these were all he saw. We were evidently in advance of the deer, so another delay was decided upon.

On May 5 we moved on fifteen and a half miles.

It took us a long time in the evening to find water, but eventually discoloured and not very palatable water was struck seven and a half feet below the surface of the ice.

The reader may wonder why, with plenty of ice and snow around, it was thought necessary at the cost of so much trouble to find water. The answer is that fuel in the shape of i-klu-ti, the heather before mentioned, was very scarce; the melting of ice over a heather fire is a slow process, and there were many thirsty souls in our party. The Huskies want to drink iced water constantly.

Here a snow-bird (bunting) was seen, the first harbinger of spring or summer that had as yet come our way. Snow-birds are invariably the first arrivals from the south, but their advent must not be looked upon as a sure sign of the approach of spring. So far there was no change in the face of the country, and these small birds that had pushed ahead must have had a hard time for the first few weeks.

On May 6, accompanied by the faithful Amer and Uttungerlah, I set out north to hunt deer, but, finding none nor any sign of them, we decided to hunt southwards the next day. One wolf, one white fox, and one raven were seen.

The raven, Arctic owl, and an occasional ptarmigan are the only representatives of the bird tribe which remain throughout the winter in the Northland. The ravens pick up a living off the carcases of deer which have been killed by wolves.

The next day it was blizzarding so that hunting was

out of the question. We were confined inside the iglu the whole day with nothing to do and nothing to read. On days such as these I have compassion on the man who does not smoke. Whatever may be urged for or against the indulgence in tobacco, one fact cannot be gainsaid—it does help to pass the time.

On May 8 we all went hunting except Darrell and Sandy, who collected heather for fuel. Amer and I killed two Arctic hares (a variety of the mountain hare, *Lepus timidus*, of Northern Europe), but saw no deer. Uttungerlah saw nothing. Pitzeolah saw two lots of deer and killed one small beast. About eight miles to the west, Amer and I struck a river flowing north, parallel with the river we were following. The intervening country was very rugged, particularly near the newly-discovered river.

It was here we shot the hares. These animals must be looked for in rugged country; the rockier the ground the better chance of finding the Arctic hare.

In the evening I boiled three thermometers, since our altitude would give us some idea as to our proximity to the coast. They boiled at 212°, 212°, and 212.1° respectively (corrected readings). The temperature of air was 19°, so that if the thermometers could be trusted we were about the sea-level.

On May 9 five deer were killed, all cows; in fact, for the last two weeks no bulls had been killed. The deer appeared to be moving in a north-easterly rather than in a northerly direction.

The following day I sent Amer and Uttungerlah with a sleigh and the pick of the dogs northwards to prospect.

Their orders were to proceed to the coast to search for Arctic Huskies, and, if possible, to bring a couple of them when they came back. I gave them a few presents for distribution amongst the coast natives in order to promote good feeling, and as an earnest of the friendliness of my party towards them.

As I was not sure of our longitude, I did not know

the exact part of the Arctic coast we were heading for. An observation for latitude, taken on May 2, showed that we were then in latitude 67° 18′ N. We had since travelled 15½ statute miles on a rather winding northerly course, which may be put down at ten geographical miles north, placing us in about latitude 67° 26′ N. Ogden Bay is in 67° 36′ N., and we were therefore within ten geographical miles of the most southerly point of the Arctic Ocean, provided, of course, we had been heading direct for this particular point (Ogden Bay), about which I could not be certain.

In the absence of Amer and Uttungerlah, Pitzeolah and I had to undertake the duty of keeping the pot boiling. We set out and travelled a long way from camp, about twelve miles south-east, before we fell in with a band of deer. The land was here almost flat, and a close approach out of the question. I killed four at long range, but it was hopeless for Pitzeolah to fire.

The deer at this time of the year are infested with the maggots of the warble-fly. These maggots are large, and are esteemed a great delicacy by the natives, who pluck them off the hides and greedily devour them. I daresay they are excellent; one never knows until one tries, but I never had the courage or curiosity to sample them.

Next day, May 11, the four deer were hauled. About six o'clock in the evening Uttungerlah and Amer returned, accompanied by two of the Arctic coast Huskies.

The strangers were tall, strong fellows of quiet demeanour. In appearance, features, build and colour they differed but little from the Eskimo of the Hudson Bay. Their clothes had a different cut, however. The outer deerskin coat only came down to the waist. It was cut away right round in this fashion, with the exception of two very small swallow-tails about a foot long, which were allowed to hang down behind. The sewing had necessarily been done with large clumsy copper needles, and was of course rough.

These natives appeared to be rather timid at first, but

presents of a knife and a file seemed to give them a little confidence. Information was forthcoming very slowly, but I did not wish to ply them with too many questions on first acquaintance. They volunteered some statements, most of which they contradicted next day. The following, however, proved to be quite correct. I copy from my diary :—

"The copper deposits, which I had been informed were to be found along Dease Strait, now appear to be located on some islands in Bathurst Inlet.

"The islands in Bathurst Inlet are the source of their supply of this metal.

"Driftwood is plentiful to the west of Cape Barrow.

"Musk-oxen are to be found to the east and west of our present camp."

On the following day we did not travel, as 1 wished to gain what information I could from our Arctic friends. Hŭn-ĭl-yak and Pŭn-ŭk-tŭk were their names. The latter also went by the name of Pī-tek-chi, which means a "bow."

It was no easy matter to gather information from them, they had themselves so much to say, and imperfectly understood Amer and Uttungerlah. It was difficult to get them to give direct answers, and they seemed not to adhere to their original statements, probably because we had not correctly understood them.

I could only make out a few of their words; but Amer, Uttungerlah, and they conversed freely, and spoke so fast that they seemed to understand one another perfectly. This was not the case, however, as I afterwards discovered. There was much talking; but little of it was intelligible to either party.

I copy from my diary a few items which were of great interest to us at the time :—

"The river we have been following from Ti-her-yuak Lake is called Arm-ark-tŭk, and the river running parallel with it, where Amer and I shot the hares, is the Pi-tok-kek River.

"There is no open water or 'flaw' during the winter time on the inland Arctic Sea, between say 99° and 105° W. longitude and 68° and 69° N. latitude.

"The ice in this part does not wholly disappear before the middle of September.

"Whales must frequent this part of the ocean, for the bones of stranded ones are found along the coast. Wavey geese (*Chen rossi*) pass over this part of the coast in June.

"Caribou are found on Kent Peninsula, at Cape Barrow, and near the coast on Victoria Land all through the winter; but there are none to be found in winter between Cape Barrow and the mouth of the Coppermine River, nor in the vicinity of Ogden Bay.

"Musk-oxen are to be found to the east and to the west of Arm-ark-tūk River.

"Kent Peninsula is reported to be almost an island, for they say that we shall cross from salt water to salt water in an easy day's travel.

"In making the traverse from Cape Croker on the east side of Bathurst Inlet over to Cape Barrow on the west side, we shall pass the islands where the copper deposits exist.

"There is no open water in Coronation Gulf during the winter, but Dolphin and Union Strait is kept open all winter by a very strong tide.

"Polar bears are reported scarce in this part, but they are numerous in Coronation Gulf later in the season.

"Lind Island, about seventy miles north from Ogden Bay, is indicated as a very favourite resort of bears, but whether in winter or summer I failed to discover. It is most unlikely that polar bears would remain all winter where there is no open water.

"Barren Ground bears (*Ursus arctus richardsoni*) are reported to be scattered all along the Arctic coast, but they do not emerge from their winter quarters till June. They are not numerous.

"We shall have plenty cold weather yet, shall be able

to haul across Kent Peninsula on the snow, and the ice will still be good on Bathurst Inlet, so that we shall easily reach Cape Barrow with dogs and sleighs if we so desire."

This was about all, and most of it was welcome news to us.

Our visitors were not old enough to remember Collinson wintering in Cambridge Bay in 1852, but they had been told about it by their fathers.

These two natives had travelled considerably. Pŭn-ŭk-tŭk had visited the Coppermine River, but had not been to the mouth of it. Hŭn-ĭl-yak had journeyed along the coast of Wollaston Land and Victoria Land and had been to Cambridge Bay. He mentioned that salmon were very numerous at this place, a fact which I see indicated on the chart.

On my questioning them about their plans for the summer, they replied that they intended to journey to the Ark-i-lĭnik River to procure wood for their sleighs. They would take their dogs but not their kyaks. During the summer they intended to construct their sleighs and would then wait for the "freeze up," when the return journey would be made with dogs and sleighs.

I at once suggested that as driftwood was plentiful west of Cape Barrow, and as the distance was not greater than to the Ark-i-lĭnik River, they should accompany us along the Arctic coast. They understood what I said perfectly, considered for a moment, and then without hesitation Hŭn-ĭl-yak stated that he was willing to come, but that of course he would have to bring his wife and family. Pŭn-ŭk-tŭk was not far behind in expressing his willingness to accompany us. Of course he also possessed a wife and family that would have to come along. The whole affair was arranged in a very few minutes. I then produced a few presents, which were supposed to clinch the bargain, and do duty for the signing of a contract.

An observation for latitude placed us in 67° 29′ N., a little to the south of Ogden Bay.

The next day, May 13, we started north again and made fourteen miles by account, but not on a very straight course. We still followed the Arm-ark-tŭk River, which took many small turns. Land was low, which I took to indicate the proximity of the coast. At camp-time our guides, as I may now call Hŭn-il-yak and Pŭn-ŭk-tŭk, stated that we were half-way to their iglus, which were out on the ice.

On May 14 we travelled ten and a half miles by account and struck the coast ice. Another seven miles brought us to the Husky camp.

The river widened considerably, and the land got very low as we approached the coast.

I tried but failed to obtain an observation for latitude. Even now I did not know exactly where we had struck the coast. Since the observation taken on May 12, we had travelled, but not in a direct line, fourteen miles on May 13, and ten and a half on May 14, coming out on to the coast. By dead reckoning this would give our present position as 67° 44′ N. This latitude, however, answered equally well for several places on the coast between Johnson Point and Blackwood Point.

The camp consisted of two iglus and three deerskin tents, which were pitched on snow foundations and so raised. There were five families and some visitors, about forty-five persons altogether at the camp.

They appeared to be the same strong, hardy-looking, good-natured and happy people that I had met in other parts of the Northland. They differed very little except in the cut of their clothes, and in the dialect they spoke, from the Huskies of my own party.

I was able to understand them to a certain extent; but they had a habit which caused a difficulty in our learning their language. They appeared to have a sort of slang of their own, which they spoke only amongst themselves. This habit is common among Huskies generally, and I picked up many words from hearing my Husky companions talking together, which, when I employed them in conversation, I was told were wrong. "That word," they would say, "we only use amongst ourselves; it is not right; so-and-so is the correct word for the white master to use." The fact is they do not wish you to learn or understand their own jargon.

A great dance was held in the evening to celebrate our arrival.

CHAPTER XI

THE NORTH COAST AND ITS INHABITANTS FROM OGDEN BAY TO MELVILLE SOUND

MAY 15 was spent in talking with the natives, photographing them, trading a few articles, and generally taking it easy.

These Arctic coast natives were very friendly, although this was their first meeting with white men. I took the measurements of several men and women, and the process seemed to afford great amusement. They did not exhibit the slightest hesitation in posing for the camera. There was no sign of any sickness amongst them. The Eskimo as a race enjoy the best of health, and this in a great measure accounts for the exuberance of their spirits, which even starvation and intense cold do not suppress.

They informed me that they lived on the ice during the greater part of the winter and spring, spearing seals through their blow-holes. Just before the ice breaks up they go inland, where they remain during July, August, September, October, November, and December, killing and spearing deer at the crossing-places. In the latter part of December, they return to the coast and remain there till the following June, seal's meat and blubber being their sole sustenance.

The older women were tattooed on the face in the manner common amongst all the Huskies I have come in contact with. They were also tattooed on the hands, wrists, and the lower part of the arm in a manner that I had not seen before.

The men wore their hair either cropped very short, convict fashion, or it was left long with only a small, circular, closely-cropped patch on the crown. In this they do not differ from the Huskies of Hudson Bay. The men all had large stomachs, but this is characteristic of the whole of the Eskimo tribes, and probably results from their eating enormous quantities of meat at one time.

With the exception of a few strings of beads, traded on one of their journeys on the Ark-i-lĭnik River, the women wore no articles of personal adornment, but their deer-skin clothes were ornamented with strips of white deer-skin worked in between that of a darker colour. Sealskin appeared to be used only for making footgear.

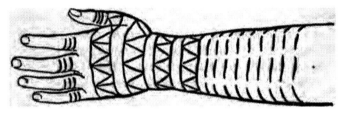

Tattooed hand and arm.

Their habitations, both iglus and deerskin tents, were clean and well looked after. One naturally expected the usual strong smell of the seal-oil lamp, which is kept burning day and night to melt ice for drinking-water.

Bows and arrows, and spears tipped with native copper, were their weapons in hunting deer. A special kind of spear was used for harpooning seals. Stone kettles and stone lamps were their only cooking utensils. At this time, being out of seal meat, they were living on oil and blubber, a diet that evidently agreed well with them.

Ki-li-nek-meūt was the name of this tribe.

Another tribe, further east, near King William's Land, I fancy, was known by the name of Net-ti-ling-meūt. About this latter tribe I was told terrible tales. They were reported to be very bad men, and very savage; but this I do not credit. I was informed that in the previous winter, food being very scarce, murder and cannibalism had been the order of the day.   Such horrors had never occurred amongst the Ki-li-nek-meūt.   But it is always so ; the Huskies one happens to be amongst invariably tell horrible stories about another tribe, but always deny having participated in the orgies they describe.

It is significant that one rarely meets with an old man or an old woman. With the poor Huskies the struggle for exist-ence must be very keen, and old age is of short duration.

The presents I gave delighted them, and they jumped about for joy.   In return they seemed eager to present me with everything they possessed.   It was a pleasure to give to them, for though in want of the first necessaries of life, no matter what they saw or how much they needed or desired anything they saw, they never begged.   I wished to make a favourable impression on them, in order that the way might be smooth for any future wanderer in their land, but I was not reckless in giving.

In order to remove any misconception as to this matter, I append the list of what I gave and what I received.

Given.	*Received.*
2 snow-knives.	2 pairs deerskin pants—men's.
4 butcher-knives.	1 pair deerskin pants—woman's.
2 pocket knives.	6 pairs sealskin moccasins.
3 files.	2 deerskin coats.
1 axe.	3 large sealskins, undressed.
4 packages needles.	3 large sealskins, dressed.
2 thimbles.	300 lbs. blubber.
2 pairs scissors.	2 bows and quivers complete.
1 small iron plane.	2 seal spears.
	1 copper snow-knife, and some copper needles and other curios.

Business was not concluded till late.   We then held a council of war, when it was decided to start the fol-lowing day.

The guides, Hŭn-ĭl-yak and Pŭn-ŭk-tŭk, whose names

K

I really must shorten to Hun and Pun, informed me that we would have to travel west along the coast for four nights before we could expect to find deer, and it would take us ten nights to reach Kent Peninsula, where we would again come on deer.

A good observation of meridian altitude of the sun gave our latitude as 67° 50′ 25″ N.

We had struck the coast in the latitude 67° 44′ N. reckoned from the observation taken on May 12, and we had travelled seven and a half miles by account north-north-west on the ice after striking the coast. Thus our reckoning was almost correct.

Still I could not place our position in longitude. A glance at the map will explain the difficulty. Any spot on the coast between Blackwood Point and Johnson Point would have suited our latitude, 67° 50′ 25″ N.

Our supplies of biscuit, pork, and sugar had some time since come to an end, but we still had nine pounds of the very best tea and enough tobacco. To run out of tobacco in the north causes general discontent in the party. It is always possible to take along a sufficient supply of this most necessary article as long as one is travelling with dogs and sleighs or by canoe. When it comes to packing on one's back, then let every man look out for himself.

We still had a large reserve of ammunition and plenty nets, on both of which we depended to furnish us a living until we should reach Fort Norman on the Mackenzie River.

On May 16 we set out at a late hour on our journey to the west. Our party consisted of twenty-one persons, of whom eighteen were Huskies, as follows: Uttungerlah, his wife and two daughters; Amer and his wife; Pitzeolah, who had no encumbrances; Hŭn-ĭl-yak, with wife and four children; Pŭn-ŭk-tŭk and his wife and three children. We now had twenty-six dogs, for Hun and Pun each had a sleigh and a few dogs. This was a large party to keep supplied with meat. However, there were deer reported ahead, and the seals would soon be discovered on the ice. For the present, Hun and Pun brought along enormous sealskin bags filled with blubber.

The nights were now so light that we found difficulty in sleeping. We often lay awake the whole night, and dropped off to sleep when it was about time to be rising.

Going due west for fifteen miles, we passed numerous small, rocky islands quite destitute of vegetation. The distant mainland was just visible as a continuous, low, undulating ridge of rocks. Next day we made thirteen miles, still due west. The going was excellent, the thawing snow presented a surface like grease.

We camped at a group of rocky islands over which the ice sheet had evidently moved in a northerly direction. Deep grooves had been scooped out of the rock, which to the north was broken off abruptly.

On May 18 the minimum temperature was 2°, and the maximum 36° Fahr. The weather was cloudless, with a moderate south-south-east wind. We made fifteen miles, and camped close to a rocky island. The ice was still smooth and the going splendid. Here I at last puzzled out our position in longitude. We had struck the Arctic coast a little to the west of McTavish Point. We saw one seal on the ice, and an Arctic owl. At camp-time we spied Husky tents in the distance to the west on our course.

May 19 was warm, and we began to have trouble with the runners of the sleighs, from which the mud came off in large chunks.

At noon when we approached the Husky tents, Hun ran ahead waving his arms, apparently making signs, and then holding them above his head, "hands up" fashion. This was the custom when approaching strangers, being a sign of peace, and evidence of being without arms. Amer and Uttungerlah were requested to do likewise, and Darrell and I conformed to the custom. In this fashion we advanced slowly, the strangers remaining grouped together near their tents. As we drew near, they all advanced to meet us, and we soon established friendly relations.

We then had a long talk, the subject of course being the visit of the white men, of whom they had heard. They were very inquisitive as to the names of the Hudson Bay Huskies in my party. They informed us that, the day before, one deer had been killed on the mainland, and musk-oxen and their tracks had been seen inland.

I got the strangers grouped for a photo, to which they did not show the slightest objection, and they proved good subjects, remaining absolutely still in whatever position they were placed.

These Huskies bore a marked resemblance to the Mongolian type, seldom seen among those of Hudson Bay. Although they appeared to be friendly enough, they did not invite any of our party into their tents. We were a very strong party and well armed, but I should not care to ask for a night's lodging from them, if alone and unarmed in the dead of winter, during a period of starvation. I distributed amongst them a few knives, files, awls, needles, fish-hooks, &c., and they were delighted. In return they presented me with a few copper implements, and some much-needed fuel in the shape of driftwood which they had collected along the coast.

There were six men and six women with their families in their camp, and, as usual, there was not a single old man or old woman amongst them, though there were plenty of youngsters of various ages. There was only one explanation of this fact.

Bidding farewell to the strangers, we continued on our course, making straight for a point of land about north-west, and after going twelve miles reached White Bear Point (Au-let-ti-wig-yuak), where we camped. Here the land was low, with numerous stony and rocky knolls, between which were stretches of flat ground.

Hun and Pun proved themselves able and willing workers. They used to pitch their tents in a few minutes and then come and assist in the building of our snow-houses. Their wives in the meantime would have the oil lamps employed in the long and tedious process of melting ice and snow for drinking-water. Taking a stroll, while the iglus were in course of construction, I noticed plenty of fresh deer tracks, and a little later I spied four of the animals. It was decided to hunt next day, but rain and sleet spoiled the sport and no deer were killed. In the night our snow-houses caused much anxiety. The weather was warm; the sides of the house commenced to bulge inwards in a very threatening manner, and many supports were required to prevent a total collapse.

The following morning it was still blizzarding, but cleared up in the afternoon, and Amer and I together shot eight deer out of a band of twelve, the only band we saw.

It was a great pleasure to hunt with Eskimo. I have shot in many lands, but of my many happy recollections I think the happiest are of caribou hunts with the Huskies. On unfavourable ground, and when deer are difficult to approach, they hold much consultation, and prepare deeply thought-out plans for the circumvention of the animals. An Eskimo, who is a good hunter, can always be depended upon to do the right thing, and he never shows the least jealousy. One fact gives much interest to shooting in the Great Northland, and that is that every pound of meat is absolutely required. Our large party with twenty-six dogs this day depended entirely on the rifles of Amer and myself.

Some ptarmigan that we came across had already commenced to assume their summer plumage.

The snow was drifting again on May 22, but we hauled the deer we had killed, and thus had a supply of meat sufficient, we hoped, to last us to It-ib-lēr-yuak, the lake on the portage across Kent Peninsula.

I obtained a good observation for latitude, which placed us at 68° 5′ N. This was, of course, where we expected to be.

On May 23 we did not travel. The weather was not favourable, and we were in no great hurry. All the mud fell off the runners of the sleighs, but they still had whalebone. Hun and Pun's sleighs were shod with short pieces of deer-horn, cut flat and riveted on with bone.

Our cooking was now done over seal-oil lamps, for there was no fuel of any kind on White Bear Point. It used to take three hours to boil our kettle of meat.

Next day we cut across White Bear Point, holding a course about north-west, but travelled only eight miles, for the going was very bad, the recent rain and sleet having been formed into a slippery crust on which the dogs could not get footing. In the afternoon three Husky tents were spied to the south, and I detached a couple of men to pay them a visit and to procure some wood if possible.

It was easy to take the bearing by prismatic compass, for we always made either for a point of land or an island which was visible at the start.

During the night three Husky men and one woman arrived. They had all been in the Husky camp I had found on the Ark-i-linik River on my journey in 1899. I could only recall the face of one of them, but they all remembered me. They gave us a little wood and a few copper implements. I presented them with a knife, a file, a thimble, a mirror, and a few needles. Needless to say they were delighted.

On May 25, shortly after starting, we spied four Huskies out on the ice with their dogs. Two of them came towards us, but were evidently afraid to come close. After the "hands up" performance had been gone through several times on their part and on ours, they came up and we had a talk. They were out hunting seals. The dogs were employed to discover the seals' houses, and, in the event of success, for hauling the seals back to camp. During the winter the seals inhabit small houses scooped out of the snow over their blow-holes. In walking on the snow-covered ice, it is possible to pass right over these without discovering them. The seal takes alarm very easily, and beats a safe and hasty retreat down his blow-hole. In the late spring the heat of the sun begins to have some effect, and ultimately it melts the seal's house away and the animal lies exposed to view. On Hudson Bay the seal-hunting Husky, by very patient crawling, and by imitating the movements of a seal, approaches inch by inch until he is within ten or fifteen yards. Beyond this range he does not care to risk a shot, for the seal must be at once killed stone dead. One flip of its tail is sufficient to send it down its blow-hole. The Arctic coast Huskies, having no firearms, are obliged to crawl up close enough to throw a harpoon with some chance of success, and they suffer many disappointments. Very often, just as they are about to throw, down pops the seal, and the fun is over.

This was the first day that could really be called a spring day. The snow which, under the powerful rays of the sun, was turning into slush, made heavy hauling for the dogs.

We camped on one of the Fitzgerald Islands, where we could easily recognise the coast-line from the chart, which appeared to be quite accurate. I have already remarked on the importance of adhering to the local names of places. In this case, had I found on the chart the Husky name for White Bear Point, Au-lit-ti-wig-yuak, I should at once have been able to fix our position in longitude.

Shortly before we reached our camping-ground, we met other Eskimo belonging to the same tribe. Among them was one oldish man who remembered Collinson wintering in Cambridge Bay in 1852. These natives appeared to be very friendly and exhibited not the least fear. One man possessed a musket, which he had traded from another Husky whom he had met on the Ark-i-linik River. He had no powder, nor caps, nor lead, and did not know how to fire the thing off, still he was quite proud of it, and packed it along wherever he went.

I obtained a good many copper articles from them, such as snow-dags, ice-chisels, &c. They appeared to be rich in copper implements. They stated that some of their copper had been obtained in Victoria Land, and some from the islands to the north.

One man had a polar bear's skull and a large hide. The bear had been speared during the winter with the aid of dogs. They corroborated the statement made by Hun and Pun about the polar bears on Lind Island, and they stated that they were numerous all through the winter.

I was surprised at the honesty of these natives. "Stuff" (which in Canadian parlance means everything that we possessed) lay scattered about outside our snow-house, but, though they handled and examined things with much curiosity, they took nothing.

Several of these natives accompanied us when we resumed our journey next day, May 27.

Although the maximum readings of the thermometer in the shade at this date were generally below 32°, in the sunshine it was very warm. We usually managed to obtain enough drinking water from cavities in the rocks close to our camps, and were thus saved the tedious operation of thawing ice and snow over the seal-oil lamps every night.

We camped on the west side of the portage across Brown Point, and here the tent was pitched for the first time. Although we had hitherto been able to build snow-houses, we had been obliged for the last fortnight to build them of special construction. The sides were made almost perpendicular and only about five feet high, waterproof sheets and the tent being then thrown over the top to answer the purpose of a roof. Four deer were seen soon after we camped.

We were favoured with the most glorious weather at this time; cloudless skies, gentle breezes, and bright hot sun during the day, though the nights were cool, even cold. The minimum thermometer read 2° on the night of May 27.

The following morning an early start was made, for I was determined, if possible, to make half-way to the portage across Kent Peninsula, where we were promised plenty of bull caribou by our guides Hun and Pun.

Passing Dease Point, we camped at some island rocks a short distance to the west.

A native who came to pay us a visit in the morning, accompanied us on our journey for a short distance, and lent a willing hand in helping the sleigh along. He took a notion to depart in rather sudden fashion I thought, when I discovered that he had taken one of my snow-knives, but in its place he had kindly left his copper one. This was the first case of theft that I had come across, and even this thief had been conscientious enough to leave his own copper snow-knife in place of my steel one, which he appeared to prefer. We camped at some rocky islands a short distance to the west of Dease Point. Here we saw many female deer, but shot none, for we were anxious to push on and reach Kent Peninsula. On this night we saw the midnight sun for the first time. Had we had a good horizon, however, I fancy it would have been visible some nights before.

The mainland to the south appeared to be high and very rocky. The land on Melbourne Island, which we had raised soon after passing the Fitzgerald Islands, appeared as a long low streak to the north.

On May 29, after travelling about ten miles, I obtained an observation for latitude which gave 68° 29' N. Three miles more brought us to the east coast of Kent Peninsula, or rather to a small inlet of the coast, where several Huskies were fishing with their copper fish-hooks through holes in the ice.

In the evening they brought me seven of the fish they had caught, which proved to be codling, the same in appearance and size as those we have around the coast of Great Britain. I was surprised to see these fish, for the Hudson Bay Huskies had always denied the existence of any sort of cod in the Hudson Bay. The Arctic Husky name for these codling was u-wŭk, and they were reported to be very plentiful all along the coast at this time of year.

Numerous deer tracks were seen as we approached the shore, and in the evening a large bull was shot.

The weather was now almost like summer. The sunshine during the noonday hours came blazing down. Already a great change was observable on the land, bare patches of ground appearing here and there. Pools of water and a few seals were to be seen on the ice. Snowbirds were increasing in numbers. In the evening Pun killed a ground squirrel. When these small hibernating animals appear it is a sure sign of summer, for they feed on grass. I may not be quite right in saying this, however, for on my last trip I observed them to burrow up through a foot of snow. But that was an exceptionally late spring, and, going back to sleep, they did not reappear till two weeks later. They are queer little brown animals, with much the same habits as the marmot. When caught at some distance from their burrows, they are easily taken by the hand and do not appear to be at all alarmed. They form the chief food of the wolverene or glutton during the summer months.

The following day, May 30, it was decided to halt in order to hunt deer, and the Huskies started at an early hour with dogs and sleigh on which to bring back the spoils. Early in the afternoon they returned with four large bulls, the horns of which were one foot high. I remained at the camp busy with photographic and geological matters.

Fuel, in the shape of moss and heaths, which had been so very scarce since leaving Pelly Lake on Back's River, was now more abundant. Several species of heaths were procurable, even a few stunted willows could be gathered, but the dwarf birch was still absent, although our guides had promised a plentiful supply at this place.

In the evening a council of war was held to decide

future plans. I was particularly anxious to gain information about the climate, and about the state of the ice in
these regions during the summer months. The statements
of the guides, Hun and Pun, appeared to be of a very
contradictory nature. It was evident that we would soon
be compelled to delay somewhere to allow time for the
slush and water to clear off the ice. It would be necessary
also to kill seals and give the women time to make sealskin
boots for all hands, or rather feet. To travel with sleighs
through deep slush is not possible ; the runners sink so
that the load breasts the slush, and the sleigh becomes
hopelessly stuck. After the slush comes the water stage,
which also is impracticable.

It was proposed to delay somewhere in the vicinity of
Cape Croker, on the east side of Bathurst Inlet. We hoped,
however, to be able to continue travelling on the ice across
Bathurst Inlet to Cape Barrow, and possibly also to the
mouth of the Coppermine River. In that case we would
be able to reach Fort Norman on the Mackenzie River,
our objective, by September 5.

Hun and Pun, on being questioned as to how late in
the season travelling on the ice could be carried on with
safety, replied "always till August 10th, and very often
till the last week in that month." These dates are easily
set down on paper, but they were only reached after much
trouble and many references to the growth of the deer's
coats and the appearance of their horns, for the Arctic
coast Huskies have no names for months, as far as I could
discover.

With my Eskimo from the Hudson Bay I never had
any difficulty in making myself intelligible in this respect,
for they have a name for each of their thirteen moons.
Each name has a meaning ; thus "mŭn-it" (eggs) is their
name for June, the month in which the birds lay their
eggs. Then the month can be divided into quarters or
weeks, and that is near enough for general purposes in
Huskyland.

Starting from Labyrinth Bay from the head of the small inlet which, although its size scarcely justifies a name, I have called Portage Inlet, we travelled one mile overland, and reached a fresh-water lake about six miles in length. We travelled to the foot of this lake, which is called It-ib-lēr-yuak, and camped. From this lake a stream flowed to the head of an inlet from Warrender Bay on the west side of Kent Peninsula. This arm or inlet from Warrender Bay, which is not marked on any map or chart, is called I-lu by the natives.

Kent Peninsula is thus almost an island. It-ib-lēr-yuak Lake, the stream, and the I-lu Inlet form a complete waterway, except for the one mile overland between the lake and the head of Portage Inlet. There is thus a first-rate canoe route, shorter and better sheltered than that round the north shore of Kent Peninsula.

The country near It-ib-lēr-yuak Lake is very rocky, and in places hilly. About a mile to the south-south-west of our camp, at the foot of the lake, stood a hill of basaltic formation, precipitously cut on the east and south.

Shortly before camping we met an aged Husky and his wife fishing through the ice on the lake. They accompanied us and camped alongside. The woman well remembered Collinson wintering in Cambridge Bay. The appearance of old folk, alone and far away from their tribe, may explain what I have already hinted at. When the old are unable to hunt, travel, and keep up with those of the younger generation, they are left behind in an iglu to starve and freeze to death during the winter. However, this old couple had "toughed" through the winter by fishing. Though decrepid they were in wonderful spirits, and healthy in appearance.

One hawk was seen in the evening.

On the morning of June 1 I told off three hunters to procure meat. They returned early with seven bull caribou, so Hun and Pun's information about the bull caribou being plentiful in Kent Peninsula was now fully confirmed. I sent the old man to fish in the lake, and in the evening he returned with five good-sized trout, one of which scaled ten pounds.

The day being perfect and the sun hot, advantage was taken to empty all the bags and boxes and lay the contents out to dry.

In the afternoon of June 2 Darrell and I ascended the hill not far from our camp, to which I have already referred. By Watkin aneroid I made the altitude 360 feet, which is certainly not very high, but this hill, Har-li-ar-li (precipitous), is the most prominent landmark for miles round. From the summit we obtained a magnificent view. To the west lay I-lu, the long inlet from Warrender Bay, which was just visible beyond. Turning to the north and east we could see the whole of It-ib-lēr-yuak Lake, Portage Inlet, and Labyrinth Bay. I scanned the ice on I-lu eagerly with my binoculars for seals lying on the ice, but there was no sign of any. No seals meant no boots for our party.

Large patches of bare ground were now appearing in all directions; the snow was fast disappearing from the flat country, but it still lay in deep drifts in sheltered spots and in gulches; some of the latter we should have had difficulty in crossing had we not brought our snow-shoes.

Many summer birds, mostly of the lark species, and another hawk were seen. In the evening two wavey geese (*Chen rossi*) passed overhead, bound for the north. The summer, long delayed, had at last arrived, for there is little or no spring in these regions.

On June 3 the weather was so hot that large pools quickly formed on the ice, threatening to flood us out; so it was decided to strike camp on the following day.

I happened to have with me the diaries kept during my journey of 1899, and it was interesting to compare meteorological notes, and such incidents as the arrival of the different summer birds. It seemed to me that the present summer was a few days in advance of that which

I had experienced on Chesterfield Inlet in 1899, though we were now five degrees of latitude further north. But the spring of 1899 was exceptionally late, and this fact must be taken into consideration. I did not possess sufficient data to form a just comparison. However, I think I am correct in saying that in these regions a considerable difference in latitude makes little or no difference in the seasons. The winter is invariably prolonged, and when summer comes it comes with a rush.

In many parts of the northland there occur beds of marine shells in elevated places such as the tops of hills and ridges, &c. Such beds were very noticeable in the neighbourhood of It-ib-lēr-yuak Lake.

Lyell ("Students' Geology," page 168) gives the following explanation of such formations :—

"The occurrence of patches and beds of marine shells at altitudes varying from a few feet to 500 feet is probably due, i.e. their present elevated condition, to the action of great glaciers or ice sheets, pushing up portions of the sea-floor possibly in a frozen condition to the hill-slopes on which they are now to be found."

At an early hour on June 4 we broke camp and moved south-westwards for three miles, passing over one small lake three-quarters of a mile in length, and reaching the head of the inlet from Warrender Bay. I shall adhere to the Husky name, I-lu, for this inlet. It is one of the few short Eskimo names that I have heard.

The scarcity of seals on I-lu made it advisable to push on the next day. Starting at an early hour, we travelled nearly eighteen miles south-west and camped about a mile beyond a hill called U-wei-yu-ŭllu, situated in a small bay on the south shore. The weather having cooled considerably, the travelling was good. It did not thaw all day.

Amer succeeded in killing the first seal of the season. A few deer were seen and three Huskies were detached in pursuit, for we wanted meat badly. One swan was seen at camp-time. The deer hunters returned during the night, each man carrying the meat of one deer on his back.

On June 6, after travelling three miles in cool weather, we passed another hill, very similar in size and shape to U-wei-yu-ŭllu, precipitous nearly all round. Although the altitude of either of these hills does not exceed six hundred feet, they form prominent landmarks.

Twelve miles south-west was our day's travel.

I-lu, which at its widest part I should judge to be about twelve miles across, now narrowed to one and a half miles at the spot where we camped, and I at once jumped to the conclusion that we were approaching Warrender Bay. In these parts it is exceedingly difficult to know if one is on the open sea or an inlet only. Rocky islands abound which are not marked on the chart; they appear in the distance as continuous land, and are easily mistaken for the mainland.

We found an abundance of willows at camp-time, but they were not dry and did not burn well.

The following day, after travelling eight miles, we reached Warrender Bay. The entrance to I-lu is hidden from view by islands overlapping one another. This fact readily accounts for the surveyors of Melville Sound having passed it unnoticed.

Crossing Hope Bay we directed our course nearly south-west to the south shore of Melville Sound.

The ice was smooth, the hauling good, and we accomplished twenty-two miles. This was a very good day's journey, for with the Eskimo quite half the day is generally wasted in smoking and talking. Having travelled with Eskimo several thousand miles, I call ten miles an average day, fifteen miles a good day, and twenty miles splendid work.

Six seals were seen on the ice, the first flock of ducks was observed, four bands of deer were spied. Pun killed five Arctic hares with his bow and arrow.

The land on the south coast of Melville Sound is rocky and mountainous in character.

As soon as we had camped the Huskies started off to hunt. They returned during the night, having killed three bulls, and each man carried a heavy load of meat.

Whatever may be said about the Huskies' rate of travelling, the charge of laziness cannot be brought against them in hunting. All the Eskimo are good packers, *i.e.* carrying loads on their backs. They think nothing of packing two hundred pounds, which is what the body, head and legs of a large bull caribou weigh. A Husky may be lazy during the day while travelling, but then he is willing to work all night, and very often, during the summer months, he will go for days without desiring to take a good "turn in." The horns of two of the bulls killed measured two feet. The animals were fat inside, and the backfats were already commencing to form.

On June 8 we moved a short distance westwards, along the coast of Melville Sound, and camped at a river, or rather a small creek, called Sarker-wark-tūk, where there was a Husky camping-ground, to which perhaps the name properly belonged. Here I decided to remain till the slush cleared away.

CHAPTER XII

ACROSS MELVILLE SOUND—COPPER DEPOSITS

I HAD expected to see a large river at Sarker-wark-tūk, for the Huskies had been talking about it for days, but the river was nothing but the little creek which flowed into the small bay on which we had camped. The place was evidently a favourite camping-ground of the Huskies, and between it and Cape Croker there were several other Husky camps.

The maximum readings of the thermometers were now above 32°, but it still froze at night, in spite of the midnight sun. The ice had been already broken away at the mouth of the small creek.

During the days we spent here we killed some deer, but they were not very plentiful. No seals were seen on the ice in our neighbourhood, but, as we required sealskin for footgear, we arranged expeditions in search of them. Amer and Uttungerlah set out armed with rifles, and Hun and Pun accompanied them with harpoons. One day (June 10) they returned with three common seals, and another day with two ūgyūk or large seals. Darrell shot a female Arctic hare which, in a fortnight, would have given birth to five leverets. We saw birds of a considerable number of species, geese, ducks, gulls, &c. On the evening of June 9 I noticed a sandpiper which behaved as if it had its nest close by. Cranes, uttering their peculiar cry, were numerous and were always paired, but I never found their nests. On June 12 Amer shot three eider-ducks, one of which, a male, weighed 4½ lbs., and the other two, females, 3¾ lbs. each. They were all very handsome.

and in perfect plumage. It has often occurred to me that the Huskies might be encouraged to collect eider-down, at least on Hudson Bay, where, on the rocky islands, the birds nest in thousands. This industry is carried on in Norway with, it may be presumed, advantage to those who follow it. If Norwegians can make anything by it, Huskies would find it highly profitable, for starvation wages to a European would mean vast wealth to the native of Hudson Bay. Could not the missionaries take the matter up?

Ptarmigan were common and so tame that they could be knocked over with a stone. Hun and Pun killed a few with their bows and arrows, but I could not compliment them on the accuracy of their aim. At one bird ten arrows were shot, at distances varying from six to ten yards, but it flew away unharmed. On June 14 I saw one loon (great northern diver) passing overhead, the first of the season.

The Huskies fished for u-wŭk or codling, and were very successful. They brought back a big sleigh-load of hundreds, perhaps thousands, some of them weighing as much as two pounds.

We observed salmon (June 14) ascending the Sarker-wark-tūk River, which flows from a lake not far off.

Flies, spiders, and other insects were noticed on June 10. Fuel was abundant in the shape of dwarf birch, but no plants had as yet shown any sign of growth. I spent some time in examining the rocks in the region, and found them marked in an interesting manner by ice action. One afternoon I took the altitude of a longish hill or ridge overlooking our camp, and found it 840 feet high.

One day I had a long talk with Hun and Pun with whose dialect I was now fairly familiar. They told me, and this information was corroborated by others afterwards, that the wavey goose nests in large numbers on Kent Peninsula, and across Dease Strait on Victoria Land, but none are found to the west of Cape Croker. I write this because the nesting habits of the wavey goose are much discussed. It is a common belief among the traders of the north that the wavey nests beyond the limit of human beings, and that an egg has never been found.

I was desirous of visiting the Barry Islands in the southern portion of Bathurst Inlet where copper was reported to be plentiful, and, as the last few days had made a great difference in the snow, I arranged to set out on June 15.

I took two companions, Uttungerlah and Hun, who acted as guides. Riding on the sleigh and driving the pick of our dogs, we travelled for seven hours, but it was difficult to say how far we went. There was much slush and water on the ice, and the dogs' pace was variable. When we camped we were half-way to Barry Island, our guide said.

Cape Croker is an island, a narrow gut of from half-a-mile to one mile wide separating it from the mainland.

We met some Huskies about camping time, so we made for their camp, where we found five tents.

These natives were most friendly; they helped to pitch our tent, and they brought fuel, while one of them started off to catch u-wŭk to feed our dogs.

Most of them belonged to the same tribe as Hun, but two belonged to the War-li-ark-i-yŭk, the tribe on the west side of the Coppermine River. The tribe, of which only a few now exist, between Cape Barrow and the Coppermine, is called Ku-yak-i-yuăk.

Deer in this vicinity were reported to be scarce.

Uttungerlah informed me in the evening that both Amer and he wished to accompany me to Fort Norman on the Mackenzie River, if I would give them a canoe in which to return.

I ascertained that we were camped five miles north of Everitt Point, called Ŭming-mŭktor by the natives.

We travelled seven hours the following day, but it was again difficult to say how far we went. The ice was fair in places, but at times the slush lay deep. However, we reached the north part of Barry Island. During the day

Hun informed me that copper on Barry Island was not nearly so plentiful as at another place, indicating a spot near Fowler Bay. At this place a block of pure copper, weighing one or more tons, was reported to be lying on the shore. If we had gone to this place I felt quite convinced that Hun would have said it was at some other place that copper was really plentiful, so I did not think it worth while to alter our course.

Along the north shore of Barry Island we picked up some drift sticks which evidently must have come from Hood River.

Two small fragments of copper were picked up by Uttungerlah in the evening.

One small flowering plant was already in blossom.

Among other things Hun had promised us were abundance of dwarf birch, and a large number of deer on Barry Island. The drift sticks provided a fire, but the absence of deer suggested that we should have to beat a hasty retreat.

The next day we devoted to examining the rock formation and searching for copper. As the occurrence of this native copper,[1] and a full description of the formation in which it is found, has been written by an eminent specialist from my notes and specimens, there is no occasion for me to say any more on the subject.

We were successful in finding the copper, which appears to be abundant and widely distributed. Whether it would ever be worth working is another matter, and one on which I am not competent to give an opinion.

We saw one deer; I shot an Arctic hare, and Hun caught some u-wŭk, which served for supper. Grass was observed to have begun growing at the roots. The ice was becoming very blue, most of the snow having disappeared.

Barry Island is called Iglor-yu-ŭlling. The island on which the block of copper was reported is called Kŭn-ū-yŭk.

[1] See Appendix.

On the shore I noticed a chip of wood, which had evidently been chopped off with a sharp axe. It must have come down Hood River, to which the Indians doubtless resort in the summer time.

Next morning, June 18, we started on our return journey. We made for the nearest land on the eastern shore of Bathurst Inlet, distant from our camp about twelve miles. Hun and I then took to the land to hunt deer. There was still considerable snow in places, but it was melting fast, and the whole country was running with water. The land was high and very rocky, almost mountainous. We must have ascended 1500 feet or more. Small grass flats lay between the hills and ridges, and in these hollows we carefully spied for deer. But it was difficult to distinguish them with a glass for they were commencing to shed their coats. If they were standing or feeding one could make them out, but if they were lying down the colour of their coats, a dirty white, harmonised so perfectly with the surrounding rocks and boulders and discoloured patches of snow, that it was very easy to pass them over.

Eventually we spied seven bulls, but we had bad luck. I got within range after making a long circuit, and had a long but absolutely steady shot. They were all lying down. I took the nearest, which happened to have his head so turned round that his horns covered his body. The bullet knocked off one horn close to the skull. They all jumped up and made off at a great pace, never giving an opportunity for a second shot. The stunned beast staggered along in a very drunken fashion, and several times ran against his mates, nearly knocking them over, but he recovered completely after going a short distance.

We camped again with our Husky friends at Üming-mŭktor. I do not know what the last syllable means, but üming-mŭk is Husky for musk-ox, which used to be and still are fairly numerous here. They are to be found a day's journey from the coast. I measured the ice at a crack and found 5 ft. 6 in. of solid ice still.

Leaving the Huskies' camp at nine o'clock on the morning of June 19, we reached our main camp at Sarker-wark-tūk at 5 P.M.

During our absence only two seals and one deer had been killed. A few salmon had been taken by the net.

Before starting in the morning, I had a long talk with a native who was reported to be familiar with the coast between Cape Barrow and the mouth of the Coppermine River. I again endeavoured to elicit some definite information as to how late in the season we should probably be able to travel on the ice. After much talk in reference to the condition of the deer's coats, length of hair and horns, and the appearance and disappearance of the mosquito, I understood that, in ordinary years, travelling on the ice was good till August 20, but that this was an early year.

I was now more than ever determined to reach the Coppermine River on the ice. If we waited at Cape Barrow for open water, as was at one time proposed, we should have to wait till September. We might expect to meet with stormy weather then, when coasting along in our small craft. Difficulties and possible accidents in ascending the Coppermine River, and again in crossing over the divide to Great Bear Lake had to be taken into consideration. Should we delay at Cape Barrow for open water, we might possibly not reach the shores of Great Bear Lake until it was too late in the season to navigate with canoes. In any case I was anxious to reach Fort Norman with as little delay as possible.

Should we be fortunate enough to reach the mouth of the Coppermine on the ice, it would be possible to reach Fort Norman some time before the ice commenced to run in the Mackenzie River. We should then be able to accomplish part of the long return journey up the Mackenzie River by open water. It is a long and tedious journey with dogs and sleighs from Norman to Edmonton, a distance considerably over 1000 miles. We hoped that with luck we might reach Fort Mackay on the Athabasca River before the "freeze up." We should then be within 400 miles of railhead.

June 20 was devoted to a general refit; cartridges were reloaded, bullets cast, and the women were kept busy making sealskin boots. I was occupied in changing photographic plates, and then in overhauling all the "stuff." I found that I still had more than sufficient trade articles and also tobacco.

In the afternoon I had a grand bath, an old kerosene can serving the purpose of a tub. It is not often that the traveller in the Northland has an opportunity of indulging in this luxury. In winter it is too cold, and in the summer the mosquitoes are on the warpath, so that one seldom or never washes even his face on a journey through the Northland of Canada. This may possibly sound very dirty to people who stay at home, but habit is a second nature; one soon forgets about washing. It is a long time between tubs.

In the afternoon I issued thin summer clothes to all hands; I had sent these up on board the whaler. It was a great relief to get out of the deerskins which had now become oppressively warm.

June is the one perfect month in the Northland. The temperature is just right; there is not a fly or mosquito to trouble one. The land is clear of snow, with the exception of a few deep drifts and banks, and the walking is good, for the land dries with wonderful rapidity. The ice is still good to travel over.

Plenty of salmon were now running.

Pun, who had started off in the early hours to hunt deer with his bow and arrow, returned in the evening with a small bull. This was the first occasion (while with me) on which he had drawn the blood of a deer, and feeling correspondingly proud, he brought the whole animal to me.

I had made no promises of payment either to Hun or Pun. They came along of their own free will, but they did whatever they were told and worked hard, as did their wives.

In the afternoon I had a long talk with my Hudson Bay Huskies about their plans, and I asked their intentions. Uttungerlah, who acted as spokesman, replied that he, Amer and Pitz wished to accompany me to Fort Norman, but that the women and children would be left at some place west of Cape Barrow, with Hun in charge to look after them. Hun had been taught to shoot with a muzzle-loader, and was now quite a good shot at short ranges. He was to have the use of a gun while in charge. Pun expressed a desire to accompany me.

The Arctic coast Huskies informed me that cow caribou came right to the coast at and east of Ellice River, but only bulls were to be found east of the river. The southern coast of Bathurst Inlet, however, was an exception; there cow caribou were to be found in the summer months.

The grass was now rushing up, and what is termed the "Barren Ground" looked fresh and green, a welcome change from the vast expanse of snow. It was a great relief to the eyes.

Several flowering plants were already in blossom, birds were singing day and night. Fond as I am of the cold weather and winter travel in the north, I confess to a keen sense of appreciation of the first glimpse of summer. It was a welcome change and a great relief from the monotony of the apparently never-ending dark days, on which the sun at noon had just showed clear of the southern horizon.

We did not now experience any difficulty in sleeping, but, though sound sleepers, we were early risers.

We fed but twice during the twenty-four hours. This was from choice, not on account of scarcity of meat and fish, of which we had abundance. The net was very

successful during the night, and early in the morning
(June 21) the Huskies brought twelve salmon.

I give their weights and measurements :—

WEIGHT. lbs.				LENGTH. ins.				GIRTH. ins.
$8\frac{1}{2}$	.	.	.	$29\frac{1}{2}$	.	.	.	—
$4\frac{1}{2}$	.	.	.	25	.	.	.	—
7	.	.	.	29	.	.	.	—
$4\frac{1}{2}$	.	.	.	26	.	.	.	—
$5\frac{1}{2}$	.	.	.	26	.	.	.	—
$4\frac{1}{4}$	.	.	.	24	.	.	.	—
4	.	.	.	23	.	.	.	—
7	.	.	.	$29\frac{1}{2}$	.	.	.	—
$5\frac{3}{4}$	.	.	.	29	.	.	.	$11\frac{1}{2}$
$5\frac{1}{4}$	.	.	.	$27\frac{1}{2}$	.	.	.	$11\frac{3}{4}$
7	.	.	.	$29\frac{1}{2}$	.	.	.	$13\frac{1}{2}$
$7\frac{1}{2}$	.	.	.	$29\frac{1}{2}$	.	.	.	13

These salmon were bright and silvery on the belly; on
the back they were of a greenish colour; the sides were
sparsely speckled with circular pink spots, varying from the
size of a small pea to nearly the size of a threepenny bit;
with one exception they all had the grilse tail. They were
not shapely fish, having no depth through the shoulders.
They proved most excellent eating, but a diet of salmon
"straight," as we found on my former journey, is rather
rich and apt to disagree, indigestion usually following. I
could see no difference between these salmon and those I
had caught in Hudson Bay. Our nets were of five-inch
mesh. This was about the right size for the larger fish, but
it allowed fish of from one to three pounds to pass freely
through, and there were many of this size.

It was decided to start for the west the following day,
and in the morning (June 22) we were early astir. The
women were so slow in packing up the endless rubbish
which they insisted on taking along, that we were four and
a half hours in getting under way, and it was half-past

eight before we finally bade farewell to our Sarker-wark-tūk Husky friends and set out for the west.

Having travelled for ten hours, including "spells," we made eighteen miles, and camped on the west side of Cape Croker.

Amer and I hunted on the land back from the shore, but we saw no deer. There must be many on this ground in winter, for the shed horns are to be found in considerable numbers.

I was surprised to see so few small birds. Apparently the majority of birds that migrate to the north do not come so far as the Arctic coast to nest. Golden and gray plover and the waders, locally known as yellow-legs, were absent, and only a very few sandpipers were to be seen, though all these birds are very numerous along the Hudson Bay coast in the summer.

We were out of deer's meat, but had a small store of salmon, which we were taking along packed in ice. The Huskies were living on seal's meat and blubber. We found sufficient driftwood at camp-time to boil our fish.

The next morning we continued our journey west. We were now crossing Bathurst Inlet. After travelling some distance we approached a flat-topped precipitous island, which in the distance very much resembled a kopje. On nearing it a different formation of rock was at once noticeable. A bed of limestone, fifteen feet thick, underlay the basalt, which was precipitous and columnar.

This Limestone Island, as I called it, is one of the many Porden Islands between Cape Croker and Lewes Island.

Directly we camped, Amer started off to hunt. He met with success, and killed three large bulls, which were badly wanted and came rather as a surprise. Hun and Pun informed me later, that bull caribou are numerous on these islands in winter. This was proved to be correct the next day, for we found the shed horns numerous.

It was decided to halt next day. The three deer had

to be fetched, and I was anxious to examine the limestone and search for fossils.

We had fairly good travelling on the ice, but shortly before we reached Limestone Island the water lay in deep pools in many places. These had to be waded or splashed through, and we now felt the benefit of our long sealskin boots, which the women had made, for the water at this time of the year is terribly cold. The Hudson Bay Husky women are excellent needlewomen. If they choose to take the trouble, they can make sealskin boots which reach to the hips, absolutely watertight.

On June 24 we halted. I examined the limestone bed, which I found to be in places as much as sixty feet thick. Fossils were diligently searched for, both by myself and by Darrell, but we could find no traces of any.

Uttungerlah killed one seal. Amer, Pitz, and Sandy went for the meat killed the day before. Hun and Pun went to inspect the ice ahead and to collect drift-wood, for we expected to have deep water to travel through the following day. The wood was to be placed on the sleighs underneath the loads.

Deer were seen travelling on the ice, but all hands were busy.

To illustrate the strange customs of the Huskies, a performance which I witnessed in the evening is worth recording.

Nanau, Amer's wife, was troubled by a small white speck or growth on one of her eyeballs. Hun's wife, Hīmiak, was operating on it. She had caught a head-louse, about which there was no great difficulty. It was tied or hitched on to a long hair, but was allowed the full use of its legs and arms, for this was essential. It was then dropped on to the eyeball and the lid of the eye was drawn over it. In its efforts to escape the louse kept scraping and scratching the surface of the eyeball. The idea, which seemed novel, was of course to loosen and remove the offending white speck. I cannot say that the operation was very successful, but the woman affirmed that she felt considerably better after it.

On June 25 our journey was resumed. We did not meet with such deep water on the ice as we expected, for we were fortunate in striking a long crack running west. By keeping close to this we avoided most of the deep pools. Such cracks drain the water off the ice for some distance on either side, but, on account of the small rise and fall of the tide, which in the Arctic Ocean does not exceed one foot, they were not very numerous. Later we came across too many of them, and experienced great difficulty on occasions in effecting a crossing.

Pun informed me in the evening that the ice beyond Cape Barrow was usually very hummocky, and that we should probably not be able to travel over it. Reaching an island where copper was reported, I decided to halt for a day.

Young birds were found already hatched out in the nests. The small birds lose no time in getting to work. They well know the shortness of the summer season in these regions. It seemed only the other day when the first summer arrival was noticed.

Next day, June 26, with Pun as guide, we walked about eight miles across the island to the south-west shore. The formation appeared to be the same as that of Barry Island. We did not find very much copper, for we had but a short time in which to search, but the green stains on the rock bespoke the presence of the metal in considerable quantities. We went to the part of the island where Pun stated he knew of a large chunk or slab of copper about three feet long and three inches thick. There happened to be too much snow and ice at this spot to let us have a chance of finding it, but I have no doubt of its existence.

On this island we shot three bull caribou, so we were all right for meat.

Sandpipers' and larks' eggs which we found were all hard set. The first butterflies were seen here.

We started again at 7.30 A.M. on June 27. After hugging the north shore of Lewes Island we passed along the south shore of Chapman Island, and camped at an island marked on the chart, just at the south-west point of Chapman Island.

At the north-west point of Lewes Island we stopped to smoke. The formation of rock being similar to that on Barry Island we commenced to search for copper, which proved to be very plentiful. First of all only a few flakes could be found, but the longer we searched the more plentiful did the copper become. Finally it got too common and we resumed our journey. The metal occurred in flakes and small chunks, the former were wedged in the rock always vertically. The rock was easily knocked to pieces by a light tap with the axe, the cleavage being both vertical and horizontal.

Between two and three pounds of this native copper were picked up in the course of half or three-quarters of an hour, while we rested.

Travelling on the ice was good. We made fifteen geographical miles in a straight line as measured on the chart, which is about right. Our estimated distance was twenty statute miles, and we were unable to hold an absolutely straight course.

Plenty of butterflies were now to be seen, and I commenced to collect specimens.

I also commenced making a botanical collection of the flowering plants, several of which were now in blossom. I saw a mosquito in the evening; it was very small and black. These creatures always appear to me to look very smart and well dressed when they first appear. As they attain maturity and commence to age, they become brown in colour. When they are full grown and become very brown their time is almost up. Their attacks then become very feeble, and a few days later they disappear altogether, when another and far worse tormentor, in the form of the black fly, makes its unwelcome presence felt. I do not now refer to the coast. On the Hudson Bay coast black flies are not known.

We killed one caribou, one ūgyūk, and one seal, while travelling along the shores of Lewes and Chapman Islands.

The next day, June 28, we continued our journey across Bathurst Inlet.

The going on the ice was excellent. Most of the water had by this time disappeared, and we were fortunate in meeting with no large cracks. These cracks, when too wide to span or straddle with the long sleigh, were a great nuisance. It was necessary then to follow them until a suitable crossing-place, where they pinched in, could be found, and, on occasions, this took us several miles out of our way.

The traverse across from the island on which we had camped to Cape Barrow was fifteen geographical miles, and there were no islands.

The scare about the hummocky ice beyond Cape Barrow seemed to be mere moonshine, as far as we could judge from our camp, and I expected to have good travelling on the ice for another month. In this opinion I was supported by Amer. Uttungerlah stated that, in ordinary years, the ice on the coast of Hudson Bay was good to travel over for sixteen nights beyond our present date.

The formation of the islands lying off Cape Barrow is similar to that observed at Limestone Island, precipitous columnar basalt. Inland from the coast at Cape Barrow the land is very rugged. Pun informed me that deer were very scarce.

We proceeded on our journey the next day. Following the coast we travelled six miles. This brought us to a place called Ūt-ku-shik Karlūk.

Ūt-ku-shik is the Husky name for a kettle. At this place was a deposit of the peculiar soft stone out of which they make their kettles. As I was anxious to examine this rock, it was decided to halt on the following day.

The coast along which we had travelled was very rocky and barren ; there was little or no soil anywhere.

Deer were seen, one seal shot. Up to this date ten seals and four ūgyūk had been killed.

We had heavy rain during the night, but the morning of June 30 was fine enough, and we started at an early hour to inspect the "kettlestone," as I called it. We walked five miles due south from our camp, Hun and Pun acting as guides.

The peculiarity of this rock, which was quite soft and easily cut with an axe or knife, is that it occurs among granitic rocks. There was just this one spot or patch of it. It appeared to be *in situ*, but it was difficult to say. It did not give one the impression that it extended to any great depth. In appearance it was grey and powdery looking. To the touch it had a peculiar soft feel. Its origin is not very apparent.

Mosquitoes were getting very thick in the middle of the day.

On July 1 we started at 7 A.M., and did not camp till 7 P.M., but we only made twenty-two statute miles in a straight line.

We were much troubled by long and broad cracks in the ice, which were now opening in every direction. We must have travelled considerably over thirty miles, for the " spells " for smoking and fooling had by common consent been relinquished. The Huskies having made up their minds to accompany me to Fort Norman, on the Mackenzie River, were as anxious to get forward as I was.

We were now making for a river called Ūnī-a-lik, which had a reputation for salmon-fishing. We failed to reach the river, and camped a short distance east of it. Here in Gray's Bay there was a noticeable difference in the state of the ice. In many places it was getting very rotten, and we observed many holes. Along the shore, except at certain places, there was already a strip of open water about thirty feet broad. Our prospects of reaching the mouth of the

Coppermine did not look so bright as they had done a few days previously.

It was out of our course to go into Gray's Bay, but it had previously been decided to leave the women and children with Hun in charge at the Ŭni-a-lĭk River, where both fish and deer were procurable.

CHAPTER XIII

FROM MELVILLE SOUND TO THE COPPERMINE RIVER

ON July 2, after travelling but a short distance, we reached the Ŭni-a-lik River, which, with a volume of water great enough to deserve the name of "river," flows into the head of Gray's Bay.

We experienced considerable difficulty in effecting a landing. Between the ice and the shore there was a strip or lane of open water, about thirty yards broad, and to get our stuff across this it was necessary to launch one of the canoes. The dogs swam and the sleighs were towed.

Here we found three Husky families in camp. These natives belonged to the Ku-yak-i-yuak tribe, who frequent the country between the Coppermine River and Cape Barrow. They reported deer in fair numbers and musk-oxen plentiful a short distance inland; they had seen a few salmon in the Ŭni-a-lik River. They said that the ice to the west was very hummocky and broken by many broad cracks or lanes of water, so that it would not be possible to proceed to the mouth of the Coppermine River on it.

They also reported a total absence of deer, musk-oxen, and fish. To corroborate this statement they said that none of their tribe ever frequented that portion of the coast lying between Hepburn Island and the mouth of the Coppermine River.

They strongly urged me to remain with them at the Ŭni-a-lik River, where fish, deer, and musk-oxen were procurable, and to proceed at a later date by open water. This all sounded reasonable enough, but I was not satisfied. Whatever was to be decided upon, I could not help feeling somewhat elated that we had accomplished so great a distance on the ice. We had been extremely fortunate, for had we encountered hummocky ice directly we struck the Arctic coast, it would have been impossible to proceed any distance. Of hummocky ice I had had experience enough on my former journey. That alone is sufficient to stop the best equipped party, although some progress may be made for a time. We had been favoured with smooth ice from the start, and though we had certainly had some difficulty in crossing, or avoiding by long detours, broad cracks or lanes of water in the ice, these were troubles that could be surmounted. Except for a few days we had had but little trouble with deep water lying on the ice. We had also been singularly fortunate in coming across deer, and we had not starved a single night. Neither had we been without fire of some kind for cooking purposes, but for this I had chiefly to thank Hun and Pun's wives for the use of their seal-oil lamps.

Looking back on the journey along the Arctic coast we had good reason, I thought, to congratulate ourselves on our good luck.

It was certainly a disappointment to be now told that our attempt to reach the mouth of the Coppermine River on the ice would have to be abandoned, but about this information I was somewhat sceptical, and determined to satisfy myself the following day.

At an early hour on July 3 I started with Pun as companion to inspect the condition of the ice to the west. Paddling across the mouth of the Ŭni-a-lik River which had broken away the ice for some distance from its mouth, but was too deep for wading, we landed on the east shore of the peninsula, which extends in a north-easterly direction towards Hepburn Island. This peninsula or promontory goes by the name of Ŭgi-ŭk among the natives of the Arctic coast. At one place it is quite narrow. From its western side we obtained a splendid view of the ice to the west. From what I could make of it, looking through my powerful deer-stalking telescope, there was nothing to be feared. Smooth ice, uninterrupted by any bad cracks, extended away in the distance as far as the eye could reach.

Pun immediately exclaimed that when the Huskies had spoken of hummocky ice, they did not refer to the ice at the west at all, but to that on the north side of Hepburn Island, on which they had been encamped during the winter. There had evidently been some stupid or intentional lying on some one's part, but the guilty parties I did not discover till later.

I returned to camp at once, fully determined to proceed west with as little delay as possible, but it was necessary to wait for a day or so in order to procure a supply of salmon sufficient to enable us to reach the Coppermine without having to hunt or fish on the way.

I argued in this manner. Suppose that we delayed for open water, which would at first only be a narrow lane between the main body of the ice and the shore, the distance which we would have to travel to the mouth of the Coppermine River would be about two hundred and fifty miles, for we should necessarily be obliged to hug the shore, going round all the bays and inlets, and we would in all probability have to make portages at places where the ice was still fast to the shore. On the other hand, the distance to be travelled in a direct line was only about ninety-five geographical miles, which could easily be accomplished in five days, barring bad cracks in the ice, of which at present there was no sign.

There was another side of the question of course. If we proceeded and only managed to get half or part of the distance to the Coppermine, and if the Eskimo's information about the absence of deer, musk-oxen, and fish should prove true, then our situation would be critical indeed, for we should be in a starving country, unable to proceed either on the ice or by water, and equally unable to retrace our steps.

Many flowers were now in blossom. Uttungerlah shot an ūgyūk, and I shot a wolf and a seal. Seven salmon and a flounder were taken out of the nets in the evening. Two of the salmon weighed 11 lbs. and 9 lbs. respectively.

Late in the evening my Hudson Bay Huskies came to interview me, and told me they could not make up their minds to accompany me further. They repeatedly asked the distance to the Coppermine River. I referred them to the chart which, I remarked, had, along the Arctic coast, proved to be quite correct, with the exception, of course, of the inlet from Warrender Bay into Kent Peninsula, and about this they readily understood why the white men had failed to observe the entrance to I-lu. I also told them that the decision as to accompanying me further west rested with themselves, but that I did not intend to delay, and that their women would have to set to work at once to make socks for the dogs, as the ice had now become very splintery, and was very hard on the dogs' feet in consequence.

Next morning, July 4, Uttungerlah, Amer, and Pitz being still undecided, I determined to leave them behind and proceed with Darrell and Sandy, taking only one sleigh, which was all the three of us could manage. Spare dog-harness and footgear were procured from the natives, for I intended the journey to the Coppermine to be a short and a quick, if not a very merry, one.

About noon Uttungerlah appeared to announce that on reconsideration they thought that they had decided to accompany me. These natives were the veriest children to deal with; they appeared to be quite unable to continue in the same mind for two minutes.

It was necessary for two of them to accompany me as far as the mouth of the Coppermine in order to bring the dogs and sleigh back, and I proceeded to make them a speech, endeavouring to make it quite clear to them that, in having accompanied me from Depot Island in the Hudson Bay to Cape Barrow on the Arctic coast, they had fulfilled their part of the contract, that they were now their own masters again, free to go where and when they pleased. I told them I was very well satisfied with their conduct and the services they had rendered me, and I reminded them that they had received all the pay which was due to them at Mawr-en-ik-yuak before starting. This, it may be remembered, had been done in order to lighten the loads on the sleighs. I then went on to say that ammunition for the return journey would be given out, also some nets, for these had been promised. The dogs, sleigh, and canoe would be handed over when I had no further use for them. All this was according to agreement.

They appeared to be under some foolish delusion that I intended to make them a present of the remaining tobacco, and of the articles which had been brought solely for purposes of trade with the Arctic Eskimo. I gave them to understand that I should be very pleased to give them more presents in "trade" and tobacco, but that more pay meant more work first, and that they would have to help me to pack our "stuff" across the divide from the Coppermine to Great Bear Lake.

This was rather a long-winded oration for me to make in the Eskimo language, and I paused to take breath and observe the effect of my remarks.

The emotions of the Huskies are very sudden and short-lived. Uproariously happy one moment, they are almost crying the next; their faces now wreathed in smiles, now pictures of woe. The transition is remarkable in its rapidity. A hanging underlip and a peculiar low moaning or humming, which they affect, give these children of the north away at once. They are angry then and feel injured, but it is quite impossible to discover the grievance, which generally is purely imaginary. In this instance they had behaved just like children who cry when a cake in a shop window, through which they have been gazing, is suddenly and unexpectedly removed.

The Huskies had seen the "trade" that I carried for so many months that they regarded it as their own, and as we were not likely to meet with any more Arctic coast natives, they jumped to the conclusion that the happy moment had now arrived when they would be put in formal possession. I held other views, however, and at length they understood and realised how foolish they had been, and how well they had been treated.

I bade them bear in mind that I, on my part, had fulfilled every promise made to them on board the schooner *Francis Allyn* in October; that the journey had been of the length agreed on; that, as arranged, they had had their wives and families with them; and, as to payment, they had received twice the amount promised. I made them distinctly understand that white men always kept their promises with natives, a statement which I regret to admit is not strictly true. The only reason I could think of why they were not satisfied was, that they had received everything beforehand; but I wished to hear from themselves what their grievance was. They looked to one another; their faces lit up, and they replied that I had given them "angikūni mai" (much much), and that they were all now agreed to accompany me and assist in packing our stuff over the portages across the divide to Great Bear Lake, as they felt sure that the white masters would find it tough work alone. I promised them a keg of tobacco, and so much of the "trade" as I did not wish to keep in reserve for dealings with the Indians I expected to meet on Great Bear Lake. So peace and happiness reigned once more in camp, and we spent a merry evening in getting everything in readiness for a start the following day.

I cannot stand a sulky temper, and the Huskies, unfortunately, have something of this very objectionable trait in their character. They appeared always to be afraid to come and tell me of a grievance which, if by chance discovered and inquired into, always turned out to be purely imaginary. They seemed to find satisfaction in nursing a grievance, and preferred this to having matters set straight. On the other hand, I have never yet seen an exhibition of violent temper, either amongst the natives of the Hudson Bay or of the Arctic coast. I do not for one moment presume that cases of violence never occur, but I should say that they are rare. The Husky character is naturally easy-going, happy and content.

To counterbalance an occasional display of sulks the Husky has many good, even noble, qualities. The good Husky knows no fear and never gets excited, either on land or on water, in attacking a polar bear with spear or ancient musket, or in standing out to sea in a whale-boat in a gale of wind.

Only one salmon was taken out of the nets in the evening. There were plenty of fish running, but the water at the mouth of the Ŭni-a-lik River was not of a suitable depth for the nets.

A theft of an axe was committed in the evening. Of course one of the Ŭni-a-lik natives was the guilty person, and, as I failed to discover him, they were all forbidden to approach our camp. This was quite a severe punishment to people so overburdened with curiosity.

It was arranged to leave all the women and children at this river with Hun in charge. I gave out fishing-nets and some trade articles, Hun being put in temporary possession of a muzzle-loader. With seals, musk-oxen, deer, and salmon plentiful I felt no anxiety about the women and children.

On July 5 we were delayed at the start by having to carry all the stuff to the ice by canoe across the intervening lane of water.

The ice in Gray's Bay was getting very rotten, and I was relieved from anxiety when we got well outside.

We ought not to have gone into the bay at all, but should have kept right on our westerly course. It was only to deposit the women and children that we entered it. When we got out beyond the point of the promontory Ŭgi-ŭk, the ice was firm and solid, and we made good progress. We travelled fifteen miles, in the course of which we met with but one crack, which, luckily, the long sleigh was just able to span. Using this as a bridge we carried all the stuff across, and were delayed only forty minutes. We camped close to Tree River Bay.

In the evening I discovered the true cause of the recent exhibition of sulks on the part of my Huskies, and the reason of their difficulty in making up their minds to accompany me. All the Huskies at the Ŭni-a-lik River had told them, that it was the same distance from the Ŭni-a-lik River to the mouth of the Coppermine as it was to the Arm-ark-tŭk River, where we had struck the Arctic coast, and they had spoken of the route as through a starving country where we should all die. The exact distance is one quarter. I was now quite able to understand the hesitation shown by my Husky friends, and they had my sympathy. Now it was all changed. I showed them the chart again. They already understood that I could find my position in latitude by sextant. They now said that white men knew and could do everything, and that they were always right, but that the Huskies were liars and knew nothing. Good-humour and laughter prevailed in spite of their having to starve.

Salmon-fishing at the Ŭni-a-lik River had proved a failure, the water being too deep for the nets, and we certainly could not afford to delay. A very fine specimen of the great northern diver, however, had been taken out of one of the nets when they were lifted in the early morning.

The canoe had to be used for landing ourselves and stuff at camp-time. In taking back the empty canoe for the balance of the stuff Sandy succeeded in capsizing it. He was pulled out gasping, but beyond a very cold wetting received no harm. There was a cairn at the place where we camped. It was about fifteen feet high and looked like the work of white men.

Pun, who had made a great boast in the early morning of how he was going to act as guide to the Coppermine, did not turn up in the evening. His heart had failed him, and he could be seen with the glass, slowly wending his way back to the tents at the Ŭni-a-lik River.

On July 6 the minimum thermometer reading was 30° and the maximum 48° Fahr. The weather was cloudless with a light westerly wind.

We started at an early hour, but a broad crack stopped us before we had travelled a mile.

As cracks in the ice occasionally extended only a short distance, it was our custom to send two men in opposite directions to discover either the end of the crack or a suitable place for crossing. Waving the arms was the signal of success.

A photograph will show how we crossed them better than written words.

We put in a hard day's travel, but only made fourteen geographical miles during the twelve hours we were on the ice. We did not stop once, either to eat or smoke. Eating was out of the question, for we had nothing to eat.

We camped two miles east of Epworth Point, and I immediately sent Amer off to hunt. He killed and packed back a large bull caribou late at night. This meat was a godsend, for we had completely run out of supplies.

The land here was very barren and rocky, the rocks being much smoothed and striated by glacial action. I have not made a record of the direction of glacial striæ at every point where they were noticed; it was hardly worth while. The general direction in which the ice sheet moved was south-east, as is generally admitted. Occasionally, very often I may say, the direction of the striæ was contradictory, for, naturally, there was lateral and retrogade movement due to pressure at certain points. The whole of the Northland of Canada gives one the impression that a mould has been pressed on the surface of the land, so striking is the smooth and flattened appearance of the rocks.

The next day, walking on the land in order to hunt deer, I was obliged to go round the large bay just west of Epworth Point. Close to the shore I observed numerous salmon in the clear water. They were feeding on minute flies on the surface, and were swimming along in large schools. I fancy that a net at this time of year would be successful if set anywhere along the shore, provided the depth of water were suitable. At Port Churchill, I remember, the nets were set straight out from the shore. With the flood tide came the salmon; at the ebb they were taken out by men on foot, for the nets were staked up and the salmon left suspended.

During the day I had the men and sleighs in view the whole time, and noticed that they were having considerable trouble on the ice. Following the shore I travelled over thirty miles, but saw no sign of deer. This looked bad. I added several specimens to my butterfly and botanical collections.

In the evening when I arrived in camp I heard very bad reports of the ice, which was described as much honeycombed and very rotten. My men had come a distance of fourteen geographical miles, but had all been through several times, and at one place the large sleigh had almost fallen through.

Ascending the rocks at the back of our camp I obtained a good view of the ice to the west. There were many islands, and between them I could see no ice at all, but open water everywhere. By keeping outside all the islands it might be possible to travel on the ice, but in what condition we should find it close to the shore, where we might wish to land, was difficult to say. If it should be too rotten to permit us to land, we should be obliged to camp on the ice and make for our former camp on the following day, by which time, judging from the warm weather prevailing, the ice would in all probability be too rotten to permit us to effect a landing, and we should then be in what is vulgarly but expressively called a "mess."

Moreover, both Darrell and Sandy were suffering from snow blindness, and another day on the ice would probably put them *hors de combat*. They had worn spectacles of a talcose substance of an inferior make, which had by mistake been sent with the supplies on board the schooner. Their surface paint had peeled off and left the eyes exposed to the glare of the snow. I wore Eskimo wooden spectacles with narrow, horizontal slits, and they were perfectly satisfactory. Glass spectacles become dim with moisture from the face and require frequent wiping.

With much regret we abandoned all hope of reaching the mouth of the Coppermine on the ice ; we were now distant from it only about fifty-five geographical miles.

Young birds were now fully fledged and well able to fly.

To be stopped here was specially disagreeable, as there appeared to be no deer along the coast. Even ptarmigan, which are numerous and widely distributed over the Northland, appeared to be absent. During the summer months, however, in the north, absolute starvation need not be feared, provided one has a plentiful supply of ammunition, for gulls, loons, hawks, and small birds can be shot, and ground squirrels are plentiful in many places.

The following day, July 8, we moved our stuff a short distance along the coast to a small river, where we hoped to be able to set our nets with some chance of success. Fish were observed here, but they did not look like salmon. Uttungerlah was sent to hunt, but returned without having seen anything. One ptarmigan was killed. Mosquitoes were getting thick, but I had taken the precaution to bring along a plentiful supply of netting for veils.

On July 9 we had the large canoe washed and laid out to dry, preparatory to being varnished and white-leaded. Anxious to lose no time in reaching the Coppermine

River, I determined to start by canoe on the first opportunity. If the main body of ice broke up, the prevailing north wind would drive the whole of it in against the shore, and we should then be completely cut off as long as the wind continued to blow from the same quarter.

The three nets took two salmon and eight white-fish, the latter species appearing to be fairly plentiful. I had brought a fishing-rod and a few flies from England for the express purpose of ascertaining if these Arctic salmon or salmon trout could be taken with a fly. I had been too busy to put the rod up, so far, but here was my opportunity. I failed to get even a rise, but there might have been no salmon in the river at the time. They appeared to come along in schools. They ran into the mouths of all the rivers and creeks. The majority of these they were unable to ascend, and they then passed right along.

On July 10 Amer and Uttungerlah were sent off at an early hour to hunt. I and Sandy were busy with the canoes. I had brought along both varnish and whitelead for fixing them, but the latter would not harden. Whitelead always must be carried mixed with turpentine and ready for use. In the afternoon I went through the whole of our stuff, and divided it into suitable loads for lifting in and out of the canoes. Loads ought not to exceed 60 lbs. This weight can be handled with ease, and in portaging a couple or three of these "pieces," as they are called, can be taken at a time. Amer returned in the evening without having seen any deer or tracks of them. Uttungerlah did not return. The nets only took two white-fish and one salmon.

On July 11 Uttungerlah returned in the early morning with a bull caribou, which he had killed about fourteen miles inland. There appeared to be no deer near the coast, but I expected to find them when mosquitoes became so numerous as to drive them towards us. The nets took four salmon and four white-fish.

In the evening I went to inspect the ice along the coast.

It was quite calm, and we paddled along the strip of water between the main body of the ice and the shore for over a mile, and we could have continued ; so we decided to make an attempt to proceed the following day.

The country now looked very picturesque, decked gay with pretty wild flowers of various hues.

In the morning at 8.30 we made a start. I had discarded everything that was not absolutely necessary. The balance of the "trade" was given out to the Huskies, who left it in cache at this place until their return.

Here we left all the dogs behind, with the exception of Uttungerlah's favourite dog and one bitch with her little pup. As this proceeding has been criticised and described as cruel by people whose experience of travel has been confined to railway journeys in England, I simply state that we had either to abandon or to shoot the dogs. I am always loth to shoot dogs. I would rather give them a chance of their life, and in this instance their chances of surviving until the return of my Huskies was good, for ground squirrels were very numerous, and on these the dogs could get a living.

We made good paddling for several hours, the ice being sufficiently broken up to permit us to paddle in and out among the loose sheets. When we had gone about twelve miles by account the tide turned and an east wind sprang up, which brought the ice against the shore, and most effectually put a stop to our paddling. By much winding in and out, and by shoving the large pans of ice to one side, we managed to push on for another mile and a half, and then camped.

I immediately went ahead to examine the ice, and discovered that we had camped close to two fair-sized rivers. I returned at once to order a start, but found the tents already pitched and all hands busy cooking, so we had supper. After passing Cape Barrow we had always found an abundance of driftwood along the shore.

Supper concluded, we struck camp and proceeded to

a spot on the more westerly of the two rivers, which gave good promise as a fishing station.

When deer are plentiful one can camp where he pleases, but at this time our fish and meat supply was from hand to mouth and most uncertain, and our camping ground had to be carefully chosen.

We found some signs of Huskies on the banks. A fire had been made and a deer killed.

The country here was very beautiful. The water in the river was quite clear, and the shores were sand and gravel. Inland a long, grassy, gently-rising slope stretched away in the distance. Vegetation was very luxuriant, and the ground showed a profusion of blossom. The miniature rhododendron with its mass of red blossom, the white blossom of our old friend the i-klu-ti, the heather which had served us for fuel for so many days on the Arm-ark-tūk River, and a white anemone were the most conspicuous. With my telescope I could sweep the whole of the country for miles around. The ground looked suitable for deer, but with the exception of some old dung there was not a sign of a beast. It was difficult to account for this.

From our camp Bloody Fall on the Coppermine River could be easily reached in two days' paddling, provided we had open water.

Slate of good quality was observed along the shore.

The weather turned bad in the evening, and we pitched our tent just in time to escape a deluge of rain. Very heavy rain fell at intervals during the night. During a fine spell, mosquitoes came forth in clouds. We had scarcely noticed them before, but now the vast army seemed to spring into existence as if by magic.

With a light north-west wind and fairly open water, we set out next morning at 7.30. The appearance of the ice and the state of the weather gave every promise of our being able to make a long day's travel west, but unfortunately we were stopped after paddling only six miles. The wind suddenly changed to the north-east, and, with a flooding tide, brought the ice in a compact mass right against the shore, completely choking a bay we were just about to cross. With some little difficulty we effected a landing by getting on to the pans of ice and pushing them aside. Great care must be taken of canoes among ice, for they are easily damaged. Ice appears to have a particularly tearing effect, even more so than rocks.

The wind blew moderately from the same quarter the whole day, and kept us on shore. Late in the evening, when the tide had turned and the wind had dropped, I walked hopefully along the coast, but found that the ice had been packed and jammed against the shore, so as to present a hopelessly impenetrable barrier to our progress west. It would have required an "ice-crusher" to make any impression on it. This was just what I had all along been afraid of. We were prisoners for as long as the wind should blow from the same quarter, and we had an opportunity of exercising that most necessary of qualities in a traveller—patience.

Having left our river we now had no place to set our nets. We would have returned the six miles we had come had we been able to do so, but the ice made retreat as impossible as advance. A few deer tracks were noticed in the afternoon, and these inspired hope. Ever since leaving the Ŭni-a-lik River we had been on short rations, but were able to get along well enough. Now I began to fear a starving time, and I knew that my Huskies shared my fears.

The following day, July 14, we were still unable to proceed.

Amer and Uttungerlah set out early in the morning to hunt. Amer returned unsuccessful. Uttungerlah returned during the night with a large bull caribou, the only one he had seen, though he had walked a long distance. I should not have objected to being delayed in this manner, if we could have employed our time in putting up a supply of dried meat or salmon, which would have saved delay further on, but that was quite out of the question where we now were. Till now we had not wanted a single meal, but had been on short rations, insufficient to satisfy our appetites. The behaviour of all, however, was quite correct, and no remarks were made.

On July 15 I was awakened at one o'clock in the morning by the flapping of the tent; a bulge in the canvas on the south side showed the direction of the wind. We had been waiting for a south wind, and I soon had the men up; it took but a few moments to dress, and we then commenced to pack up and load the canoes. The ice had already commenced to move off the shore, and it seemed just possible that we were to have a free passage right to the Coppermine River.

The southerly wind, however, was merely a local puff and lasted but a short time. After we had paddled four miles it fell dead calm, and the flooding tide brought back the drift-ice, which forced us to put ashore again and camp.

Shortly afterwards a deer came quite close to us, but gave no chance for a shot, as it was half mad from the attentions of the warble-fly and soon vanished in the distance. I spent most of the day adding to my botanical collection. Darrell collected butterflies for me. It did not appear as if I should be able to add largely to either collection, for both butterflies and flowers seemed to be nearly over. A blue Lupin (*Lupinus nootkatensis*), which is very common in the Northland, was still in flower.

The object of the journey had now been attained. We had explored the land between the head of Chesterfield Inlet and the Arctic coast; we had visited several of the copper deposits on the Arctic coast, and our collections, entomological, botanical, and geological, were as complete as it was possible to make them. Mosquito time was now in progress, when but few photographs could be taken. We really had nothing further to do in the north, except to get out of the country, and that at present was not possible on account of the barrier of ice.

The hills on the west side of the Coppermine were clearly seen from the rising ground behind our camp, and appeared but a short distance away.

Signs of former Husky camps were plentiful. The tribe of the Ku-yak-i-yuak must have been numerous in former times, but had now all gone, except the three families encamped at the Üni-a-lik River.

The rise and fall of the tide was just one foot. The water in the Arctic Ocean (on the surface at least) appears to be but very slightly saline. We used to drink it straight out of the sea.

On July 16 we were still icebound, and there appeared to be but a remote chance of getting further west for some days.

The ice loosened somewhat with the ebbing tide, but not sufficiently to permit of the canoe being launched. The flood-tide, I knew, would immediately pack it in on the shore again.

After a slim supper I decided to spend the night in hunting, for we were still very short of meat.

Before starting I gave my men instructions to keep a sharp look-out on the ice, and if, owing to a favourable change of wind, there was a possibility of moving forwards, to lose no time in striking camp and proceeding. I expected to keep the movements of the men in view from the high land where I proposed to hunt deer.

As I ascended the rising ground to the south mosquitoes were in clouds, their incessant buzzing amounting to a roar which was most annoying. It was on account of this plague that I decided to hunt on the heights, where it was cooler and where mosquitoes were fewer. After four hours' walking I sighted a female, which, after considerable difficulty, I was successful in shooting. The difficulty was to make an approach, as, owing to the plague of mosquitoes, she was continually on the move. When I did arrive within reasonable distance and raised my veil, I was assailed by such a swarm that I could not distinguish the

N

sights on the carbine. The bullet was effective, more by good luck than steady shooting.

The deer were now shedding their winter coats. Between the old white hair, which still hung in bunches from their sides, patches of new black hair was showing. When an animal was at rest, these black patches on the grey and white looked exactly like a piece of black moss on a grey rock, and it was exceedingly difficult to pick up a beast with the glass.

After starting a smudge fire with wet moss to keep the insects in check, I skinned and cut up the beast. This wretched animal was one mass of mosquitoes, and its coat was specked with tiny beads of blood from each puncture. Consequently, it was in very poor condition.

Packing back the quarters, loins, shoulders, and tongue, I made for the nearest part of the coast, for in the event of the men having been able to move forward, I should have cut them off. In pursuing this deer I had lost sight of our camp.

On arriving at the coast, I found the ice along the shore still set hard and fast, and at once concluded that my men were in camp and unable to move. Knowing that they were almost without meat, I decided to pack my load of meat to camp rather than leave it in cache on the shore, but, on arriving at the camping-ground, I found that the men and canoes had departed. There was only one conclusion to be drawn from this fact, and that was that while I was hunting the ice had loosened ("gone abroad" is the correct expression) and given them a clear passage of which they had not been slow to take advantage, and that, shortly after they passed, the ice had closed in again.

As they had received instructions to pay no attention to me, but to push right on to the mouth of the Coppermine River if possible, I cached my back load of meat and made haste either to catch them up or meet them at the Coppermine, a longish walk on the top of my night's hunt.

I walked for three hours, and found them in camp at a point distant ten miles from our last camp. The three Huskies had gone off to hunt, fresh deer tracks having been seen.

Having been on my feet for thirteen hours, part of which time I had been packing a heavy back-load of meat amidst myriads of tormentors, it was a welcome relief to get inside the tent, stretch out my weary limbs at full length on the ground, and indulge in a pipe without interruption from the infernal mosquitoes.

This was July 17, and I reckoned we were now only eighteen geographical miles from the mouth of the Coppermine—so near and yet so far, so long as the ice barred the way.

In the evening at the turn of the tide we made two unsuccessful attempts to get through the ice, and were eventually obliged to relinquish our efforts and to camp —having only advanced half a mile. It was useless to attempt to force our way through the ice. We might perhaps have done more chopping with the axes, and then hauled the canoes through or over the heavy floe-ice; but we should probably have damaged the canoes beyond repair in so doing. Our patience was again called upon.

Amer killed a very large bull caribou, which was in fairly good order, so for the present our minds were relieved from anxiety about starvation.

Next day I discovered that the small peninsula or point of land on which we had camped was almost bisected by two small salt-water lakes, connected by a small tidal stream. One short portage would have brought us to these lakes; the small tidal stream was deep, and would have offered a waterway to the next bay, which happened to be clear of ice. It is invariably a wise plan to have a good look ahead before deciding where to camp. One may be within a short distance of a good river for fishing, and not discover it till after the camp is pitched and everything unpacked. This, it may be remembered, happened in our case on July 12.

After making a short portage we launched the canoes and paddled across a small bay, on the west side of which we landed. Then by making another portage, we avoided the next point of land. It was always against these points of land that the ice rested compact. The small bays remained fairly clear of drift-ice.

The latter portage was 620 paces, the ground being hard and level. It took two and a half trips without the canoes to carry all our stuff over. The small bay we thus reached was quite clear of ice, but the next bay and the point of land beyond were set fast with drift-ice.

The tide was now on the turn, and the weather threatening, so we cooked supper and took a rest, hoping that after a short delay the state of affairs would be more favourable. We were in luck, for from the heavy thunder-clouds which had been gathering in the south-west sprang a steady breeze, accompanied by rain. When the rain stopped, the ice had drifted clear of the point. From a small rise in the ground I could see that the next point, and also the point beyond, were clear, and my fear of being penned in for an indefinite time was dispelled, but, to show that my anxiety was not groundless, I may remark that Back was detained by drift-ice near Montreal Island at the mouth of Back's River at the end of July 1834.

We lost no time in launching the canoes and getting under way. The further we proceeded the less drift-ice did we encounter. It was all open water ahead, and we hastened along the free passage towards the mouth of the Coppermine River.

We passed the mouths of two rivers, which appeared to be outlets of the Coppermine. Thinking that by ascending either of them we might escape Bloody Fall, we paddled close inshore, but the river mouths were very shoal, and moreover, we had no wish to explore further. I knew from the chart the exact position of the main outlet of the Coppermine, so we pushed on.

We had a stroke of luck in bagging a large bull

caribou which I shot at long range, and which the Huskies skinned, cut up, and stowed in the canoes within ten minutes. When deer were scarce, as they had been since we had left the Ŭni-a-lik River, the killing of a caribou meant so much to us that it always found a place in my diary.

A couple of small grey geese (barnacle) were shot by Darrell as we approached the mouth of the Coppermine River. We were getting into a country where food supplies promised to be more plentiful.

After passing the last two small islands marked on the chart, we sighted what I took to be Mackenzie Point and Cape Kendall; but, owing to the mirage, we could not with certainty distinguish between islands and points on the mainland.

The land on the shore along which we paddled consisted of gently-rising, grassy slopes, dotted with occasional very green willow-beds; and small outcrops of dark rock here and there gave the whole a very picturesque appearance in the early morning light. Altogether the country left a favourable impression on my mind.

The mouth of the Coppermine River seemed a little further west than I expected, but the chart in my possession was on such a reduced scale that it was difficult at times to recognise headlands, bays, or islands. The eastern branch was plainly visible a long distance off, and for this our small crafts were headed. This was not the main outlet, however, as we discovered when the canoes grounded on a sand-bar which extended right across. This channel was wide and shallow, but there was evidence that at some former time, if it was not the main outlet, it had at all events carried a considerable volume of water.

We had been nine hours at the paddles when, at four o'clock in the morning of July 19, we put ashore to breakfast on the bull caribou and then go to sleep.

We camped at the foot of the Fall on the east side. Immediately on landing we discovered a large cache of salmon, besides salmon-spears, bows and arrows, and other gear, all showing that the Huskies of the region were not far off and intended to return.

My Huskies discovered and brought me a large bone, which could only have belonged to a very large bear, probably a grizzly. There are "Barren Ground" bears all along the Arctic coast, from Kent Peninsula to the Coppermine, but they are not numerous. At several places I came across their "hooking" for roots, occasionally quite fresh, but none of the party happened to get a sight of a live bear.

Having discovered that portaging would be easier on the west side, we, on the morning of July 20, crossed the river and began to make the portage, which was about half a mile in length, the walking being fairly good, but through thick willows in places. The weather was fine in the early morning, but clouded up later, and there were thunder-showers in the afternoon. We discovered that the coast Huskies had been in camp on this side only the day before; in fact, we must have surprised them. They had slipped off in a great hurry and very quietly, leaving their stone kettles full of half-boiled salmon. They apparently had just had time to haul down their tents, throw their half-dried salmon in a heap, and decamp. Spears, bows and arrows, cooking-pots, clothes, &c., lay around just as they had hurriedly left them. They had evidently been very successful in obtaining salmon, thousands of which had been killed with a very long-handled spear, with double prongs made of native copper. I had not seen such spears before, and I took one for a specimen. I also took a supply of their dried salmon, leaving in exchange some knives, files, needles, awls, a looking-glass, and a pair of scissors.

These natives must have belonged to the War-li-ark-i-yuk tribe, who frequent the coast to the north and west of the Coppermine.

Above the Fall we encountered a long stretch of rapid and shoal water, where the river spread out over a wide, stony bed in many different channels. Tracking was here out of the question; the water was too swift for poling, and we were obliged to walk the canoes up. The water in some places was too shoal for the canoes; in others, almost too deep to wade against. It was generally about thigh deep, but very often it took us up to our waists, and at these places it was with difficulty that we kept our feet. It was excessively tiring work, walking against this heavy water. Though it was continued all day, we made only five miles. By the evening the outlook had not improved, and it was evident that we were in for a tough time. There was silence in camp that night, due possibly to fatigue, but no doubt also to depression of spirits.

It was fortunate that we had taken time by the forelock and had pushed ahead, for, at this time of year, the water was of an agreeable temperature for wading. Had we been a month or six weeks later, we should probably have been unable to withstand its temperature. With a good head of water in the early summer the river would be easy to run, but it proved most difficult to ascend.

The country was flat or undulating and grass-covered, with willow beds on either side. The river wound between low banks or in places without banks.

Deer tracks were seen as we camped on the east side.

The morning of July 21 broke dull and threatening, but it soon cleared up and a start was ordered. We crossed the river at once, and then waded and walked the canoes up as we had done the day before. However, we were soon able to put out track lines, and after three miles of uninterrupted tracking we reached the second rapid about two o'clock in the afternoon. I did not understand why this was marked on the chart as a "rapid." There was only rough water, which could be very easily run at any stage of water and in any kind of craft. At a high stage of water it would probably be not even rough. It ap-

Not Escape
(8 mi from
Bloody
Falls)

peared at first that we might manage to track up this piece of water, but a cut bank, below which there was no place for the trackers to walk, effectually put a stop to this operation. We were obliged to make the portage, and for this we took the east side of the river. The distance was about a thousand yards, and the going was good. This occupied the rest of the afternoon, and we camped when all the stuff was across.

After supper I walked about three miles up the river to examine ahead. It appeared that tracking might be possible for a short distance, after which another portage would have to be made.

At our camp here we saw stunted spruce for the first time in this region. Vegetation of every kind was becoming more luxuriant.

I saw a large bear's track and fresh dung.

Next day, July 22, a very thick mist, accompanied by rain, obscured everything, so that we could neither travel nor hunt, and we lay in tent the whole day. I was getting anxious about food, for we had only one full day's supply in camp. The signs of deer that we had seen were old. Bears are always a doubtful quantity. They appear difficult to find in every country except perhaps Kashmir and a few other places in the Himalayas. The river so far was unsuitable for net-fishing.

The following morning the weather was still bad, and it was with some hesitation that I ordered a start. Our tent was soaking wet and very heavy, as was most of our other stuff, and I knew that we had to make a portage a short distance ahead. However, our present camp was in a bad position, and there appeared to be no deer.

Following the eastern side of the river, we were enabled to pass a line underneath the first cut bank. It required five men to handle a single canoe at this place, and therefore only one could be taken up at a time. We accomplished a mile, partly by tracking and partly by wading, and then another cut bank stopped us.

When, in ascending a river too swift to paddle against and too deep for poling the canoe, one encounters a steep and high cut bank which is too high to track from and which leaves no footing beneath for the trackers, one of two alternatives has to be chosen. One is to cross the river, for it is rare to find cut banks precipitous on both sides. When on account of rough water it is not possible to cross, then the other alternative must be adopted, that of making a portage on the side of the river where one happens to be. In the circumstances I am describing not even portaging is possible until a suitable place has been found for getting the stuff and the canoes up the bank. One has, in short, to go back and look for a slope where a landslip has occurred, or a stream has cut through the rock. The place which we chose for scrambling up the bank, though it was the best we could find, was not an easy one, and it took all six of us to handle one canoe. We had, in fact, to climb the steep ascent, and I was in fear and trepidation for the safety of our canoe, for one bad slip would have meant ruin ; the men and the canoe would in an instant have been at the bottom of the cliff.

The Huskies were excellent at this work—strong, careful, and patient—and so were my own men, Darrell and Sandy, but they would hardly wish their excellent services to be mentioned. The portage accomplished, we had fair tracking for about a mile, after which we camped at the foot of the first real bluff of spruce that we had as yet seen. This was on the west side of the river.

We saw very few deer tracks, and these were all very old. Signs of bear were plentiful. We could only make two more meals out of the remnants of the now putrid salmon found in the native camp at Bloody Fall. We ought to have spent a day in hunting, but I was anxious to push on and reach the Sandstone Rapids. I had an idea that there would be a better chance of coming on deer and bear further south. Below the Sandstone Rapids we might be able to set our nets.

We resumed our journey at seven o'clock in the morning next day, July 24.

The river was very crooked, the water being shoal in some places, rough in others. We were a man short in each canoe. To track a canoe up swift water four men are necessary. Two are required on the track line, one should be at the bow with a pole, and one acts as steersman. The man in the bow ought to have a knife ready to cut the track line should the canoe broach to. For if a canoe gets broadside on to the current, and the trackers continue to haul on the line, they will pull it over.

We were now on sandstone formation, and although we had precipitously cut banks to deal with, there generally was a ledge of rock on which the trackers could find footing.

At one place Sandy, when tracking, was jerked off a ledge of rock without serious injury. I was in the bow of the canoe with pole, and Darrell was steersman. In such cases it is foolish to attempt to turn the canoe. A Peterboro' canoe is very nearly of the same shape in the bow and in the stern, so in taking a run downstream the men's places are reversed, the bowsman acting as steersman. One word of advice, which should be remembered by those who canoe in dangerous waters, is, "Do not get excited."

We had very swift water the whole day. Since leaving Bloody Fall we had only found half a mile of placid water where the paddles could be used, and there we had seen numbers of white-fish. During the day we observed one duck and two loons. I was surprised that we came across no geese. I was delighted to observe a number of fresh deer tracks along the shore in places where there was sand or gravel. My mind was relieved of a great anxiety, for should we have been without food I could not have expected my Huskies to remain with us, and without their assistance, owing to the unexpected difficulties, I should not have known how to manage. It is not possible to make four men out of three, and it required four men to a canoe at every place where the water was very rapid.

We made about fifteen miles, which I considered a very good day's work. We were now not far from the Sandstone Rapids. One of the canoes having sustained damage on a rock, it was decided to halt the following day in order to repair it, and also to dry everything.

Mosquitoes had given us but little trouble, and we had not as yet had occasion to erect our mosquito bars. The mosquito plague is regulated by the weather. During a cold and wet summer there are scarcely any.

On July 25 Amer, Uttungerlah, Pitz, and Darrell sallied forth to the chase; Sandy busied himself fixing the canoe with spruce gum, which could now be obtained from the stunted spruce trees; and, as the day was perfect, I took the opportunity of laying everything out to dry in the blazing sun.

I boiled three thermometers which read 211.5°. Temperature of the air, 74°. Corrected altitude, 273 feet above sea-level.

The meridian altitude of the sun gave our latitude as 67° 30′ 28″ N.; we were therefore within a few miles of the Sandstone Rapids.

Amer returned at five in the afternoon, having killed a large bull caribou. The hunters' return was anxiously awaited, for we had absolutely nothing to eat. Uttungerlah returned later, having also been successful. Darrell announced that he had seen the Sandstone Rapids, which he said were about five miles distant.

The following day, July 26, we were obliged, owing to rough water or cut banks, to make four portages, varying from a quarter to half a mile in length, and, in the evening, we camped opposite the south end of the large island, which is marked on the chart close to the Sandstone Rapids.

We had come very near to having a disastrous canoe accident at a dangerous "chute." Considering what a canoe accident would have meant for us, I realised the fact that we had taken a foolish risk merely to save time and trouble, and I decided to take no such risks in the future. If we had lost everything, we should have been obliged to return to the Eskimo at the Ŭni-a-lik River. For myself I would not have cared to tackle the long walk from the Coppermine River round Great Bear Lake to Fort Norman on the Mackenzie River, though I suppose it could have been accomplished.

Resuming our journey in the early hours of July 27, we had a fair piece of tracking to begin with. The river, however, was still very crooked, and was here about one and a half miles wide. Owing to the position of two small stony islands, we were obliged to go considerably out of our way. Two large bull caribou were seen, but they had already got our wind, and were bound for other parts. It was pleasant to know that deer were not far off. We were surprised to find not a sign of musk-oxen. This was a place where they might have been expected; they had not been killed out by Indians or Eskimo, and I could not account for their absence.

We had passed the two small stony islands by noon. Here the sandstone formation ceased. We were soon obliged to make a portage of about 300 yards to avoid a rough piece of water, which, like most others, could have been easily run. In the afternoon the character of the river changed. The precipitously cut banks gave place to low, sloping, stony shores; but the current was still swift. The walking on shore for the trackers was good, and our progress was fair. We travelled fifteen miles by account, and camped two miles north of a large bend which the river makes, first to the south-east and then to the south-west.

Spruce were increasing in size and number, and when we camped, we were actually in the woods once more. Still they only amounted to a fringe on each bank, and did not extend any distance from the river.

While tracking, Sandy was nearly tripped up by a chunk of native copper on the shore. It weighed about twelve pounds.

My Huskies were commencing to show signs of impatience at which I was not at all surprised. When making arrangements with them, I had told them the distance from the Ŭni-a-lik River to the Coppermine, and also the distance I proposed to !ascend the latter river. I had given an estimate as to the number of days they would probably be absent from their womankind. This time limit had already been exceeded, owing, in the first place, to the unexpected and premature break up of the ice, and in the second, to the difficulties of navigation presented by the Coppermine River. I told them in the evening that I should only take them as far as the headwaters of the Dease River.

The following day, July 28, we made better progress. The tracking was good, and there was no more sign of precipitously cut banks. Low sloping ground, covered with grass and provided with an edge of rounded stones close along the shore, afforded excellent footing for the trackers. The current was steady and swift, about five miles an hour, the river being about 300 to 400 yards across. We made eighteen statute miles by account, and camped opposite the small creek which is marked on the chart as coming in from a small lake on the west side.

Deer tracks were numerous and fresh. I can hardly explain with what satisfaction I regarded the presence of deer in the neighbourhood. Darrell and Sandy apparently took the presence of deer as a matter of course, and seemed to trouble their heads but little about the food supply, but the whole journey had been an anxious one for me. I *knew* what a starving time would have meant. Temporary inconvenience and suffering do not count for much, but prolonged starvation now would have necessitated the abandonment of the greater part of our stuff, and we should have been compelled to escape from the country with nothing but our rifles, nets, and ammunition.

Moreover, I could not have expected to retain the valuable services of my Huskies.

All had gone admirably up to date in spite of the unexpected difficulties, and our anxiety about food was shelved for the moment, for we spied deer shortly after camping on the west side of the river.

All the deer that we had seen lately were bulls. They were apparently travelling from the east side of the Coppermine to the west side and, then going in a south-westerly direction, probably to meet the migrating bands of deer from the north, but I have given up attempting to solve the mystery of the habits, range, and movements of the "Barren Ground" caribou.

At 6.30 in the morning of July 29 we were under way again. The minimum of the thermometer was 31°; the maximum, 65°; the sky was cloudless; we had a light westerly wind; the weather was very enjoyable.

The river held a south to north course and was fairly straight. The water was quiet, and the tracking along the shore excellent. After travelling five miles we came to an island which is marked on the chart to the north of Mouse River. This island is of considerable extent, and much larger than is indicated by the chart. Having passed it I kept on the look-out for the river (Simpson's Kendall River) coming in from the Dismal Lakes. There was no appearance of it.

When we camped I sent Uttungerlah to explore. I went west and ascended a rising ground, thinking I might possibly get sight of the Dismal Lake or indications thereof. Uttungerlah returned and announced that he had discovered the river from Dismal Lake, about two miles further south. He reported that it appeared to be navigable for canoes, and also that at its mouth he had noticed an ancient Indian grave and old marks of chopping on the trees. I now had no doubt that we were on the right track towards the divide between the Coppermine and Great Bear Lake.

Shortly after we started in the morning, I shot a large bull caribou on the banks of the river. Killing deer in this manner saved much time and hard work. This animal was in good order, and it was a simple matter to place it in the canoe and proceed.

The woods were now continuous. Robins and other small birds which are strangers to the barren Northland were now plentiful. It was a lovely cool morning on July 30. There had been slight frost during the night (three degrees), and in the very early hours a heavy mist hung over the river, but this was quickly dispelled by the rising sun. After tracking along the western bank for about one and a half miles, we came to the mouth of Kendall River, which was a much larger stream than I had expected to find, and we left the Coppermine River without much regret. The latter is a difficult river to ascend, but would be splendid to run, so far as we travelled on it. There would only be one portage, that at Bloody Fall. We had been ten and a half days in ascending the river, which was very crooked. It is difficult to say how far we travelled; probably over eighty miles. On one of the days we had not travelled.

We had not experienced any starvation in the ascent. Although we saw fish in numbers at every suitable place, we never set the nets, for we did not happen to camp at these particular spots.

The Kendall River was about thirty yards broad at its junction with the Coppermine. Its waters, which were beautifully clear, ran over a clean gravel bottom.

We paddled up the first three hundred yards, but then this method of advance was stopped by a small cañon and swift water. This at first looked a more serious obstacle than it actually was, for we were able to wade and walk the canoes up.

Looking east across the Coppermine, I could see nothing of Mouse River, the mouth being probably hidden from view by an island. I inspected the Indian grave of which

I had been told, and the marks of axes on the trees close by. The grave seemed that of a child and appeared to be very old, as did also the chopping marks.

Kendall River proved to be very crooked, and we were obliged to make so many twists and turns, that I do not think that we made more than four miles in a straight line the whole day. It was confined by low banks, thickly grown with willows, which made it difficult for the trackers to walk, but we did not have to make a single portage. Land on either side of the river was low, and supported by a stunted growth of spruce trees. Deer tracks were plentiful, but we saw no animals. Ptarmigan were very numerous in the willow-beds. The young birds were about the size of "cheepers," but well able to fly. The old birds looked very handsome in their full summer plumage of rich brown. We saw two young wolves, which appeared almost as large as their parents. I collected a few butter-flies, but they were now hardly worth taking. They had been much knocked about by wind and weather, and a large number of them could scarcely fly at all.

Some delay was occasioned on the morning of July 31 by my Huskies, who requested permission to leave at this place the canoe which I had promised them for their return journey to the Ŏni-a-lik River. I assented to their request, and, when the canoe had been placed in cache, I took the opportunity to discard some superfluous stuff, including our mosquito bars, which we had carried the whole way from Fort Resolution without ever having had occasion to erect them. Mosquitoes were now on their last legs. Black flies had appeared, but up to date their attacks had been mild. Generally speaking, black flies cease their attacks when the sun goes down.

The larger of our canoes easily held all our stuff. Two men, a bowsman and a steersman, manned it; two were placed on the track line, while one was told off to keep the line clear of bushes and snags. Five men in the place of

O

three on a single canoe made a great difference, and I was free to go ahead to hunt.

The river again proved very tortuous in its course. We certainly travelled over nine miles, but I do not think, that, in a straight line, we advanced more than five or possibly six miles.

I noticed that large numbers of bull deer had already gone westwards. The tracks appeared to be about ten days old, and they were all of the same age. Having sighted Dismal Lake from a small outcrop of limestone on the south side of the river, I waited for the canoe to come up, and then taking my shot-gun in place of the carbine, set out to shoot ptarmigan. While walking along the banks of the river, I perceived numerous fish in the pools. They were remarkably tame, and I shot fourteen of them as they rose to the surface to feed on small flies. They proved to be Arctic trout (Back's grayling) and excellent eating.

The Arctic trout, which appears to be widely, but not universally, distributed throughout the Northland, is a handsome fish, dark in colour, and averaging in weight from 1 to 1½ lbs. The head is small and neat; the scales are coarser than those of the ordinary trout; the flesh is always white, so far as my own observation has gone. The peculiarity of this fish lies in its large dorsal fin, which is spotted, and, when seen upright in the water, is of a very pretty colour. The sides of the fish are also spotted, but, owing to the dark colour of the skin, the spots are not easily discernible. When the canoe overtook me I decided to camp, as the water was very suitable for fishing. A single net which was set took three large lake-trout and several toolabies almost immediately; the trout weighed 17 lbs., 18 lbs., and 20 lbs., respectively.

Blueberries, now commencing to ripen, promised an addition to our food supply, though not a very important one. Far north these berries appear to be very watery. At Fort Churchill it was found impossible to make jam of them.

On the last night of July I was haunted with unjust
suspicions of the Huskies. One of the canoes and most of
their stuff having been left behind in cache, what was to
hinder them from running away before morning? If they
secured one hour's start and reached the canoe, no man on
foot could catch them up. Once on the Coppermine they
could run the eighty miles to the Bloody Fall in a single
day easily; there were no portages to stop them. I could
have secured their rifles and so made sure of them, but
this step would have been unwarranted by any act on their
part, so I resolved to watch. They had left their canvas in
cache and were now without a shelter of any kind, so I
suggested to them to sleep in our tent; but my proposal
was instantly rejected, and I became more uncomfortable.
They slept peacefully under the open sky, while I, guarding
their slumbers through the night, became more and more
ashamed of my suspicions. In the morning I felt humbled
when the Huskies, ignorant of all that had been in my
mind, set about their work as usual. The Husky is simple
and manly, and the last thing he would think of would be
to sneak off. If he wants to leave, he will inform you of
the fact, and perhaps change his mind five minutes afterwards.

Starting at 6 A.M. on August 1 we continued up the
Kendall River, which is a rather pretty stream to navigate.
With a good head of water in the early summer, the whole
distance from the Dismal Lake to the Coppermine could
be run in a couple of hours. In ascending, we had not
been obliged to make any complete portage, though at a
good many places part of the load had had to be portaged.
This was on account of the low stage of water. It was a
great and a welcome surprise to me to find the river navigable at all. I fully expected to be obliged to portage the
whole distance from the Coppermine to Dismal Lake,
which would have meant packing our canoe and stuff at
least twelve miles through the bush, although the charts
indicate only five miles.

After tracking about 1½ miles further we entered the foot of Dismal Lake, where we coiled and stowed away the tracking lines and resorted to paddles. It was indeed a relief to get out on the open and quiet water of a lake. The ascent of a dangerous river, or rather, I should say, a river where continued caution is absolutely necessary to prevent an accident, is apt to "get on the nerves." Every day the attention is strained, and every night you are obliged to pitch camp close to the thunder and swish of the rough, heavy, and rapid water, which you know you will have to tackle the following morning. Very old hands may not experience these feelings, and very young hands are ignorant of the real danger that awaits them in the event of a bad canoe accident.

For my own part, I have not yet got hardened to risks which, from ample experience, I know to be serious. A canoe accident within reach of civilisation does not mean much. As a rule the crew get safely out with a wetting, and the loss of the stuff can always be partly made good at the nearest post. A canoe accident in the wilds, however, has a different meaning altogether. By the total loss of canoe and stuff death may stare the crew in the face, and an uncommonly unpleasant death; for the party, having water to drink, would probably survive a long time to wander about, living on berries and pushing forward in the vain endeavour to circumvent some of the large lakes of the north in order to reach the nearest Hudson Bay post. Rifles, ammunition, axes, and everything of vital importance should be, but not always are, lashed to the thwarts, and the whole lot might go. A few years ago a white man went astray near Great Bear Lake in the early Fall. He was rescued by the Indians when death had almost claimed him. In the winter time it would not be so bad. One would soon freeze up.

At the lower end of Dismal Lake a large creek comes in from the south-west. This has formed a shoal bar which extends across the foot of the lake.

This no doubt was the place visited by Dr. Richardson on August 14, 1826, and described in the following passage of his report to Franklin :—

"In endeavouring to *get round the south end of a small chain of lakes which lay in our route, we were stopped by a narrow stream about six feet deep, flowing from them to the Coppermine River, but, on sounding the lake a little way from the head of the stream we found it was fordable without difficulty.* We marched to a late hour in search of fuel to cook some deer's meat, which M'Leay had procured in the course of the day, and were fortunate in at length finding a wooded valley on the banks of a small stream that fell into the chain of lakes which we had crossed. It is probably this river, and chain of lakes, that the Indians ascend from the Coppermine River in canoes to the height of land which they cross on their route to Bear Lake" (Franklin's "Narrative of a Second Expedition to the Shores of the Polar Sea," pp. 272, 273).

The words in italics undoubtedly refer to the foot of Dismal Lake. I forded the lake at precisely the same spot. Richardson's latitude here was given as 67° 10' N. At "the narrows," about eleven miles to the north-north-west, I found my latitude to be 67° 21' N. These determinations agree so closely as to confirm and establish the identification.

In Richardson's time the chain of lakes was unnamed, and remained so until they were visited in March 1838 by Thomas Simpson. That traveller, in his report to the Hudson Bay Company, used the descriptive expression, "the dismal lakes," and in his book, published seven years later, the epithet "dismal," applicable in March, but certainly not in August, was raised to the dignity of a name. The native name for the lakes, or rather lake, is Tesh-i-ĕr-pi, a name to which I adhere.

Amer and Pitz were told off to hunt along the shore. Uttungerlah, Darrell, Sandy and I, working the paddles, seemed to make the canoe fairly fly through the water, but our apparent speed was chiefly the result of so much very slow travelling previously.

It was my intention to reach the head of the lake as quickly as possible, and then, taking Uttungerlah, to begin exploring possible routes to the west. The charts now proved quite useless.

After paddling for three miles, we appeared to have reached the head of the lake. This was not the case, however, as a little exploration showed. Our progress here was almost blocked by low, sandy, willow-grown islands, between which were shoal channels with considerable current in places. After a couple of shots at channels which proved too shoal for our canoe, we came out on the larger part of the lake, and then paddled seven miles north-north-west against a stiff head-breeze. Again I thought that we had reached the head of the lake, but on landing and ascending a knoll I saw an inlet to the west.

On continuing up this bay or inlet we were all much surprised to observe three figures, which were undoubtedly those of human beings, and we discussed the question whether they were Indians or Eskimo. Not expecting to meet any more Eskimo, I naturally concluded that they were Redmen, but the glasses brought to bear on the strangers soon satisfied us that they were Eskimo, and a kyak lying on the shore soon put any doubt to rest.

These natives appeared to be very timid and on the point of running away. Fearing a repetition of what had occurred at Bloody Fall, I told Uttungerlah to hold up his hands and shout that we were Huskies. This caused them to hesitate, but did not prevent their beating a hasty retreat inside their tents, which were pitched at the top of a small hill. We landed and pitched our tent, and while a kettle of trout was boiling I went up to pay them a formal visit.

There were four tents, but only one man, a woman, and a youngster at home. The others were away hunting deer. The man told us his name was Ig-li-khi, and his

fears were allayed by a few small presents. I was anxious
to obtain some information about the country to the west,
especially how far off and in which direction the divide
lay. I gathered this much : Ig-li-khi had never met white
men before ; neither had he met Indians, but he had seen
the smoke from their camp-fires on the other side of the
divide. His party belonged to a tribe who inhabit the
islands of the Duke of York's Archipelago. This tribe
was called the Nuggi-yūk-tūk, and comprised but five
families. They had travelled hither with their dogs and
sleighs in the spring, in order to fish and hunt deer during
the summer and fall, for this was a place where the deer
crossed. They intended to return to the Arctic coast in
the winter.

Ig-li-khi stated that he did not know the region very
far west, but had heard that it was a long distance to the
country where the water flowed in the other direction,
i.e. west into Great Bear Lake. He knew that there were
some small lakes on the far side of the divide, but could
give no further information. He had heard of Great Bear
Lake, however, which he described as an enormous stretch
of water—"tēr-ē-ōk-tē-met-nar" (like the sea). The lake
we had just paddled up continued for some distance west.
It was all one piece of water, and was called Teshi-ēr-pi.
This is the Dismal Lakes of the chart.

We were now camped at a place where the lake pinched
in, what I have called "the narrows."

On my questioning him whether some of the absent
Huskies had not been over the divide and seen Great Bear
Lake, he replied that they had ; his two sons were camped
a day's journey to the north, where they were killing deer
and drying the meat. One of these lads had not only seen
the Great Lake, but had been to its shores and knew the
way across the divide well. He had been forced to visit
the Indian hunting-grounds during a starving period. This
information was more promising. I suggested that he,
Ig-li-khi, should start early the next morning to hunt up

and bring back this son to act as our guide. The promise and exhibition of an axe, a knife, and a file caused him to give a ready assent to this proposition, and he undertook to leave at daybreak in his kyak and return without delay.

Amer and Pitz turned up in the evening, having killed a bull deer and seen several others. Four female deer had been speared by Ig-li-khi at this crossing-place on the previous day. There were numberless large trout and toolabies where we were now encamped. In fact, we were on an ideal spot. There were deer in fair numbers quite close at hand; the lake was stiff with fish; musk-oxen were to be found not far off.

We were at a considerable height above the sea, our altitude (according to the boiling-point thermometers) being 860 feet; but this altitude must be taken as only approximate, as the thermometers were not absolutely trustworthy. At this elevation the hot weather now prevailing was tempered by a cool and pleasant breeze.

We were now again on the " Barren Ground," *i.e.* in a country where there was a total absence of trees. These we had left behind when we entered on Teshi-ēr-pi Lake. We had, however, an abundance of dwarf birch, moss, heaths, and willows for cooking purposes.

The surrounding country was flat or undulating ("rolling" perhaps best describes it), and gave promise of holding lakes, which, it was hoped, would give us an easy route over the divide. There were very few rocks visible. The country was mostly covered with grass.

CHAPTER XV

TROUBLES ON DEASE RIVER

IGLIKHI made an early start on the morning of August 2 in his kyak. We remained in camp, taking life easily. The net was most productive. Many large trout, Arctic trout, and toolabies were taken. The last named were very large; six of them scaled just over five pounds apiece, and they proved most excellent eating, superior to any white-fish that I had ever tasted. This is most unusual. By many Indians the toolaby is considered a very inferior fish, and I have frequently seen them thrown away. All the fish we caught at "the narrows," and also in Kendall River, had that firmness of flesh which constitutes the difference between a first-rate fish and one that is not worth eating.

At noon I took the meridian altitude of the sun, which gave our latitude 67° 21' N. The observation was excellent.

Iglikhi returned in the evening, having failed to find his son. He (the son) had left the place where he was supposed to be, and Iglikhi, having no proper footgear, did not care to prosecute the search on land. This was a disappointment. However, Iglikhi's wife volunteered to try her luck the following day.

Iglikhi informed me later that his son had only been to Great Bear Lake with dogs and sleigh in the early spring, so I decided, even in the event of the son being found, not to employ him as a guide, since we were compelled to find a canoe route.

Having failed to get any satisfactory information about the head-waters of Dease River, and not expecting any serviceable information from Iglikhi's son, I decided to search for a different route across the divide. We were already too far north, judging from the last observation. If we proceeded up Teshi-ēr-pi Lake, we should be travelling still farther north. How far we should then have to portage from the head of Teshi-ēr-pi Lake over to a point on Dease River whence it would be navigable for a canoe, was a very doubtful question, but it appeared that the farther north we proceeded, the longer a portage we might expect. I decided to move back about six miles down Teshi-ēr-pi Lake, and try to discover a route thence over the divide. From the charts there appeared to be a possible route, along which several small lakes which would be of the greatest service to us were indicated.

Iglikhi promised his services on the portage for one day only, but he said that his wife and two sons would accompany us further and assist in packing our stuff across. How far, he did not state. We acted on the decision arrived at over night, and had everything packed and loaded in the canoe by an early hour on August 3 ; but Iglikhi, at the very last moment, gave me information which caused me to change all the plans at once.

This information was to the effect that, during the previous summer, three Indian tepees had been seen on a lake about four miles (as nearly as I could guess) from the head of Teshi-ēr-pi Lake. This statement naturally led me to conclude that the Indians had a route over this way, and that probably the head-waters of Dease River were at no great distance from the head of Teshi-ēr-pi Lake. The Indians doubtless frequented the head-waters of Dease River at this time of year in order to spear deer. They would not be without their canoes when thus employed, and it seemed reasonable to suppose that Dease River was navigable more or less.

Our canoe was accordingly unloaded and the tent repitched. I proceeded up the lake in the canoe, accompanied by Amer, Pitz, and Iglikhi to explore.

It was difficult to judge how much to believe of the information furnished by Iglikhi. Of one thing I was certain, my Huskies but very imperfectly understood the dialect he spoke.

We walked along the shore in order to spy for deer, which were not numerous, and Iglikhi informed me that there was a portage of from three to four miles between the head of Teshi-ēr-pi Lake and a longish, narrow lake in a south-west direction. The water from this lake, he said, flowed south-west into Great Bear Lake. On this portage of three or four miles were either two, three, or four small lakes (Iglikhi could not give the exact number). These were at the height of land or right on the divide. It was on the longish, narrow lake before mentioned that the three Indian tepees had been seen.

Darrell had been sent to explore the country to the south-west, but he reported it to be very rugged. He also reported having seen the smoke of a bush fire. I regarded this as probably the work of Indians on the other side of the divide. My Huskies did not take this view, but thought it more probably the work of one of the Husky deer hunters making a fire for signal purposes.

Iglikhi's wife, who had started at a very early hour to hunt up and bring back her two sons, returned in the evening, having failed in her search.

Now that the tough work of portaging was about to commence, it was natural to expect some one to fall sick. This is invariably the occasion chosen by Indians on which to plead sickness. Pains in the heart, lame backs and sprained ankles are common complaints. I always expect such, and in the present instance I was not disappointed.

Uttungerlah's turn had come. He stated that he was sick unto death, and he lay groaning on the moss. I could not believe that he was shamming, for he was the last man to play such a low game; but I remarked to him in jest that the time for portaging was always chosen by the Indians for placing themselves on the sick list. Poor

Uttungerlah could not repress a smile. He replied that I ought to have known him better by this time, which of course I did.

On August 4 we made a start for the head of Teshi-ēr-pi Lake, and Iglikhi accompanied us. I bade good-bye to Uttungerlah with much regret, and left him behind with Iglikhi's wife to look after him. He was really very ill from a liver complaint to which he was subject, and from which he had almost died a few years before. He was a splendid specimen of an Eskimo, very powerfully built, and as strong as an ox. He was absolutely to be relied upon to carry out orders. He never could do too much work; in fact, he had abused himself in this direction, both by carrying enormously heavy loads on his back, and by exposing himself and starving during the intense cold. He could not stand heat; on the few fairly hot days we experienced he was quite useless, and much ashamed of himself in consequence; but he made up for lost time when the weather cooled.

We paddled eleven miles north-west, six miles west-south-west, and seven miles south-south-west to the head of Teshi-ēr-pi Lake, the upper portion of which thus makes a very considerable bend. I am quite satisfied that I did not over-estimate the distance travelled. We kept four paddles at work; Pitz and Iglikhi were walking.

In the afternoon, the wind being dead aft, the canoe was put under canvas. The breeze freshened very quickly, and we soon had all we could carry. The small craft appeared fairly to fly, but when close down to the water one gets a very exaggerated idea of the speed.

Spruce we found to be fairly plentiful at the head of the lake. I had not expected to find any so high up. Indian tepee poles were also observed.

On landing and taking a short walk, we saw from the numerous beaten paths that large bands of caribou had passed at this end of the lake, on their migration south, about ten days previously. Quantities of old musk-ox dung were noticed, and also fresh bear signs, so that there was promise of food supply in crossing the divide. Nevertheless, we all regretted leaving Teshi-ēr-pi or Dismal Lake. It certainly did not appear "dismal" to us, but quite the reverse.

I do not remember ever having coming across a lake where fish were so numerous. Large trout, some of which ran up to twenty-five pounds, could be seen swimming in the clear water as we paddled along. The toolabies we caught averaged nearer five pounds than four pounds, and, as before remarked, were most excellent eating. Arctic trout were numberless.

The lake is shoal in most places, with sand or gravel bottom. There must be grand feed in it, for all the fish taken were in splendid condition; but what it consisted of we did not make out. The large trout fed exclusively on the Arctic trout, which is called Back's grayling by Richardson.

Altogether, at the narrows on Teshi-ēr-pi Lake we had passed a very pleasant time. The weather had been perfect. Deer had been shot as we required them.

The total length of the lake I put at thirty-six miles. The distance could easily be paddled in one day. One ought to be able to track a canoe up Kendall River in two days, so that three days are sufficient for the journey from the Coppermine River to the head of Teshi-ēr-pi Lake. It would take less than two days the other way, for the entire length of Kendall River could be run in a few hours with a good head of water.

There were many signs of Indians having of old resorted to this place to hunt. Tepee poles, both erect and lying on the ground, were to be seen. Several old pieces of birch bark, such as Indians always carry to mend their canoes, gave evidence that in former times they used to come to the head of Teshi-ēr-pi Lake in their canoes.

We had the prospect of hard work within the next day or two, for our number was reduced to five, and our canoe and stuff had to be portaged to a navigable part of Dease

River. I hoped, however, that the good fortune which had attended us hitherto would continue. We had had no sickness, except in the case of Uttungerlah; we had not been without food for a meal on a single day, and we had always been able to light a fire for cooking. We could now have meat and fish diet varied, for there was a plentiful crop of berries of different sorts.

On the morning of August 5 we decided to spend the day in searching for the shortest and best route. Pitz and Iglikhi were missing, and the delay would give them a chance to join us if they so wished.

I sent Darrell and Sandy to explore to the south and east. Sandy's instructions were to search for the headwaters of Dease River, which he was to follow until the stream gave promise of being navigable for a canoe. Darrell was told off to find the long narrow lake marked on the chart on the north-west side of Dease River.

Sandy returned at seven in the evening, having travelled a long distance to the south and east. On his way back to camp he had discovered the desired creek, one of the many head-streams of Dease River. He had followed this for about half a mile, and he now reported that, though very narrow, this stream was of fair depth and offered a waterway for some distance at least. The length of the portage which would have to be made from our present encampment, he put at about five miles. This was welcome news indeed. Since this stream could only be one of the many small head-streams of Dease River, I thought we had a good chance of finding fairly navigable water. Other streams would probably be adding their waters as we descended.

I took Amer with me to hunt and to spy out the country with my long telescope.

From the head-waters of Teshi-ēr-pi Lake a narrow swampy gulch ran south-south-west, bounded on either side by a high sloping bank, and along this gulch lay a small chain of lakes; perhaps it would be more correct to describe them as shallow ponds.

The divide between the waters flowing east into Coppermine River and those flowing west into Great Bear Lake
lay between two of these ponds. At the present dry stage
there was no water perceptibly draining either way, but it
was very easy to see that the water, during the wet season,
did flow in both directions.

The gulch or ravine ran in a fairly straight course for
about three and a half miles, and we walked along the
high sloping bank which confined it on the right hand side.
Beyond its south-south-west extremity, where the high
banks also came to an end, lay an extensive flat plain,
dotted with lakes and ponds. I must rely on a rather
poor photograph to give a better idea of the country than
verbal description can supply. The whole of this flat was
drained by the Dease River. It was mostly grass-covered,
though sandy, and showing many small sandy knolls and
ridges. The flatness of the country promised depth of
water, and the absence of outcrops of rock led us to hope
that the stream would be unbroken by rough water.

From the high bank at the head of this ravine we
obtained a splendid view of the region. The course of
the main Dease River, as indicated by a continuous growth
of spruce, could easily be followed with the aid of the
telescope. Great Bear Lake was still a long way off, but
I could locate it, although its waters were not visible. The
creek discovered by Sandy—which I may as well call
Sandy Creek, both in honour of the discoverer and as
indicating the character of its banks and bed—could not
be discerned from this spot, although we looked right
down on its banks.

Deer could be seen in large numbers making their way
south across the plain. As there appeared to be none near
us we decided to remove the camp, but, first of all, only
to Sandy Creek. We had no meat, and only three fish
remained for our breakfast.

Darrell returned at six o'clock the next morning,
August 6, but he had failed to discover the long narrow

lake. However, he had shot four deer, which were badly wanted at the time, and had found fresh signs of musk-oxen.

We then commenced to arrange our packs. I had decided to take four loads right across and pitch camp on Sandy Creek, but before we had gone half-way steady rain came down, so we pitched the tent and returned to our old camp for other loads of stuff. Darrell was despatched to fetch a big back-load of the meat he had killed and cached the previous day. Sandy, Amer, and I returned to our old camp at the head of Teshi-ēr-pi Lake for another load of stuff. On arrival, we found Pitz there; he had gone a little astray. Iglikhi's leg had played out, so he had turned back.

When it commenced to rain we pitched the tent at once, and camped a quarter of a mile short of the end of the ravine. As two of the ponds along this ravine were each about 300 or 400 yards in length, we decided to use these the following day.

The next day, August 7, the canoe was taken right across to Sandy Creek. Several small ponds on which we were able to launch the canoe and paddle short stretches saved us some labour in portaging it.

I hunted, for we were completely out of meat again. Going west, I travelled over the hills for about four miles and struck the small round lake, which is marked on the chart as the source of the north-eastern branch of Dease River. The stream flowing out of this lake proved to be Sandy Creek. The lake appeared to be about three miles long.

Following the stream slowly down, and spying the ground most carefully for deer, I brought my glass to bear on an object such as I had not seen for many months, an old musk-ox bull. He was lying absolutely still on the bank of the stream, and it required a second look to assure me that it was really a musk-ox and not a low bunch of scrub spruce. With good cover and a steady wind I had no difficulty whatever in making an approach. As we were badly in want of meat, I took no risks, but fired eight bullets into him as fast as I could. Poor brute! he could not make out what was up. He kept turning round as each bullet struck him, until he finally toppled over dead. He was a very large bull and in splendid condition; in fact, he was the only really fat musk-ox I have ever seen killed. The old hair was already all shed, and his robe looked in good order.

We were now assured of at least five or six days' supply of meat, by which time I hoped and expected to be some distance down Dease River.

To skin and cut up a big bull musk-ox single-handed is no light task, and it is a slow one, except to a Husky. I commenced on this fellow, but got rather tired of the job and contented myself with "gralloching" the beast. The paunch contained nothing but willows. I packed some of the fat and meat, and on my way back I met Pitz, who returned at once to dress the carcase and place it where it would be safe from the wolves.

When musk-oxen get away into a quiet secluded little place, it is extremely difficult to find them. This bull had been here the whole summer, and had not strayed half a mile.

The deer appeared to have all passed. I did not come across a single fresh track.

We had bad weather at this time, strong winds and much rain. The winds were always north-north-east or north-west. I could not help thinking where we now might have been had we not pushed forward from the Ŭni-a-lik River. These northerly winds would most certainly have brought the ice in against the coast, and so kept us prisoners for an indefinite period.

The next day, August 8, the balance of the stuff was portaged early. Amer and Pitz then returned to the head of Sandy Creek for the remaining musk-ox meat. We procured about 60 lbs. of fat from this animal, and I rather

P

think that the Huskies ate their share. I did not blame them. We were all starving for fat. When a musk-ox is in really prime condition, layers of fat are to be found on the neck, which is then the best part of the animal to eat. Fat does not form on the back as it does with the caribou.

The distance we portaged was about three and a half miles or about three miles straight in a south-westerly direction. Owing to bad travelling in places, it was not possible to keep a quite straight course. There were several lakes close to the route we followed, but these were not discovered till too late. It is no waste of time to explore and have a good look ahead, before commencing to make a portage, or even before pitching camp. It saves a deal of extra work in many instances, as we had already experienced.

On arriving at Sandy Creek, we found it to be only about fifteen feet broad. However, it was deep, with scarcely any current, and it offered an excellent waterway as far as we could see.

The water was most beautifully clear. Our camp was pitched on a good, hard, grass-covered spot with a thick clump of spruce for a background. It looked most picturesque.

This spot struck us as a most desirable one on which to spend a month or so. Musk-oxen were numerous, although we had only come on one. Bears likewise, although we had failed to come on any. The bull caribou were daily expected to arrive, and fish (Arctic trout) were plentiful in Sandy Creek. This was a sportsman's paradise, but too far distant for the majority of pleasure seekers. There were neither mosquitoes nor black flies to bother one.

In the evening, I told Amer and Pitz that they could return the next day. We expected to have many portages still to make, but I had promised to allow them to return as soon as we struck the head-waters of Dease River.

Their time was up, and I well knew their anxiety to go. It was most fortunate that we had been enabled to avail ourselves of their services for so long. We should have had a terribly tough time without their able assistance in making the ascent of the Coppermine.

We had a large amount of rain during the night, and, on the morning of August 9, everything being soaking wet, a delay was decided upon, until the weather cleared and the tent and stuff got a chance to dry.

We then packed up, loaded the canoes, and bade farewell to our faithful Huskies, Amer and Pitz. We parted with much regret on my part, and with, I may hope, a little on theirs. They had been in my service for a year, and had behaved like the manly fellows they were. They were now a long distance from their homes. After picking up the dogs and sleighs, women and children, they had planned to paddle their canoe to the head of Bathurst Inlet, and there to await the "freeze up," when they intended to start with dogs and sleighs across country to the Ark-i-linik River, whence they would have no difficulty in finding their way back to the inhospitable region on the borders of Hudson Bay.

I had made Uttungerlah a present of a couple of duplicate charts I possessed. He seemed to prize these more than anything else that I had given him. He was never tired of producing them and pointing out to the other Huskies our position and the different places marked.

Sandy Creek was in places only six to nine feet in breadth. There was a sluggish current here and there; in deep holes the water was quite dead. Where the water was of sufficient depth, we experienced no difficulty in spite of the many sharp crooks and turns, but where the small stream spread out over a sandy or gravel bed there was less than four inches of water.

Our canoe was fairly heavily loaded, and at these shoal places, some of the stuff had to be taken out and portaged, until the water got deeper again. By the evening I reckoned that we had travelled eight miles by the stream, and had made but two and a half statute miles in a straight line, so erratic had been the course of Sandy Creek. Small as this stream was, it was of great assistance. Portaging is not only very hard work, but it takes much time. We were on the right road, anyhow, for marks of old Indian chopping were to be seen on some spruce stumps hard by.

Sandy Creek took us in a south-west direction on to the large flat plain, which we had swept with the telescope a few days before. We were leaving the hills and the spruce woods, and our chances of getting musk-oxen on the open plain were nil. However, we still had a fair supply of fat musk-ox meat, and when that should be finished, well, we could only hope that something would turn up to take its place.

The next day, August 10, we proceeded, but our trouble was now about to commence.

Taking a pack in order to lighten the canoe a little, I walked ahead to see what was waiting us. Sandy Creek, which promised so well at the start, now commenced to lose its good character. Stuff had to be taken out at several places in order to lighten the canoe sufficiently to permit of its being dragged over shoal, sandy, and gravel stretches. We then encountered a succession of miniature rapids. The stream spread out over a stony bed, necessitating a portage of three-quarters of a mile, which we did not finish till noon. Further progress was made under similar conditions. The water in the stream would be good for a short distance, after which we would again come on shoal and stony places.

I ascended some rising ground in the afternoon to obtain a view ahead. As far as I could see along the stream, there was shoal water flowing over a stony bed, and quite unnavigable. I could also see at the distance of about three miles the junction of Sandy Creek with the main branch of Dease River, which flows in from the north-east. This was conspicuously marked by a small kopje-shaped hill, which I had seen distinctly when spying from the high bank on the divide.

I decided to portage the whole of this distance. It was mere waste of time taking all the stuff out of the canoe and reloading in order to travel a few dozen yards on the water. It being fairly early still, we portaged the stuff about one mile towards the junction of the streams and then camped.

Altogether, in a straight line we had travelled three and a quarter miles south-south-east. We had, of course, actually travelled very much farther. I reckoned that we were now twelve statute miles in an air-line from the head of Teshi-ĕr-pi Lake.

We were now about two miles from the junction of Sandy Creek with the main branch of Dease River.

In the event of Dease River proving unsuitable for navigation, instead of portaging along the river it would be wiser to make a straight cut over to the long narrow lake which is marked on the chart to the north-west of Dease River. Our camp was distant from this lake about six or eight geographical miles, as measured on the chart.

After supper, I gave Sandy instructions to proceed to the junction of the streams, then follow Dease River down for some distance and report on the navigation.

Darrell and I were to hunt up the easiest and straightest route to the long narrow lake, which for present convenience I shall call Long Lake. I should have named this lake, but that I felt certain that it bore an Indian name, though I failed to ascertain it on our arrival at Fort Norman, all the Indians who frequented the north-east end of Great Bear Lake being then absent.

Large numbers of female deer were seen at camp time. They were feeding and travelling south-east.

The next morning, August 11, Sandy followed Sandy Creek down to its junction with the main branch of Dease River, and returned early, for it seemed there was no doubt that Dease River was navigable. Even Sandy Creek he reported to improve about a mile farther down, where it would be navigable for the canoe half loaded at least.

Darrell and I, having struck south-west in search of Long Lake, travelled about five miles over very difficult ground, and then found ourselves in the vicinity of Dease River. It was a temptation to go and have a look at the river and know the worst, so we yielded and went. We were surprised and delighted to discover a river fully twenty yards wide. It appeared to be deep, but the water was very muddy. It flowed with a very sluggish current, which in places was imperceptible, between moderately high, alluvial, steeply sloping, and occasionally cut banks. Paddles could be used to good advantage.

There being every appearance of the river maintaining this character for a long distance, we did not prosecute the search for Long Lake. We were hunting for a waterway to Great Bear Lake, and to all appearance Dease River promised this. The course of this river was very erratic, but that did not matter, so long as we were spared making portages. We were all in high spirits in the evening, for there was every hope of having an easy journey to Great Bear Lake.

Had we been compelled to make the portage direct to Long Lake, we should have had a very tough time, for the country, although fairly flat, was very lumpy in some places, swampy in others, and mostly covered with a strong growth of black birch reaching to the waist. Forcing one's way through this was most tiring work, even without a load. We should not have been able to hold a straight course, owing to small intervening lakes. The portage would probably have taken us ten days. One mile and a half a day would have been our limit.

Deer, all cows and calves, were very numerous and quite tame. Not being in want of meat, we left them unmolested; but it was decidedly comforting to know that meat was around if we were in need of it. Bear tracks were seen, but they were not numerous.

The following morning, August 12, at six o'clock, we commenced to portage. Taking the canoe first we carried it just one mile, to a place where there was sufficient water to float it rather more than half loaded. Returning, we portaged three loads to the canoe, and returning once more, we portaged three loads right to the junction of the streams. Sandy and Darrell then went back for a few remaining things, and, having loaded up, brought the canoe safely to the junction, where we camped.

The flat-topped kopje before mentioned had a strong growth of stunted spruce on its summit. Although of no great height it is a conspicuous landmark.

The country here was very pretty. A scattered growth of stunted spruce fringed the river on either side. "Stunted" is rather an ugly word, and possibly may leave a wrong impression. "Young" spruce gives a better idea of the growth. There were numerous small lakes a short distance from the river. An ever-present strong growth of black birch made walking laborious.

In the afternoon I hunted for bull caribou and looked for musk-oxen, but without success. It seemed as if we should have to fall back on the wretchedly lean meat of the cow caribou, which, after the calves are dropped, is not worth eating.

On August 12 my thoughts naturally turned to the land of the red grouse. I observed the young ptarmigan, of which there were large numbers. The young birds were strong on the wing in spite of the very short and late nesting season. They were fully as forward as young grouse in Scotland at this date, and would have afforded good sport, except for the fact that they were worthless to eat. The weather was warm, and black flies very troublesome.

We started shortly after six the next morning, August 13. The men paddled the canoe along while I went to hunt, as our fat musk-ox meat was almost finished. I shot a young bull caribou, packed most of the meat to the river bank, and there left it to be picked up by the canoemen as they passed. Cows, calves, and young bulls were numerous, but there was not a single old bull to be seen. It was evident that bulls did frequent this part of the country in the fall, for every spruce of about 6 ft. or 8 ft. in height showed marks where they had rubbed their horns. Bears must be scarce along Dease River, for I walked a long way, and spied over a very large extent of country, but found none, and but very little sign of them. Musk-ox sign was plentiful, but old.

The men with the canoe got along splendidly in the morning in spite of the erratic course of the river. In the afternoon, however, shoal and rapid water was encountered and but little progress could be made. By the evening they had reached a place where the river cut its way through a bed of rock, making a short portage necessary. It was too late to commence portaging, so they camped.

I sighted Long Lake while hunting.

Dease River carried but little water at this time. Where the water was deep and the current slow it had the character of a river, but where it widened and spread out over a bed of rock it was not worthy of a better name than a creek.

By account we had come six miles, but it was difficult to keep reckoning of distance travelled. To look back and estimate the distance by the eye was the best plan.

At camp time I shot a female wolverine as she was swimming across the river. She carried a ground squirrel in her mouth, which she evidently had intended for her family.

We began portaging next morning, August 14, at an early hour; the distance was only about 200 yards, and we soon had everything across.

The men were obliged to wade and walk the canoe down for about half a mile. The river then took a sharp bend to the south. Here again a portage was necessary for a distance of 300 yards, and it had to be made on the south side of the river.

Having given the men a hand at the portages, and having observed that the river improved further down, I went off to visit Long Lake and to kill deer. After walking a short distance I came on four old Indian camps which had been occupied the previous fall. Keeping north-west I soon discovered Long Lake, the outlet from which I found at its north-east end. The stream flowed east and then south, finally discharging into Dease River. It had a considerable volume of water.

My men had received instructions to signal their position at noon by making smoke. I determined to stop them if they were not too far down the river, as I could now see that, a short distance below our second portage, there was a place where the portage to the foot of Long Lake should be made. It was quite evident, from signs which I saw at the foot of Long Lake, that the Indians used this route on their journeys from Great Bear Lake towards the divide. It also appeared that, having reached the foot of Long Lake, they had chosen their camping-ground as close to Dease River as possible, as if intending to return by the Dease River route. Anyhow this was the way in which I read "the writing on the wall."

Noon came, and up went a dense column of smoke away down the river. It was too late now; we had missed the short portage of about three miles between the foot of Long Lake and Dease River.

At 3 P.M. another column of smoke showed that the men were making good headway; at 5 P.M. they showed me that they had camped. Smoke signals are very useful, and a number of things can be said by a good arrangement of them.

Dease River was completely concealed by a heavy belt of spruce. We had run past the deer apparently. I only saw one young cow, which I shot. I observed a common snipe, a rare bird in these parts. The men had to make one portage during my absence.

The weather next morning being very threatening we

did not start early. After we were loaded up I left my men to get on as best they could. They had instructions to make smoke at noon, 3 P.M., and 5 P.M., and to set the nets directly they camped, for we had nothing to eat. Crossing the height of land between Dease River and Long Lake, I struck the latter about 2½ miles from its head. From a high rock I obtained a good view of its whole length, which certainly did not appear more than eight miles. The woods between Dease River and Long Lake were now continuous, but they were still sufficiently scattered for good shooting, although they rendered spying with the glass somewhat difficult. There was just an off chance of coming across a deer, bear, or musk-ox in such country. From the number of small trees which had recently been horned, I knew that there were musk-oxen around, for the deer had not yet commenced to rub their horns. Spying from every accessible point, I was lucky enough to sight a solitary musk-ox bull. The wind was blowing directly from me to him, and I cannot understand why he did not get my wind, for their sense of smell is very keen. I lost no time in getting after him. The woods here were fairly open, and I got a good chance at him at 300 yards. Closer I did not dare to go on account of the wind. While he was busily engaged in horning a small tree I fired five bullets into him, and, after galloping a couple of hundred yards, he rolled over dead.

A musk-ox being a large animal, there is no difficulty in hitting the beast, but, at the longer ranges, it is not easy to make sure of placing the shots well, on account of his shaggy coat. It was a lengthy and tedious job skinning and cutting him up.

Black flies were in swarms, and they appeared rather to appreciate a smudge fire which I made.

I made a pack of about 80 lbs. of the meat and hung the rest on trees out of the way of wolves. I then went to Long Lake, which was but a short distance away, and cooked some choice pieces for lunch. Shouldering my pack, I then commenced to retrace my steps, and, on arriving at the height of land from which I commanded a view of the whole of the valley of Dease River, I sat down, lit my pipe, and awaited the hour of 5 P.M. for the smoke signal from my men. Smoke was to be seen to the north-east, about the place where we had camped the previous evening. To this I paid no attention. Punctually at 5 P.M. I could just discern a faint column rising through the spruce trees about the place where I judged the men ought to be. To this place, therefore, I bent my steps.

On arriving at the river I was much surprised to find, instead of my men, two Indians on the opposite side seated beside a small fire. They appeared to be equally surprised to see a white man. They had no canoe, but the sight of my back-load of meat quickly made them decide to pay me a visit. They soon pushed some dry logs into the river, lashed them together, and paddled across. The few words of Yellow Knife language at my command appeared to be quite unintelligible to them. The only word of English which either of them knew was "yes," and this was their answer to everything I said. In vain I endeavoured to ascertain if they had seen my canoe pass. I drew a canoe with two men seated in it upon a piece of paper and pointed down the river. I got the inevitable "yes" in reply, but I could place no reliance on this answer. Having seen smoke to the north-east about the spot we had left in the morning, I concluded that, for some reason, the men had been delayed, and had not moved the camp, so I decided to camp and await their arrival the next day.

We now had nights sufficiently cool to make a camp-fire agreeable, especially as I was without a blanket. The Indians acted as cooks and we had a grand feast, which lasted till a late hour, until they were filled up to the neck and could hold no more. They had had nothing of their own to eat. It was a case of the white man having plenty and the Indian starving in his own country.

They informed me that several families were encamped some distance away. They had killed a band of twelve musk-oxen, and were busy drying the meat. So much I managed to understand.

After breakfast next morning I bade my Indian friends farewell. They made tracks for their tepees, while I ascended the high ground on the north side of the river and there waited the signal of smoke which, in the event of my not turning up, my men had been instructed to make at 9 A.M.

I sighted the signal and was pleased to find that they had made good travelling, and were a long way down the river. Their rapid progress, however, implied the loss of all the musk-ox meat, for to catch them up at their present rate I had to abandon what remained of my 80 lbs. backload. It was also quite out of the question to return and fetch the rest of the meat, which I had taken so much trouble to dress and hang up on the trees. I hastened to head my men off lower down the river. At noon I was passing through some fairly thick woods, and, the land being flat, I was unable to see the smoke signal of that hour. This was also the case at 3 P.M. I hurried along and, shortly after 4 P.M., reached higher ground, whence I at once sighted a dense column of smoke. I made straight for it, and found my men in camp just above a rapid, caused by the river entering a narrow gorge or defile, where portage was necessary. The sight of the camp was welcome enough, for I had been walking very fast over very dry ground. The sealskin boots I was wearing had dried up and become very hard, and my feet were in consequence badly rubbed; in fact, I had had enough of it.

The nets had been set the previous evening, and had been successful in taking many suckers, but only one whitefish. The sucker is the most worthless fish in the north, being soft, tasteless, and full of bones. The head is the only part worth eating. Sandy had killed a goose. Our prospects in the way of food were not very encouraging at this time. We had left all the deer behind; there were now no tracks, and it looked as if we would have to depend solely on our nets. I reckoned that we were now within ten miles of Great Bear Lake, a very short distance if we only had decent navigation, but ten miles of rapids meant a ten-mile portage, and in rapid water our nets could not be relied upon to take many fish.

CHAPTER XVI

DEASE RIVER, GREAT BEAR LAKE, AND BEAR RIVER

AT an early hour on the following morning, August 17, we made a portage of four hundred yards, which placed us below the small cascade at the gorge. Navigation on Dease River then became very bad, and remained so throughout the day. We found shoal and rapid water at every turn. No sooner were we in the canoe and using the paddles or poles, than we had to jump out, wade, and walk the canoe down. Fortunately the water was still of an agreeable temperature, but to be in the water all day takes it out of a man, and I have found that nothing will make one lose flesh so fast as continued wading on an empty stomach.

I left the men and canoe shortly after we had finished portaging, in order to hunt, for we had nothing to eat. I came on fresh musk-ox sign at once, but failed to sight a beast. From a high bank on the north side of the river I saw Great Bear Lake, and a welcome sight it was. It did not appear to be very far distant in a straight line, but I could see only its eastern arm, which lay like a streak of silver between the dark spruce woods.

Hunting was now very difficult; it is always so in woods, unless there is a skiff of snow, or the ground is favourable for tracking. In woods it is quite impossible to use the glasses. The limit of one's range in thick woods is so confined, that one may easily pass close to an animal without seeing it. The chances of meeting and killing game under these conditions are very small. Musk-oxen were numerous where I hunted, as evidenced by the number of small trees which had been recently horned.

Had there been a skiff of snow, I could have killed an ox in a very short while, but without it, and with the ground as hard as a rock, the only plan was to quarter the ground systematically up wind, and keep on walking and peering through the bushes. My men put in a hard day with the canoe, and I put in a hard day's hunting without success. We went supperless to bed. This was the first day on which we had starved.'

I decided to follow the river the next day and shoot ptarmigan, as the men required assistance at the portages. For musk-oxen I would have to travel some distance from the river.

White birch and alder bushes put in a first appearance. On August 18 we did not make an early start. It had rained during the night, and the tent was soaking wet.

Dease River continued to be very bad indeed. We made four portages and camped at the fifth. The length of these portages was half a mile, two hundred yards, four hundred yards, and three-quarters of a mile; the fifth was one hundred yards. Over this we carried our stuff, but not the canoe, and then camped. To portage all our stuff and the canoe used to take four trips. The footing on the slimy stones along the shore was very bad in places, and I was fearful of some one slipping and the canoe receiving damage. We could not afford to delay.

We camped early at a quiet stretch of water, where it was possible to set a net. We had starved the whole day, for I had been too busy at the portages to shoot any ptarmigan.

Moose tracks were seen along the shore, also one rabbit. We were now in a thickly wooded fur-bearing country. Many old "dead-falls" made by Indian trappers were to be seen. Our nets caught no fish, so I took a carbine and went ahead on the off-chance of coming on a moose or musk-ox, and also to examine the river.

It was not easy to decide on the right course to take. We were starving, and there was every prospect of our starving until we reached Great Bear Lake. It was a momentous question whether we should continue travelling and starving, or call a halt in order to hunt. Had we been in open country, I should not have hesitated to call a halt and hunt, but in the thick timber the chances of success were small. A day's delay meant another day of starvation, in the event of getting nothing. I decided to push on.

The next morning, August 19, when we lifted the nets, we took out a 4 lb. pike, neither a large nor a very choice fish, but welcome nevertheless. It was soon boiled and greedily devoured ; that and a drink of tea, our last, made us feel considerably better. We then portaged the canoe, and as we proceeded the river improved. There were still numerous stretches of shoal and rapid water, however, down which the canoe had to be guided and pulled, the men wading, but there was only one portage, and that, being only about four yards, simply required the unloading and reloading of the canoe. We then had long quiet stretches of water, some of them a mile or more in length, where the paddles were used to good advantage.

I hunted again, but still without success. I shot one rabbit, which unfortunately was blown to pieces by the expanding bullet.

The mouth of Dease River was sighted at 2 P.M., and I think we all gave a sigh of relief. The portaging was over, and we had a clear course to the west end of Great Bear Lake.

The journey had taken fourteen days from the head of Teshi-ēr-pi Lake, and twenty-one days altogether from the Coppermine, a long time to accomplish a distance of about fifty geographical miles, which is all that the charts make it. That distance in an air-line is probably about right, but of course we had travelled very much farther. It is not an easy canoe route by any means. Of course the low stage of water rendered it more difficult than it otherwise would have been.

Shortly after noon we passed an Indian camp which the natives had just left. They had been catching and staging a large quantity of fish, but had taken them all away. At the mouth of Dease River we noticed several of their fishing places, and the temptation to camp and try our luck with the nets was great. About 3 P.M. we paddled clear of Dease River out on the clear quiet water of Great Bear Lake, through which the canoe seemed to us to glide at a great speed. One does not obtain a good view of Bear Lake from the mouth of Dease River, for a large island obstructs the view.

We paddled to old Fort Confidence, Thomas Simpson's winter quarters in 1837-38. The distance from the mouth of Dease River is about six miles. I expected this to be a fishing place. Our two nets were at once set, and they were anxiously looked at before we turned in, but, alas! there were no fish in them. We went supperless to bed, but in the best of spirits. It was some satisfaction to know that there was plenty of food in the lake, even if it could not be caught. Late at night we heard a shot close by, showing the presence of Indians, and we went to sleep with great hopes of falling in with them next day.

Old Fort Confidence was partly in ruins, but the chimneys still remained perfect.

In the morning two fair-sized trout were taken out of the nets, sufficient for breakfast; and we set out at eight o'clock. We paddled round the first point, expecting to find the Indians in camp, for it was here the shot had been fired on the previous night. We found the camp fires, but the natives had departed at a very early hour.

We continued on our course on perfectly calm water, and made about twenty-four miles. I possessed some trolls (spoons and minnows) which I had brought out from England, and two of these were kept out all the time. As a rule, when paddling in a canoe, one travels too fast for successful trolling. Two large trout, one of them a twenty-pounder, were hooked, but both were lost. The trolls

Q

(spoons) were much too light and fragile for these heavy fish. One requires a spoon about half a pound in weight with stout cod-hooks attached. The loss of these two fish meant no supper. After pitching the tent, we all went to eat blueberries, which were fairly plentiful, but it takes a long time to fill up on blueberries, and they are not sustaining. There was no sign of either deer or ptarmigan.

The coast of Great Bear Lake was here very barren and rocky, and the spruce very stunted in growth.

I remarked to Darrell and Sandy in the evening, that we were lucky to have a plentiful and wholesome supply of cold water to drink, but my remark did not appear to afford them any comfort.

On August 21 the minimum thermometer reading was 44°. The weather was dull but fine, wind variable.

The nets took one toolaby of 3 lbs., which when cleaned and cooked gave us a light breakfast. With a light fair wind we left at 6.30 A.M. The wind soon gave out, however, and we were obliged to ply the paddles. We kept steadily to them the whole day, never stopping except to light a pipe or take a drink of water. There was no occasion to land and go ashore; for we had nothing to eat and no tea to drink. The trolling in the afternoon was successful. Although most of the large trout broke away, we brought three (13 lbs., 7 lbs., and 5 lbs.) inside the canoe. This was quite sufficient for supper and a light breakfast. I also shot a loon and a gull, which all helped.

The shore of Bear Lake was very straight and low, quite destitute of any growth of trees. The timber commenced at a varying distance of from one to four miles from the shore.

It was my intention to camp at the mouth of Haldane River, where the nets could be set in any weather. There being practically no bays or harbours along this shore the nets, even if down, could not be looked at in the event of a storm. We failed, however, to discover the mouth of the river. After paddling forty miles we landed and had supper directly, for we were all ravenously hungry. We then pitched the tent and set the nets. No sooner had Darrell and Sandy finished setting the nets and come ashore, than they had to go out to them again. They took out fourteen white-fish and one large trout, two of the white-fish scaling almost 6 lbs. apiece. This was capital, and meant a supply to take along with us.

Fishing with nets in lakes to which one is a stranger is most uncertain work. It is only at particular places that white-fish can be caught. These fishing places are generally known to the natives, and therefore it is advisable to camp at old Indian camps. But we had evidently now struck a first-class fishing ground, which was unknown to the Indians, for there was no sign of any old camp.

The high land at Scented Grass Hill was plainly visible from this place. Fresh bear-sign was seen on the land.

Next morning, August 22, a heavy mist enshrouded the lake. We did not start till 8.30 A.M., as we had many fish to clean, for the nets had been successful during the night; sixteen white-fish were taken out, some of them very large, 7 or 8 lbs., none of them under 4 lbs. This was the largest average of white-fish that I had ever heard of. In Great Slave Lake their average weight is 3 lbs.

After eating what we wanted, we still had about 60 lbs. of cleaned fish to take along, so for the present our minds were relieved of anxiety on the score of the food supply.

We were fortunate in having the wind off the shore, and we paddled along on smooth water. We had the sail set for a couple of short spells. The act of hoisting sail on such occasions appears to have a fatal effect on the wind, which at once drops or else hauls ahead.

We stopped at 1 P.M., as we now had fish to cook for dinner. Driftwood was abundant along the shore.

Proceeding, we shortly afterwards met a large party of

Indians, who were on their way to the head of the lake to spear deer and dry the meat. One of the party spoke a little unintelligible English, but I managed to understand that he advised us not to make the portage across the peninsula or cape at Scented Grass Hill, though there is a frequented route across. These Indians were starving, as Indians, when I meet them, generally are. There is no reason why they should starve, except such as may be found in their own folly. They were now travelling in a large band. They were well provided with nets, and must have caught large numbers of fish, but possibly not sufficient for the crowd of men, women, and children who composed the party. They had hunted without success.

They invited us to camp with them, but if we had done so they would have devoured our reserve of fish at one meal. So we hastened away, and made twenty-eight miles before we camped. I estimated that we were now within twelve miles of the place where the traverse is made across Smith Bay.

Next morning, August 23, it was blowing rather too hard to proceed. The shore being still quite straight, the difficulty was to load the canoe and get safely launched in the heavy lop which had got up.

I hunted in the morning, but, with the exception of a few ptarmigan, I saw no sign of game. About 5 P.M., the wind having moderated, we loaded up and got away by 5.30 P.M. We were now travelling along the north shore of Smith Bay. Two small islands lying off a deep bay mark the place from which to begin the traverse.

The deep bay mentioned may be called Traverse Bay, and the eastern point of it Traverse Point. We paddled fourteen miles to Traverse Point, and then a little over a mile along Traverse Bay. We then camped. This part of the coast was entirely destitute of trees, and we had great difficulty in collecting sufficient drift sticks to boil our kettle. We did not pitch the tent, for we had no pole, and the timber line was a long way off. I had intended to make the traverse that night, but the weather did not give us a chance.

Next day, August 24, we were still delayed by the weather. It was not blowing hard by any means, but sufficiently so to make it prudent to remain on shore. We set the nets directly we had finished breakfast, and then paddled to the head of Traverse Bay for a supply of wood and a tent pole. Returning on foot, I noticed a little sign of bear, but there was neither new nor old sign of deer. I do not believe that this part of the coast is ever frequented by deer. A fine 15 lb. trout was taken out of the nets when they were lifted.

The wind moderated towards the evening, and at 7.20 P.M. we started across the traverse to the Accanyo Islands, which lie a short distance off the south shore of Smith Bay.

The night was cloudless and calm, a perfect night on which to make the traverse of fourteen miles. If the wind falls with the sun and the sky remains cloudless, one is almost assured of smooth water the whole night. We crossed in exactly four hours. The Accanyo Islands are very low, in fact only spits of sand. The night was dark and nothing could be seen of the land. Steering by a star, we paddled along in dead silence until the beating of the surf on the shores of the island was heard. We then swung off to the eastward, thus saving a few miles, and paddled steadily for five hours, after which we put ashore and cooked our 15 lb. trout for breakfast. All our other fish had been consumed.

Resuming our journey after the morning meal, we paddled for three hours, and came to an old Indian encampment. This place seemed to give promise of success in fishing, so we camped, the time then being 9.30 A.M.

We had paddled during the night forty-two miles in fourteen hours, including a two-hour spell for breakfast.

The nets were set as usual directly we camped, and

they took four trout by the evening, so we had supper and then turned in for a well-earned rest.

The following morning, August 26, we were under way at 6.45. Three small trout were the result of the night's fishing. Our nets were of too small a mesh. One of them was only a herring net, and the other was of a mixed mesh. Great Bear Lake is famous for its herrings (so called), but these can only be caught near the foot of the lake and in Bear River.

It was quite calm when we started, and we headed across a bay towards Gros Cap, which is the most easterly point of the peninsula at Scented Grass Hill. A head wind unfortunately sprang up, and it took us a very long time to cross the bay, a distance of ten miles. In fact we only just managed to reach the lee on the far side.

In canoeing on large lakes which have straight shores, it is most unwise to hold on too long. At the first appearance of the wind rising, no time ought to be lost in putting ashore. Directly a lop gets up there is great danger of smashing the canoe when attempting to land. I refer to wind from the lake, not of course from off shore.

We landed, set the nets, and waited for the wind to drop, intending to proceed by night again.

The wind calmed down towards evening; the nets were lifted and yielded one small trout only. We resumed our journey at 6.30 P.M. and paddled along towards Gros Cap. The water was smooth, although there was a heavy ground swell, which continued to roll the whole of the night and the next day. It had evidently been blowing hard out on the lake.

The night was perfect. Light airs gently ruffled the surface of the lake; the ground swell did not impede our progress. At ten o'clock, when the moon rose, we had rounded Gros Cap, and were running west along the south shore of the peninsula of Scented Grass Hill. We passed several fires, which we at first took to be Indian encampments. Presently, however, the fires became too numerous;

there were thousands of them; there was a bush fire all along the coast.

The first streak of dawn could be seen at 2 A.M.; at four it was daylight. We then struck south-west across Deer Pass Bay. This traverse proved to be longer than I expected—viz. fifteen miles. The weather was very settled, or I should not have ventured across by day. We landed at 8.30 A.M., having kept steadily to the paddles for fourteen hours, and travelled forty-six miles, a long way for men on one small meal a day, and we were all fairly weary. To sit in one position for so long a stretch is very fatiguing, harder even on the legs, which have nothing to do, than on the arms, which have all the work to do.

After the nets were set and the tent pitched, our solitary small trout was cooked, equally divided and solemnly eaten. We filled up, or attempted to do so, with blueberries, and then turned in and slept soundly.

As we had been living pretty toughly and working fairly hard for many days without luxury of any kind, even tea and salt, we were all fairly thin; the work was beginning to tell. We were almost barefooted, and our clothes were in a most disgraceful state. It was high time to reach some dépôt of supplies, where we could refit. However, our goal, Fort Norman, was and had been in sight (so to speak) since we first struck Great Bear Lake, and it was now but a short distance away.

Sandy's internals had been giving much trouble for some days, the inevitable result of eating too large a quantity of fish on the occasions when we happened to have a plentiful supply. When one who has been starving, or on short rations, abuses a time of plenty and overloads his stomach ever so little, the unfailing result is violent purging and severe indigestion.

The temptation to fill up is great, I allow, for at the time the sensation produced by a square meal is eminently satisfactory, but prudence should be exercised. Men in such circumstances should resolve to rise from each meal but half satisfied, until they become quite accustomed to full rations again.

There appeared to be a few moose along the western shore. One small trout was taken in the evening, which gave us a couple of mouthfuls each.

On August 28 the minimum thermometer showed 32° Fahr. The weather was cloudless and calm. It had been my intention to start at a very early hour, but the lifting of the nets delayed us, and it was 5 A.M. before we finally got under way. The nets provided breakfast in the shape of two fair-sized trout, one Arctic trout of the usual size, and one herring (so called), the first herring we had caught. We started with full stomachs, and paddling steadily the whole day, without a "spell" of any sort, till 6 P.M., we made about forty miles. A breeze from the north then sprang up, which did us good service, for it took us along another twelve miles. We camped after dark. It was too late to set the nets, so we starved for a change.

I may say a word or two about sailing a canoe. A sail ought never to be set unless the wind is abaft the beam. On this account a square sail with a light yard is much to be preferred to a leg-of-mutton sail. The advantage of the square sail lies in the fact that there is no temptation to set it unless the wind is really abaft the beam, for then only is it of service. The Indians invariably use the square sail, and I have never heard of their capsizing a canoe.

We had a sharp frost during the night.

We started next morning, August 29, at 2.30, for I was determined to reach the foot of the lake before the wind sprang up and stopped us. Breakfast did not cause delay, for we had none, and the nets had not been put down. Little could be seen in the early hours. About 5 A.M. I judged from the appearance of the land that we were passing old Fort Franklin. Shortly afterwards a heavy bank of mist to the south showed where the outlet of Bear River probably lay. Proceeding, we sighted many fish stages and old Indian camps on our right.

It was my intention to push right on for Fort Norman. However, as we were starving, I thought it fair to let my men have a say in the matter. I told them that by pushing straight on we should probably reach Fort Norman, where supplies were a certainty, in about twelve hours, but on the other hand, the fishing stages indicated that fish could almost certainly be caught here, as the place was no doubt the fishing station resorted to by the men employed by the Hudson Bay Company. Sandy exclaimed that he was ravenously hungry and would like to try the nets for something to eat, so his wish ruled the day. Darrell said nothing. We paddled to the fishing dépôt, landed, pitched the tent, set the nets, and went to sleep.

We had at last reached the foot of Great Bear Lake. No wind or bad weather could stop us now. For myself I did not care whether we reached Fort Norman a little sooner or later. The distance from the mouth of Dease River to the foot of Bear Lake is only about 180 statute miles on a direct course. Following the shore, as one is compelled to do in a canoe, we had travelled by account 276 statute miles. The north and western shores of the lake are very easy to follow. There are but few islands, and there is no chance of running into blind bays and inlets, which cause frequent trouble to those who navigate many of the larger lakes in the Northland. We had been exceptionally fortunate in the way of weather, for on the larger lakes in the north, especially in the fall of the year, it is of common occurrence to be detained for days, even weeks, at a time by strong winds.

Possibly we should not have wanted food at all had we possessed a good outfit of trolling gear and a couple of nets of 4 in. mesh, but of this I have some doubt, for the Indians we met were provided with the proper nets, yet they were starving.

Deer had been conspicuous by their absence. A few ducks and geese had been seen, but none shot, for we had not thought it worth while to paddle long distances out of our course in pursuit.

At noon I woke Darrell and we went to look at the nets, which had now been down six hours. There was not a fish, so we quickly pulled the nets and got ready to start.

We left at 1.30 P.M. and headed for the mouth of Bear River. After paddling a short distance we saw smoke along the shore, and with the glasses I made out two Indian tepees and a newly erected log shack.

As we felt very empty, and as there was, if not a certainty, at least a very good chance of our obtaining a supply of fish from these natives, we headed the canoe for their camp.

The tepees were tenanted by two Indian families. The men were engaged in building the log shack. Not much work was being done, however, for measles had broken out, and they were all sick, some of them being in a very bad way. They at once asked me for medicine, but I had none to give them. They treated us well; cooked us a good meal of dried and fresh fish, and then laid before us a large basket of blueberries for dessert. They even produced some tea, the last they had. What a comfort it was to put food into the empty stomach! but caution had to be exercised. I presented our host with a knife, a file, and about 1 lb. of tobacco, with which he seemed delighted. He then gave us some fish to take along for our evening meal.

This native spoke a few words of French, and he gave me some information about rapid water on Bear River, and the side of the river which we ought to keep.

We entered the river at 5.30 P.M. The current was strong, about five or six miles an hour. Paddling with the current we made good way, and camped at 9 P.M.

Bear River is from 150 to 300 yards broad at the outlet. It is of varying depth, and confined by low sloping banks covered with a stunted and poor growth, chiefly of spruce and larch. A few poplars were to be seen. Large numbers of herring were seen jumping clear out of the water at the outlet.

We were up betimes the next morning, August 30, but a heavy mist lay like a pall over the river. It was not possible to see more than a few yards ahead. As we expected to meet with some rough water, it was not advisable to start till the sun rose and dispelled the mist.

We left shortly after 8 A.M. The current continued strong, and in two hours we reached the "rapids." The Indians whom we had met the day before had given me an exaggerated idea of these rapids. There is rough water only for about three or four miles. It is advisable to keep on the left hand side of the river. With ordinary care in steering between the protruding boulders, there is not the faintest chance of an accident.

Below this rough water we came to smooth water with diminished current. A ridge of hills, through which the river at this place cuts its way, is of limestone formation. We were now more than half way to the Mackenzie River. The current improved a little lower down, and shortly afterwards we sighted Bear Rock, which lies in the northern angle formed by the junction of the Mackenzie and Bear Rivers. The banks of Bear River, which had been high and steeply sloping, became lower as we approached the valley of the Mackenzie River, behind which we saw the snow-capped peaks of the Rocky Mountains in the distance. A few miles farther, and we paddled out on the magnificent and broad waters of the Mackenzie. Fort Norman is situated on the high bank on its east side, a few hundred yards to the south of its junction with the Bear River. We reached Fort Norman shortly after 4 P.M., the passage of the Bear River, said to be about ninety miles, having taken us exactly eleven hours to accomplish. The Bear River is one of the few good rivers in Northern Canada. The Ark-i-linik is another. The current in both is good, and there are no portages.

Our long and latterly somewhat tedious and hungry journey had come to an end. We had at last reached our goal, civilisation, and supplies. For many months we had been keenly looking forward to hearing news from the outside world. In this, however, we were somewhat disappointed. There had been a hitch in the forwarding of the mail, and Fort Norman had been many months without news. The assassination of President McKinley and the termination of the war in South Africa were recent news to us.

The Hudson Bay Company's representative, Mr. Timothy Gaudette, happened to be absent, but the keys of the store were produced by Mr. Spendlove, who represents the Church Missionary Society at this post.

For the great kindness and attention shown to us by both Mr. and Mrs. Spendlove during our short stay at Fort Norman, I take this opportunity of expressing my hearty thanks.

Abundant supplies were furnished by Mr. William Elliot, and a substantial meal of bacon, fish, potatoes, bread and butter, and coffee with milk and sugar, was laid before us. It was a novel sensation to sit on chairs again with our legs under a table, within doors, and with a roof over our heads. A pipe of good tobacco following the sumptuous repast completed our happiness. I make no pretence of being in love with hard and tough times. However, these do no harm, and they certainly enhance the appreciation of the good things of civilised life on one's return.

It is remarkable how soon one can become accustomed to doing without things. To men unused to a "meat straight" diet, the absence of bread is at first keenly felt, but soon ceases to trouble. Even salt one does not miss after the first few days.

Looking back on our long journey, I could not help congratulating myself on the exceedingly good fortune which had followed us throughout. The journey, as originally projected in England, had been carried out in every detail. We had experienced no sickness or starvation, for we could well afford to forget the very few days on which we were without food while navigating on Great Bear Lake. They did not remain in our minds as a feature of the trip. In crossing the land from Ti-bi-elik Lake to the Arctic coast, I considered that we had been exceptionally fortunate in the way of food. Our dogs also had kept well and strong, though at one time the fatal dog sickness, prevalent at times in Huskyland, threatened to make a clean sweep of them.

The collections made—entomological, botanical, and geological—and the photographs taken had been landed in safety. We had arrived at our destination at a sufficiently early date to permit of our accomplishing part, at least, of the journey to rail-head at Edmonton by open water, a distance of considerably over one thousand miles.

In spite of our caution with respect to the amount of food we consumed, we all went down with severe attacks of indigestion. The stomach accustomed to a diet of fish or "meat straight" refuses at first to assimilate food to which it is unused. Bread, beans, potatoes, &c., remained on our chests like lead, and when we left Fort Norman on September 2 we were all sick men, and it was fully a week till we recovered our usual northern robust health.

The journey from Fort Norman up the Mackenzie River to Fort Resolution on Great Slave Lake is usually made in twenty-eight days. I was informed that it had been accomplished in seventeen days. We reached Fort Resolution on September 28, having thus accomplished the journey in twenty-six days. We reached Fort Mackay on the Athabasca River on October 15, and there we were frozen in. After a month's delay, the homeward journey was resumed with dogs and sleighs. Early in December we reached the Hudson Bay Company's post at Lac-la-Biche, where we procured horses, and the journey thence to Edmonton, a distance of about one hundred and sixty miles, was easily accomplished in five days.

APPENDIX

THE GEOLOGY OF NORTH CANADA

INTRODUCTION

THE vast region lying to the west of Hudson's Bay, and known as the Barren Lands of North America, was traversed in two journeys in 1893 and 1894 by Mr. J. Burr Tyrrell, M.A., on behalf of the Canadian Geological Survey, and the geological observations then made were published in the Report of the Survey for 1896.

In the first of these explorations, in 1893, the country to the west of Baker Lake and lying between west longitude 64° and 65° was reached. Further north the region extending to the Arctic Seas remained unexplored, and accordingly I determined to traverse it and the Arctic coast as far westwards as the Coppermine River to observe what I could of their geological features.

The following notes on the physical features and the rocks of this region are given only as a record of my own observations in this far northern portion of his Majesty's dominions.

FROM BAKER LAKE TO HUDSON BAY

On approaching Baker Lake from the west we passed over a generally rolling and undulating country, but rocky in places, and a few sand and gravel dunes were observed.

The land forming the shores of Baker Lake itself was low. The rocks on the northern side have been ascertained to be Laurentian, while those on the southern shore are of Cambrian age.

At a little distance from the south shore is a range of low hills running east and west between the mouth of the Kazan River and the head of the lake, and at a distance of about eight or ten miles from the shore there is a somewhat high hill called No-a-shăk.

North of Baker Lake the Ti-her-yuak-lŭg-yuak River, varying from forty to sixty yards in width, flows towards the Quoich River along a very crooked course between banks which, in the west, are low and sloping, but, as the Quoich River is approached, become higher. Here the course of the river is straighter, the country on either side being much shut in. The rocks seen were granitic in appearance on both banks of the river.

To the east of the Quoich River the country is generally level and prairie-like with a few small lakes, but near the east end of Baker Lake the surface is much broken and very rocky in places with occasional small lakes.

The region between the Quoich River and Hudson Bay on the north side of Chesterfield Inlet may be said to be typical Barren Northland, as it is full of small lakes with but small areas of sometimes rocky, sometimes grassy land between. Indeed, it is scarcely too much to say that most of the land is water, so much of the area is occupied by lakes; so generally spread and disposed are they that a route in any direction will traverse what may be called a chain of lakes. East of Ti-her-yuak-lūg-yuak Lake the country changes somewhat as it becomes very rocky, and there are typical glaciated crystalline rocks on either side of the river that flows from the lake into the head of Whitney Inlet. The river, with a straight course to the east, narrowing and widening between steep-sloping and rocky banks, has a rugged apparently granitic country on each side.

As the coast of Hudson Bay is approached the level of the land lowers, but it is still rocky and full of small lakes.

The small island near the shore of Hudson Bay, between Winchester Inlet and Whitney Inlet, known as Depot Island, consists of granitoid gneiss with the foliation very distinct; although the rocks are much smoother on this island, no glacial striæ were observed.

It appears to me remarkable that the striations, which are so frequently seen on the rocks of this region, and attributed to the action of flints in the bottom of the great ice-sheet, especially those on the softer rocks such as sandstones, have not long since been worn away by erosion and denudation.

From Hudson Bay to Ti-bi-elik Lake

I remained with the ship at Depot Island from Jan. 10 to Feb. 10, 1902, when I commenced my journey to the Arctic coast.

The first section of the route was from the coast of Hudson Bay to the Ti-bi-elik Lake, lying to the west of Aberdeen Lake, so that we had to proceed due west and revisit Baker Lake, which is about midway.

On the 17th of February we struck Armit-or-yuak Lake, which is narrow and has many arms and legs, so to speak. The river flowing into the lake has a decided fall, and comes from either the north-west or the west and not from Ti-hit-yuak Lake, while the river from the lake reaches the coast south of Whitney Inlet. The river we followed was confined by high rocky banks of red crystalline rock.

After passing Baker Lake we saw three lakes before reaching
Schultz Lake. The sandstones, so conspicuous on the south side
of Baker Lake, had given place to the red felspathic rocks of the
Laurentian pre-Cambrians.

For a long distance westwards the country was flat or slightly
undulating.

On the 18th we saw a hill of grey quartzite like the Huronian
quartzite of Marble Island, and this rock was seen in numerous
exposures on the 20th also. The country continued generally flat,
but it was rugged in places.

On reaching the Ti-bi-elik Lake, which extends westward from
the 100th meridian of west longitude, we found an undulating
country with a somewhat conspicuous flat-topped hill which is a
useful landmark.

The Region between the Ark-i-linik River and the Arctic Coast

On the 5th of April the exploration of the region to the north of
that traversed by Tyrrell in 1893 was commenced.

During three days' journey northwards from Ti-bi-elik Lake the
country was generally level, but with some low flattish ridges and
knolls giving it a somewhat undulating character. The surface was
almost clear of snow, but largely covered with fragments of red
sandstone, indicating the extension to this area of the Cambrian
rocks of the southern side of Baker Lake. In this region there was,
for the Barren Lands, remarkably little surface water, only one small
lake being seen throughout the 6th of April, on which day we made
nine miles.

On the afternoon and evening of the following day, the abundance
of granitic boulders on the surface and the absence of red sandstone
fragments, although there was no rock seen *in situ*, showed that the
geological structure had changed, and that we had now entered
upon the great pre-Cambrian region of the northern Barren Lands.
The surface configuration and general aspect were, however, very
similar to those of the area we had previously traversed, but we
were gradually attaining somewhat higher levels, and the altitude
here was found to be 515 feet above sea-level. A short distance
north of this point the surface water flowed northwards, from which
it was evident that we had now reached the divide between the
basin of the Ark-i-linik River and that of Back's River. To the
north-east of another small lake some sandy hillocks diversified
the surface.

Here, on the 8th, we found an exposure of grey quartzite resembling the Marble Island quartzite, and this may indicate the
presence at this place of Huronian rocks. .

After another day's march, during which we crossed several lakes, we reached a small river flowing northwards between low-sloping and occasionally high-sloping banks, but without any rocks to be seen *in situ*.

On the 10th we reached a small lake with, on its western side, an island with a gravelly flat top rising 120 feet above the surface of the lake, with steeply-sloping and, in some places, precipitous sides.

The river continued through an area slightly undulating, with an occasional dip or small ravine breaking the uniformity. With a width of from 300 to 600 yards the river now flowed over a shallow gravel and boulder-covered bed, the boulders consisting of a reddish granitic rock. It appeared to have a somewhat sluggish current, without rapids, but gradually the banks became more broken and the adjacent area more hilly and rocky, with exposures of granitic rocks *in situ*.

Another day's journey brought us close to the mouth of the Buchanan River, and the south-west shore of Pelly Lake, into which flows Back's River. The region hereabouts is low and generally flat, but slightly hilly or undulating in places, with much of the fragmentary country rock scattered over the surface.

The land on the northern side of the lake is very low, but stony in places, and the surface of the water was found to be only 260 feet above sea-level. We were now midway between Depot Island in Hudson Bay and the mouth of the Coppermine River on the Arctic coast, about 650 miles from each station.

North of Pelly Lake the country continued of the same low and slightly undulating character, but with much of the rock of the country exposed. This was still the same reddish crystalline rock, smoothed but not striated by ice action.

The lake with the native name of Ti-her-yuak is full of rocky islands, and its shores are formed of granitic rocks.

The river flowing from the lake at its northern end has a width of about forty yards, but widens in places and encircles numerous small rocky islands, while at others it is confined by sloping rocky banks of varying height, and sometimes, near the river, very rugged.

The rocks here appear to be gneissic in character, a specimen brought home proving to be a decomposed gneiss consisting of quartz, felspar and chlorite after biotite, and the rock shows signs of mechanical deformation. (See Description of Rock Specimens, A.) The rock had on its exposed surface a reddish or pink colour, and this is the prevailing colour of the rocks of this region.

The river flowing to the north after leaving Ti-her-yuak Lake traverses a very sterile area which here justifies the name Barren Lands. No vegetation is to be seen except a few blades of grass here and there, while rocks, both fragmentary and *in situ*, are everywhere to be seen. Small shoal lakes with sandy bottoms are formed by widenings of the river.

On the 1st of May we reached latitude 67° 12′ 37″, where the country was very low and flat, but it soon became rugged with rocky steeply-sloping banks of about twenty feet in height by the river-side, and here the river flowed over rapids.

The rocks of the whole of this district were of the same general character as those seen previously, reddish granitic rocks with a large proportion of felspar, but at this place hornblende was a constituent mineral.

The country traversed during the next few days was rugged in places, but there were small stretches of grassy land where there appeared to be a fair depth of soil. The rocks continued similar, and there was an entire absence of schistose rocks.

The photographic views will best give an idea of the surface of this region, the main features of which are a succession of glaciated and smoothed rocky ridges trending north-west and south-east. Between these ridges are either shoal lakes, grassy swamps, or dry, flat stretches of soil generally circular in shape. These last have evidently been old lake areas.

At one place there is a distinct terminal moraine, but of not more than 200 yards in extent, formed of loose rounded stones, apparently from the same rocks that form this region. The miniature valleys or gulches between the rocky ridges appear to be due to the denuding action of ice.

On the 12th of May we found our latitude to be 67° 28′ 53″, and on the following day another specimen of the country rock was taken.

This is described by Dr. Flett, after his microscopical examination, as a hypersthene biotite granulite, with apatite zircon and iron oxides present. Unlike specimen No. 1, it is not gneissose. (See Description of Rock Specimen, No. 2.)

The land gradually became lower in elevation and the river widened as the coast was approached, and on the 14th of May we had the satisfaction of reaching the mouth of our river and the shore of the Arctic Sea at north latitude 67° 50′ 23″.

The Arctic Coast from the Mouth of the Ti-her-yuak River to the Mouth of the Coppermine River

The coast-line near the mouth of the Ti-her-yuak River is formed of crystalline or metamorphosed rocks of the same general character as those of which so much was seen on the route northwards from the Ti-her-yuak Lake. A single specimen was taken close to the river mouth; for if a hundred specimens were collected they would all differ slightly but immaterially, and one was sufficient to establish the important fact that the pre-Cambrian rocks of North America extend to the Arctic coast at this place.

On commencing our journey westwards along the coast over the ice, and with the mainland shore to the south, we found that small rocky islands almost entirely destitute of vegetation were numerous, scattered at a little distance from the shore of the mainland, which appeared as a long, low, undulating ridge of rocks.

There was much evidence of the great ice-sheet having moved in a northern direction here, as there were deep grooves scooped out, and the rock surfaces of the islands were much striated. It was also noticed that the rocks, similar to those on the mainland, were all abruptly broken off to the north.

On the 18th of May, quartz rock and granitic or gneissose rocks with much quartz were conspicuously observable in bands and patches, with smoothings and deep striations.

Continuing westwards to White Bear Point in latitude 68° 5′ 27″, we found the coast-line very low but stony, with rocky knolls and intervening small flats. The rocks were smoothly glaciated, and quantities of small loose stones and sand were seen.

On the 25th three Eskimo met us with a few copper articles and a lump of native copper about 2 lbs. in weight. This native copper, from which needles and other domestic implements are made, is obtained by the Eskimo from islands to the north—Victoria Land, and other localities in higher latitudes.

At the portage across Kent Peninsula we found the rocks still similar, but giving indications of change of surface level in very recent times, as beds of recent marine shells [1] occur at about ten feet above high-tide level. Similar patches of shells were seen until June 10th, and some occur among the soil or gravel on hill-slopes as high as 500 feet above sea-level.

On the 31st of May we crossed the divide on the Kent Peninsula portage and found the country very hilly and rocky. There was one isolated hill of quite a precipitous character. Photographic views are given to show the features of this area. During our stay here, latitude 68° 32′ 46″, on the 2nd of June, I ascended the precipitous hill, Har-li-ar-li, which is 360 feet high and has a flat top. The rock was a good deal broken on the surface, and showed no evidence of the passing of an ice-sheet.

The rocks, however, had now changed in character, as the granitic or gneissic rocks that had characterised the region through which we had passed from the Ti-her-yuak Lake in latitude 66° had given place to a decidedly igneous rock, which proves to be a coarse-grained ophitic dolerite. (See Description of Rock Specimens, No. 4.) There were, however, at this place transported boulders of the previously traversed rocks.

On the 3rd of June, near a lake on the isthmus of the Kent Peninsula named It-ĭb-lĕr-yuak, many patches of marine shells were observed. The shells were similar to those seen on the 30th of May

[1] *Saxicava artica* and *Cardium islandicum*.

at Portage Inlet. The occurrence of marine shells on coastal slopes may be accounted for otherwise than by coast elevation, for sheets of shore ice are capable of pushing up portions of the seashore in a frozen condition, and thus shells may be left on the land at considerable elevations above the sea-level.

On June 5th we found the country rock like that at Mount Har-li-ar-li. It was here to be seen in a horizontal sheet and much jointed. At about four miles distance we again observed the pre-Cambrian gneissic rocks, which doubtless underlie the sheets of dolerites.

At the mouth of the I-lu Inlet, where we arrived on June 6th, the land is low on the north, but high and precipitous in many places on the south shore.

There are two unusually lofty hills on the south-western shore of I-lu Inlet, one named I-ta-wing and the other U-wei-u-ullig, the latter of which is the highest, having an elevation of about 600 feet, of which about 150 feet is formed by a perpendicular rock precipice.

On the 7th, in latitude 68° 12' 07" the coastal land was high and rocky and even mountainous in character, and on the 8th we camped at a small bay, overlooked by a hill that I ascended on the 9th, and found to be 840 feet above sea-level.

A long slope of flat rock ascends to within 150 feet of the summit, and this is a flesh-coloured granitic mass dipping west at an angle of about 30°. It is a felspathic grit containing much well-rounded quartz in grains with largely decomposed felspar and scaly secondary mica. (See Description of Rock Specimens, No. 5.) The surface of the rock is smoothed and grooved by ice action, but not striated. The crest or summit ridge of 150 feet is formed by a doleritic rock similar to No. 4 on Mount Har-li-ar-li and to that in the vicinity of It-ib-lër-yuak Lake. The rock on this summit is a hornblende diabase. (See Description of Rock Specimens, No. 6.) It is also smoothed and grooved, but not striated.

It is impossible to say in which direction the ice moved at this place. The rocks where precipitous have their faces to the east, west, south, and north-west.

On the 10th of June I examined a precipitously-cut hill about four miles from our camp. The cliffs faced due west, and were opposite to the face of the 840 feet hill that I had ascended the day before, and from which I had obtained the rock specimen No. 5. Between the two hills extends a valley of about three miles in width, containing two long narrow lakes, and through the valley the surface water flows northwards. The rock forming the valley bottom is a fine red sandstone consisting of rounded grains of quartz with a small amount of cementing material. (See Description of Rock Specimens, No. 7.)

This sandstone rock is in places conglomeratic, and is there full of quartz pebbles. The felspathic grit (No. 5) and the red sandstone (No. 7) seem to pass into each other at a certain altitude, while the summit capping of the hill is the hornblendic diabase (No. 6).

It appears to me that the valley between these two hills has been formed by ice-action, which has taken away.nearly all the doleritic rock of the summit levels, leaving only the crests of the two hills, and No. 5 has been removed also, except where it remains between No. 7 and No. 6, while the sandstone rock, No. 7, remains to form the bottom of the valley. It is to be noted that the felspathic grit, No. 5, contains quartz pebbles as well as the sandstone. Briefly, it may be stated that the crests of the somewhat high hills in this area are composed of the volcanic doleritic rock, No. 6, while at lower levels is the grit, No. 5, and at the bottom of the valleys is the sandstone, No. 7, though, it should be added, this last rock is not always exposed.

I could not ascertain in which direction the ice-sheet had moved, but from the conspicuous smoothing and grooving, it is evident these hills have been covered by it; and it seems to me remarkable that the whole of the uppermost rocks have not been removed by the powerful glacial action to which they were subjected. Possibly they were exposed before the ice-sheet made a general movement. The origin of the small, flat, generally circular, gravel terraces, which have been noted by every one who has visited the Barren North Land, is not very apparent. I noticed and watched the *débris*, gravel, grit, and sand that issue from a deep bank of snow. It ran down and was settling in and filling up a small circular hollow in the ground. One might say that a miniature moraine from a miniature glacier, the snow-bank, was terminating in this hollow. It now appeared to me that the ice-sheet had moved in a southerly direction over this area.

On the 13th the land seen five miles to the south was very rugged and rocky, and it continued so on the 15th, when we traversed the portage across Cape Croker, where we found a fine-grained granitic or gneissic rock.

On the 16th we reached Barry Island, which one of my Eskimo had described as the best place for copper. He now said copper was more plentiful on an island six or eight miles north of Fowler Bay. However, two pieces of native copper were found in the evening.

The next day we searched for copper on the north-west shore of the island.

The main rock of the island is a fine-grained basalt which Dr. Flett described as granular, holocrystalline, and non-porphyritic, and a good deal decomposed. (See Description of Rock Specimens, No. 10.) The rock, although hard, is easily broken in all directions by a tap of the hammer. The summit of the island is, however, formed of a rock of the character of No. 6, and is described as coarse-grained ophitic dolerite with plagioclase and augite, and perhaps a few grains of olivine. The ophitic structure is very perfect. (See Description of Rock Specimens, No. 11.)

The underlying basalt dips west at an angle of about 25°, and it is in this rock that the native copper occurs. The copper is plentiful, for the quantity we obtained was found after but a brief search, and on a neighbouring island, Kŭn-nu-yŭk, a mass of copper had just been found, so large that a man could hardly lift it. There also copper is often found in the tide-way. The whole of the lower levels on Barry Island are covered with *débris* from the basalt, and where the rock has been disintegrated by weathering, copper has fallen out, so that flakes of the metal may be found along the sea-shore. In many places, too, green patches indicate that nuggets or flakes of copper have recently fallen out from their matrix.

The copper-bearing rock also contains crystalline quartz, some of which forms beautiful amethystine veins, of which some specimens were taken. There is here some further evidence of coastal elevation in the occurrence of saucer-shaped lines of water-worn *débris* at from twenty to forty feet above the present level of high tides.

The question whether it would ever pay to work the native copper of these regions remains for the consideration of experts. I have always understood that native copper occurring in small flakes or nuggets and sparsely distributed, is of but little practical value, and that copper can only, as a rule, be successfully worked from ores that are rich and easy of access. Much depends doubtless on its abundance and regularity of distribution. This island, Barry Island or Iglor-yu-ullig, is several miles in length, and perhaps three or four miles across. The Island to the south-south-east, Kŭn-nu-yŭk, is still larger, besides which there is an island to the south-west which has given much copper, and there are copper-yielding islands to the north. The copper-bearing formation holds good everywhere except on the summit cappings of the islands.

On the 18th of June we reached the most easterly land of Bathurst Inlet, which is very hilly and rocky, some of the hills attaining an altitude of 1500 feet. Between the hills are grassy flats, but at present they were but swamps.

On the 23rd, on our way across Bathurst Inlet, we approached a flat-topped precipitous island very much resembling a kopje. When near to it I noticed a change in its rock formation, and saw that there was a bed of limestone about fifteen feet thick underlying a capping of igneous rock of about 20 feet thickness.

On further examination I found the limestone which is thinbedded and horizontal, in places 60 feet thick. The summit, igneous rock, is an ophitic dolerite similar to the cappings of the islands and hills previously seen. (See Description of Rock Specimen, No. 13.)

Although fossils were diligently searched for, none were found in the limestone.

The dolerite is columnar in places, and large masses and much smaller *débris* have fallen to the base of the precipitous cliffs formed by the limestone and the dolerite. Southwards from the island mass a long spit of the dolerite rock projects into the sea, and it is seen to be very much smoothed and grooved, and the striæ, all trending to the south-south-east, are very numerous.

About five miles beyond this limestone island we passed a small basaltic island on which two pieces of copper ore were picked up. It seems as if copper is to be found wherever this basalt occurs.

On the 25th June we camped on the north point of Lewis Island. With the exception of some precipitously-cut rocks near our camp, this island is formed of the same partly-decomposed basalt as Barry Island. It is described as fine-grained, granular crystalline, decomposed basalt. (See Description of Rock Specimen, No. 15.)

Although we did not find so much copper here, the green marks on the rocks were more numerous, but we did not spend an hour altogether in the search. One of our Eskimo knew of a large mass of copper on the south-west shore of the island, which he stated to be as much as five feet in length and three inches thick. It protruded from the rocks under the water, it was said, but there was too much ice for us to find the copper. A piece of quartz with copper ore and native copper was picked up on the seashore. Another specimen of the copper-bearing rock here is a decomposed basalt, fine-grained, and not unlike No. 15, but vesicular. (See Description of Rock Specimen, No. 17.)

In the bays of this island a regular succession of apparently old shore-lines can be seen. There are as many as eight, and although there are no shells, the fragmentary *débris* gives evidence of being water-worn.

On the 27th we rested at the north-west point of Lewis Island, where we again found the copper-bearing basalt, and accordingly we commenced a search that resulted in our collecting about 2 lbs. weight of copper. The metal appeared to be very persistent in its occurrence in the partly decomposed basalt of which all the islands we passed that day consisted. The flakes of copper seemed to be always vertical when in their rock matrix. The rocks of this island, where they are not disintegrated, are well smoothed by glacial action, and the striæ are numerous and distinctly trend south and south-east.

Cape Barrow was reached on the following day, and this prominent headland, pointing due north, we found to consist of the felspathic gneissic rock of which so much had been seen. It is here very red and handsome in appearance, and is rounded and smoothed.

The islands lying off the Cape are basaltic, and the rock appears to have a columnar structure, and I think it overlies a bed of limestone. The precipitous cliffs of these islands are very similar to those of the limestone island previously seen. The land behind the coast-line is here very rugged.

On the 29th June we arrived at a place called Ŭt-kūs-kĭk, where there is a remarkable rock from which the Huskies have for generations made their kettles. The mass of this rock, which we may call kettle-rock, was situated about five miles from the site of our camp, and occurred as an enclosed mass in the red granitic-looking rock. It is so soft that it can be easily cut with an axe, and is of a greenish grey colour with a smooth steatitic feel. The rock is indeed a talc chlorite schist. (See Description of Rock Specimens, No. 18.)

The country at this part of the coast is rocky in general appearance, but grassy valleys, now somewhat boggy, abound.

On the 3rd July we encamped on the south-east side of Gray's Bay. The land forming the opposite and northern side of the bay is a promontory terminating in a point to the north-east, off which lies Hepburn Island.

Our camp was on the pre-Cambrian gneissic rocks, but on the promontory across the bay four miles distant and four miles from the north-eastern termination, we found red sandstone underlying what resembled sheets of basaltic rocks which, with precipitous cliffs, prevailed at the surface both throughout the promontory and on Hepburn Island. The rock is described by Dr. Flett as fine-grained, well-foliated hornblende schist. (See Description of Rock Specimens, No. 19.)

We found the land near Epworth Point on the 6th very rocky, but the rocks much smoothed and striated.

Further west, precipitous basaltic rocks are seen overlying the felspathic granitic or gneissic rocks, and at two places we observed an occurrence of the talcose kettle-stone.

On the 8th of July we reached a part of the coast about twenty-seven miles west of Epworth Point, where the coastal country may fairly be called beautiful, with long, grassy, gently-rising slopes extending inland from sandy and gravelly shores that form the coast-line.

The rocks seen were slates with good slaty cleavage, horizontally bedded and capped by basaltic rocks, of which large detached masses lay balanced on narrow ledges of the slate.

On June 15th the hills on the other side of the Coppermine River were clearly visible from the rising ground at the back of our camp, and they did not appear to be very distant.

Doleritic rocks again formed the summit levels, and consisted of coarse-grained ophitic dolerite with augite. (See Description of Rock Specimens, No. 21.)

On the 19th of July we reached the mouth of the Coppermine River.

The country we had seen along the coast for several days was of a very pleasing character in the Arctic summer, long, grassy slopes rising from the sea-shore, with occasional patches of willows that stood out conspicuously owing to their extreme greenness.

II

ROCK SPECIMENS FROM THE NORTHERN PART OF CANADA

Described by Dr. JOHN S. FLETT, F.G.S., &c.

1. A decomposed gneiss, consisting of quartz, felspar, and chlorite after biotite. The felspar is mostly orthoclase, but plagioclase is also present, and decomposition of these two minerals has given rise to much secondary mica. Everywhere the rock shows abundant signs of mechanical deformation, and cataclastic structure is highly developed. The quartz is often crushed to powder, the felspars broken and torn up. Epidote and chlorite are frequent, probably both secondary after biotite.

2. A peculiar rock which may perhaps be best described as a hypersthene biotite granulite. It consists, for the most part, of orthoclase, plagioclase, and quartz. The quartz was proved to be uniaxial and positive, and forms lenticular or elongated masses which give the rock an indistinct parallel structure. It is not gneissose, however, but looks massive in the hand specimen. In addition to the minerals named there is a small quantity of biotite and of hypersthene. The last-named mineral was recognised by its cleavage, straight extinction, dichroism, and polarisation. It shows the usual decomposition into bastite. It is not common in rocks of this kind. Apatite, zircon, and iron oxides are present as accessories.

3. Decomposed, fine-grained olivine basalt or anamesite, consisting of lath-shaped plagioclase and small grains of augite with a small amount of olivine which has passed into dark brown serpentine. There is also a good deal of iron oxide and secondary limonite.

4. Coarse-grained, perfectly ophitic dolerite, with large irregular plates of purplish-brown augite, enclosing many small elongated plagioclase felspars. It does not seem to have contained olivine, and is a very fine example of ophitic structure.

5. Felspathic grit, containing much well-rounded quartz in grains which are sometimes 2 mm. in diameter, together with felspar, mostly somewhat decomposed. The quartz is granitic and not frequently sheared, and the cementing matrix between the grains

is full of fine, scaly, secondary mica. There are a few fragments which seem to have been derived from a felsitic rock.

6. Hornblendic diabase. Consists of plagioclase, felspar, and hornblende, which is partly uralitic, and probably after original augite, partly compact and apparently primary. There is also a little biotite and large plates of ilmenite, needles of apatite, &c. Most probably this was once an ophitic dolerite with augite and plagioclase, but if so the augite is entirely uralitised. See 13.

7. Fine quartzose sandstone, composed of rounded grains of quartz, with a small quantity of cementing material. It contains also a few bits of felspar and grains of iron oxide.

10. Fine-grained, granular, holocrystalline, non-porphyritic basalt, a good deal decomposed. The augite has all weathered into chlorite and other secondary products. The rock does not seem to have been ophitic. Not unlike specimen marked 3.

11. Coarse-grained ophitic dolerite, with plagioclase, felspar, and augite, and perhaps a few grains of olivine. The ophitic structure is very perfect. In some ways this rock approaches gabbro, as the augite often has a diallage structure, but the ophitic character resembles rather that of the dolerites. It contains large irregular masses of ilmenite and a little biotite and apatite.

13. Ophitic dolerite, similar to the preceding, but more decomposed. There is a little biotite in this rock, and dark green hornblende, some of which is secondary after augite (uralite), but part is primary, and has formed on the surface of the original augite.

14. Coarse-grained pegmatite, consisting of quartz, orthoclase, plagioclase, and chlorite. There is also some fresh dark brown biotite and a little muscovite. The rock has been sheared, and the quartz is often broken up; in the hand specimen it has a somewhat gneissose character.

15. Fine-grained, granular crystalline, decomposed basalt. It consists of plagioclase, felspar, and small grains of augite, and is neither porphyritic nor vesicular. It has probably contained a little olivine, though that mineral is no longer present in the unaltered condition, but is represented by pseudomorphs of brown serpentine. There is also a good deal of iron oxide, partly weathered to limonite.

17. Decomposed basalt, fine grained and not unlike the preceding, but vesicular. The vesicles are filled with chlorite, quartz, and secondary sphene (?) after ilmenite, and a peculiar feature of the rock is the occurrence of pale more felspathic zones around the vesicles. The rock has consisted originally of plagioclase and granular augite, but both these minerals are now much decomposed.

P.S.—The mineral referred to above as iron oxide is really a copper ore filling veins and cavities. It is dark red when fresh, but weathers into green malachite. (Soluble in HNO^3, giving green solution, precipitated by NH^3, and dissolves to form dark blue fluid on addition of excess.)

18. Talc chlorite schist with scattered grains of iron oxide.

19 Fine-grained, well-foliated hornblende schist, consisting of small crystals of hornblende, grains of felspar, and some epidote, and iron oxides.

21. Coarse-grained ophitic dolerite, with augite, olivine, and plagioclase felspar. The structure is ophitic. There are large plates of ilmenite and some apatite. The augite is weathering to chlorite. Olivine is scarce, and is decomposing into serpentine.

III

LEPIDOPTERA FROM ARCTIC AMERICA

By HENRY JOHN ELWES, F.R.S., &c.

THE collection of which I give a list was made by Mr. David Hanbury, who has appended notes on the localities and habits of the insects, which give an exceptional value to it.

Though small in number of species, it is the most interesting Arctic collection I have yet seen, and most of the specimens are in beautiful condition. The variation in some of the species is extraordinary.

Considering the difficulties under which collecting is carried on in such a region, and that Mr. Hanbury had not previously any experience in collecting, this collection does him the highest credit.

He has been good enough to present the greater part of it to the National Museum.

LIST OF MR. HANBURY'S ARCTIC COLLECTION

1. *Erebia fasciata.* (See Plate, fig. 11 ♂, 12 ♀.)
    E. *fasciata*, Butler, Cat. Sat. B.M., p. 92, Pl. II., fig. 8 (1868).

Several specimens in beautiful condition; from Point Epworth, 11, vii.; Cape Barrow, 30, vi.; Chapman Island, 27, vi.; Gray's Bay, 1, vii. These agree with the type in the British Museum from Cambridge Bay, and vary considerably in the amount of rufous in the fore-wing above, which in the females extends to the base of the wing.

The fringe in quite fresh specimens is grey.

2. *Erebia disa.*
    Papilio disa, Thunberg, Diss. Ins. Suec. II., p. 37 (1791).

Three males and a female from Point Epworth, 11, vii. These resemble specimens from Finland much more closely than they do specimens of the var. *mancinus*, Hew., from Alberta, in having the band of the hind-wing below well marked.

3. *Erebia rossii.*
    Hipparchia rossii, Curtis, Ross' 2nd Voy. App. Nat. Hist,
        p. 67, Pl. A, fig. 7 (1835).

A pair from 140° W., 67° 40′ N., 14, vii., and one from Point
Epworth, 11, vii., are perfectly fresh, and seem to show that this
species is barely separable from the Asiatic form, *ero,* Brem. *Cf.*
Trans. Ent. Soc., Lond., 1899, p. 347.

I previously had only bad specimens from Hudson Bay for
comparison. Recently I have received a fresh female taken by
Mr. Sampson in Frobisher Bay, Baffin's Land, 14, vii., 02.

The fringes of these three are all grey, which is not the case in
any of my Altai specimens however fresh, though slightly evident
in some from Transbaikalia.

4. *Œneis bore,* var. *taygete.*
    Œ. taygete, Hübner, Samml. Ex. Schmett (1816–1824).

Several pairs in beautiful condition from Barren Grounds, Gray's
Bay, and Point Epworth; vary a good deal in the breadth, shape,
and distinctness of the bands on hind-wing below. Two show the
marginal row of whitish spots on hind-wing very distinctly, these
are usually faint or absent in Labrador specimens.

5. *Œneis semidea,* var. *vel crambis,* var. (See Plate, fig. 9 ♂,
        10 ♀.)
    Hipparchia semidea, Say, Amer. Ent. III., Pl. 50 (1828).
    Chionobas crambis, Freyer, Neuere Beitr. V., Pl. 440, figs.
        3–4 (1844).

Five specimens from Barren Grounds and one from Point
Epworth, fresh and in good order, must, I think, be referred to
one of these species. I might call them *peartiæ,* Edw., or *assimilis,*
Butl., but they are intermediate between the types of those two
forms in the British Museum, being rather less conspicuously
banded on the hind-wing below than the former, and rather more
so than the latter.

Some of them show more or less trace of the marginal row of
grey spots on the hind-wing, which at first led me to think that they
were *crambis;* but in a fresh state they are much blacker than any
of the faded specimens of *crambis* I have before me. Whether that
species, which I only know certainly from Labrador, occurs also
in Arctic America, and whether when we know it better it will be
possible certainly to distinguish it from *semidea,* are points which
at present remain obscure.

6. *Cænonympha tiphon*, var. *mixturata*.
    C. tiphon, var. *mixturata*, Alpheraky, Rom. Mem. sur.
        Lep. IX., p. 326 (1897).

Two males and a female from Dismal Creek, taken 30, vii., are in bad condition, but are sufficient to show that the form found here, like that from Alaska, is nearer to the Kamschatkan variety than to any other.

7. *Argynnis pales*.
    Papilio pales, W. V., p. 177 (1776).

Three males and a female from the Barren Grounds, taken 16 and 18, vii., are the first specimens of this species I have yet seen or heard of from America, where I have long expected to hear of its discovery.

The males are quite typical, and could not be distinguished from some Alpine specimens.

The female is like some I have from Northern Siberia.

8. *Argynnis polaris*.
    A. polaris, Boisduval, Ind. Meth., p. 15 (1829); *id*. Icones,
        Pl. XX., figs. 1, 2 (1833).

Specimens were taken in all the localities visited in the first half of July, and are quite typical.

9. *Argynnis chariclea*. (See Plate, figs. 6, 7, 8.)
    Papilio chariclea, Schneider, Neuest. Mag. V., p. 588 (1794).

The most extraordinary variation is shown by the specimens of this species, which occurs in all parts of Arctic America, and was taken by Mr. Hanbury at all the places where he collected.

Among them a male from Chapman Island is almost black. Another from Dismal Creek is very small and pale, but a female from Point Epworth is a wonderful aberration, and I cannot say positively whether it is *polaris* or *chariclea*, though the size and the shape of the wings indicate the latter species.

10. *Argynnis frigga*, var. *improba*.
    Papilio frigga, Thunberg, *t. c.*, p. 33.
    Argynnis improba, Butler, Ent. Mo. Mag. XIII., p. 206
        (1877).

Several from the Barren Grounds and one from Point Epworth are like the type, and show but little variation.

11. *Lycæna orbitulus*, var. *franklinii*.
    Papilio orbitulus, Esper, Schmett. I., 2, Pl. CXII., fig. 4
        (1800).
    Lycæna franklinii, Curtis, *t. c.*, p. 69, Pl. A, figs. 8, 9.

A pair from the Barren Grounds are not so distinct from the

Arctic form found in Europe, var. *aquilina*, Stgr., = *aquilo*, Bd
as those from Labrador, and are perhaps nearer to those I ha
taken in the Rocky Mountains near Laggan.

12. *Colias hecla.*
      C. *hecla*, Lefebvre, Ann. Soc. Ent. Fr., 1836, p. 383, Pl. L
         B, figs. 3–6.

Four males and three females from the Barren Grounds, 11
W., 67° 40′ N., 13–16, vii. Agreeing well with other specime
from Arctic America, some of which were called *glacialis*
McLachlan.

Staudinger now catalogues the Lapland form as var. *sulitela*
Auriv. The specimens in Mr. Hanbury's collection differ *inter*
to a remarkable extent in the colour of the borders and discal sp
of the wings above.

13. *Colias boothii.*   (See Plate, figs. 1–4 ♂, 5 ♀.)
      C. *boothii*, Curtis, *t. c.*, p. 65, Pl. A, figs. 3–5.

This was represented by several fresh specimens, which enal
me to confirm the opinion formed on very insufficient previo
knowledge, that it is a species perfectly distinct from the last. T
variation in this species is so great that I have had to figure fi
specimens to give a fair idea of it; some of them would be suppos
by their markings to be females, but though the abdomens a
difficult to examine, owing to their hairy covering and being som
what compressed in packing, I can find only one undoubted fema
among them. None of the specimens sent are quite what Cur
figures as *chione*, in which the marginal band is faint or absent.

The species seems to have been fairly common at Point Epwort
Gray's Bay, and on the Barren Grounds.

14. *Colias pelidne.*
      C. *pelidne*, Boisduval, Icones, Pl. VIII., figs. 1–3.

Three pairs from Point Epworth, Barren Grounds, and Disn
Creek, of which the females differ *inter se* a good deal, one bei
white and two lemon-yellow.

15. *Colias nastes.*
      C. *nastes*, Boisduval, *l. c.*, figs. 4, 5.

Four males and two females from Barren Grounds, all varyir
These might be called *rossii*, Guen., or *moina*, Streck., by those w
like to try and distinguish local forms, a very uncertain task in t
case of Arctic insects.

HETEROCERA by Sir GEORGE F. HAMPSON, Bart., B.A., F.Z.S.

NOCTUIDÆ.

Hypsophila zetterstedti, Stgr., 114° 67° 40′.

GEOMETRIDÆ.

Aspilates orciferaria, Wlk., 114° 67° 40.
Cidaria, sp.   114° 67° 40′

TORTRICIDÆ.

gen. sp., Point Epworth.

IV

FLORA OF THE ARCTIC COAST OF NORTH AMERICA: OGDEN BAY TO COPPERMINE RIVER (100°–115° W. Long.)

COLLECTED BY DAVID T. HANBURY, 1902. DETERMINED BY R. A. ROLFE, A.L.S., OF THE ROYAL GARDENS, KEW.

ANEMONE parviflora, Michx.
Caltha palustris, L.
Papaver alpinum, L.
Parrya arctica, R. Br.
Cheiranthus pygmæus, Adams.
   (Hesperis Pallasii, Torr & Gray.)
Cardamine pratensis, L.
   „ digitata, Richardson.
Draba alpina, L. variety with bright yellow flowers.
Draba alpina, L., variety with pale yellow flowers.
Draba incana, L.
Erysimum lanceolatum, R. Br.
Silene acaulis, L.
Cerastium alpinum, L.
Stellaria longipes, Goldie.
Arenaria Rossii, R. Br.
   „ peploides, L.
   (Honkeneja peploides, Ehrh.)
Lupinus nootkatensis, Donn.
   (L. perennis, Hook., not of Linn.)
Astragalus aboriginum, Richardson.

(Phaca aboriginorum, Hook.)
Hedysarum boreale, Nutt.
Astragalus sp. nova?
Oxytropis campestris, L.
   „ nigrescens, Fisch.
Dryas integrifolia, L.
Potentilla biflora, Willd.
   „ nivea, L.
   „ „ var.
   „ *fruticosa, L.
Saxifraga cernua, L.
   „ Hirculus, L.
   „ oppositifolia, L.
   „ tricuspidata, Rottb.
Epilobium latifolium, L.
Aster sibiricus, L.
Matricaria inodora, L.
   (Pyrethrum inodorum, Sm.)
Arnica montana, L., var. angustifolia.
Senecio palustris, L.
Taraxacum officinale, Wigg.
Crepis nana, Richardson
Cassiope tetragona, L.
Andromeda polifolia, L.

* Not included in Arctic North-Eastern America in Hooker's "Distribution of Arctic Plants."

Ledum palustre, L. forma de-
cumbens.
Rhododendron lapponicum, L.
Pyrola rotundifolia, L.
* Primula farinosa, L.
Armeria vulgaris, L.
Mertensia maritima, S. F. Gray.

* Pedicularis capitata, Adams.
  ,,   hirsuta, L.
  ,,   sudetica, L.
Pinguicula vulgaris, L.
Oxyria reniformis, Hook.
Woodsia glabella, R. Br.

* Not included in Arctic North-Eastern America in Hooker's "Distribution of Arctic Plants."

V

METEOROLOGICAL OBSERVATIONS

SEPT. 22, 1901 TO SEPT. 23, 1902.

NOTE

MAXIMUM and minimum thermometers were supplied by Cary, and were verified at Kew prior to starting.

All readings are + unless marked −.

When travelling, it was not always possible to observe a maximum reading; and, as during the summer months we often travelled by night instead of by day, the same remark applies to some minumum readings which are missing.

All maximum readings were taken in the shade, unless specially stated otherwise.

Both maximum and minimum readings during the winter months were taken about three feet from the ground, the thermometers being laid on a chunk of snow out of the way of the dogs.

Remarks on the temperature, such as "cold," "warm," "cool," "hot," refer only to what we experienced ourselves, and have no reference to the reading of the thermometer at the time. A low or high reading of the thermometer gives no idea of the cold an individual may feel, so much depending on the force and direction of the wind, the humidity of the atmosphere, &c.

"Cloudless" does not mean absolutely cloudless in every case.

METEOROLOGICAL OBSERVATIONS.

Date.	Max. in Shade.	Min.	Wind.	Remarks.
1901. Sept.				
22	40	...	N. fresh	Fine, cool.
23	...	25	N.N.W. fresh	„ clear
24	...	20	W.S.W. „	„ „
25	...	26	S.W. light	„ cloudless sky.
26	...	27	E. & N.E. fresh	Overcast, snowstorm in afternoon.
27	...	31	N.N.W. light	Dull, wet skiff of snow.
28	...	30	N.W. fresh	Overcast, snow squalls.
29	38	28	W.S.W. light	„ but fine.
30	41	28	N.W. „	Wet snow skiff.
Oct.				
1	43	28	N.W. light	Skiff of snow last night, fine day.
2	...	24	N.N.W. fresh	Snow skiffs at times, fine.
3	24	20	„ light	„ „ „
4	28	18	„ „	Fine.
5	23	19	S.E. „	Dull, snow in evening.
6	...	26	N.W. strong	Clear sky, cold winter.
7	24	8	W. „	Overcast, snow at times.
8	20	16	„ „	Clear sky, cold.
9	22	9	W.S.W. „	„ „
10	...	19	S. light	Overcast, warmer.
11	...	28	S.E., S.W. mod.	Snow squalls and drizzle.
12	...	21	N.N.W. „	Bright, sunny, cold (Baker Lake).
13	15	0	N.E. strong	„ „ „ „
14	11	11	N. „	Cloudy, cold wind „
15	9	5	N.W. light	Clear „ „
16	10	5	„ strong	„ „ „
17	16	1	„ very light	„ „
18	15	1	W.N.W. very light	Hazy „
19	26	9	N.W. light	Clear „
20	12	− 1	S.E. „	Cloudy „
21	28	10	E. „	„ snow last night „
22	27	26	E. then W. light	Cloudy, snow at times (at foot of Baker Lake).
23	24	17	N.W. light	Clear (at foot of Baker Lake).
24	16	12	„ mod.	Cloudy „ „
25	15	11	N.E. „	„ snow at times (at foot of Baker Lake).
26	13	4	N.W. light	Clear, getting colder (at foot of Baker Lake).

Date.	Max. in Shade.	Min.	Wind.	Remarks.
1901. Oct.				
27	8	−9	E. calm	Clear, cold (at foot of Baker Lake).
28	15	−20	E. strong	Blizzarding, snow drifting (at foot of Baker Lake).
29	35	15	S.E. calm	Hazy, snow wet (at foot of Baker Lake).
30	37	35	None	Dead calm, cloudy, warm (at foot of Baker Lake).
31	25	25	N.E. then N.	Blizzarding, snow drifting (at foot of Baker Lake).
Nov.				
1	3	2	W. strong	Clear, drifting (at foot of Baker Lake).
2	5	−8	W. „	„ „ „ „
3	3	−8	W. light	„ cold „ „
4	5	−12	S.W. „	„ „ „ „
5	4	−14	S.W. calm	Hazy, sunny at times (at foot of Baker Lake).
6	18	−9	S.E. light	Cloudy, a skiff of snow fell (at foot of Baker Lake).
7	25	−1	N.E. strong	Drifting (at foot of Baker Lake).
8	11	8	N.W. mod.	Cloudy, fine „ „
9	11	0	N.W. „	„ „ „ „
10	3	−2	W. light	Clear „ „ „
11	−9	−8	S.E. mod.	Bright, clear, and cold (at foot of Baker Lake).
12	−8	−17	N.W. light	Clear, sunny (at foot of Baker Lake).
13	−11	−14	W. „	„ „ and cold (at foot of Baker Lake).
14	...	...	N.N.W. light	Cloudless and cold (at foot of Baker Lake).
15	...	...	Calm	Cloudless.
16	...	...	S.E. light	Cloudy, warmer, drifting in afternoon.
17	...	...	S. „	„ warm, looks like snow.
18	...	...	W.N.W. mod.	Mild, snow in afternoon.
19	...	...	W. strong	Cloudless, snow drifting.
20	...	...	W.N.W. strong	Drifting thick.
21	...	...	W. mod.	Cloudless, cold.
22	...	...	S.E. light	Hazy, mild.
23	−32	−40	N.W. strong	Drifting, very cold.
24	−30	...	Calm	Cloudless.
25	−28	...	S.W. light	„
26	...	...	S.E. „	Overcast and dull.
27	...	...	S.E. „	Snowstorm, mild.
28	...	...	N.W. mod.	Cloudless, cold.
29	−35	...	N.W. light	„ „
30	...	...	W. „	„ „

Date.	Max. in Shade.	Min.	Wind.	Remarks.
1901 Dec.				
1	...	...	Calm	Cloudless, cold.
2	...	...	S.E. light	„ milder.
3	...	...	N.W. strong	Drifting, cold.
4	...	...	S.E. light	Cloudy, warm.
5	...	...	N.E. very light	Cloudless, cold.
6	...	...	S.E. mod.	Cloudy.
7	...	...	S.E. strong	Drifting thick.
8	...	...	W. mod.	Cloudy, cold.
9	(−40) (mercury	−40) solid)	W. „	„ very cold.
10	−34	...	Calm	Cloudless, cold.
11	mercury	solid	„	„ coldest day as yet.
12	−12	...	N. light	Cloudy, warmer.
13	...	...	N.N.W. strong	Drifting and cold.
14	−33	...	N.W. strong	„ „
15	...	...	N.W. „	„ „
16	−25	...	N.W. „	„ „
17	−25	...	N.W. „	„ very cold.
18	−23	−29	W. mod.	„ cloudy.
19	−18	−25	W. light	Fine again.
20	−20	−27	E. „	Cloudy.
21	−8	−20	E. in A.M., N.W. in P.M.	Clear, colder.
22	−35	−35	W. light	Cloudless, cold.
23	−36	−39	W. „	„ „
24	−37	−41	E. „	„ „
25	−35	−40	E. very light	Clear and cold.
26	...	−36	S.E. mod.	Dull, drifting and not cold.
27	−11	...	N. very light	Cloudy, very warm travelling.
28	...	−14	E. „	Foggy, mild.
29	...	−7	S.E. light „	Misty, warm.
30	...	−4	E. „	Warm, cloudy.
31	...	−3	E. „	„ „
1902 Jan.				
1	...	−18	N. very light	Clear, getting colder. Then −30 at 4 P.M.
2	...	−33	N.W. light	Cloudless, cold. Then −32 at 3 P.M.
3	...	−33	S.E. strong	Snowing and drifting. Then −8 at 4 P.M.
4	...	−22	N.W. mod.	Cloudless, light snow last night.
5	...	−36	S.S.E. „	Fine morning, drifting in afternoon.
6	6	−10	S.E. light	Cloudy, warm.
7	...	5	E. „	Two in. snow last night. Then +8 at 3 P.M.

Date.	Max. in Shade.	Min.	Wind.	Remarks.
1902 Jan.				
8	...	−12	N. very light	Clear, warm. Then −3 at 3 P.M.
9	...	−7	S.W. light	Getting colder, cloudless. Then −25 at 3 P.M.
10	...	−39	N. light	Cloudless, cold.
11	−36	−41	N.W. „	„ „
12	...	−43	N.E. „	„ „ wind S. in evening and drifting.
13	−12	−18	W. „	Fine, wind rising in evening.
14	−25	−38	W. „	Cloudy, light snow.
15	−36	−38	N.W. strong	Blizzarding, snowing and drifting.
16	−42	−46	N.W. light	Cloudless, cold.
17	−39	−46	N.W. in A.M., N.E. P.M.	„ „
18	−38	−48	N.W. mod.	„ „ light drift.
19	−30	−38	N.W. „	Wind increasing in evening.
20	−23	−36	N. strong	Blizzarding.
21	−35	−40	W.N.W. mod.	Cloudless, cold.
22	−23	−46	N.W. light	„ warm.
23	−44	−50	N.W. strong	Coldest day yet.
24	−49	−54	W. light	„ „
25	−37	−57	N.W. strong	Blizzarding, coldest day of the winter.
26	−26	−38	N.W. mod.	Drifting, thick.
27	−29	−42	N. light	Fine, clear.
28	−24	−37	N.W. „	Cloudless.
29	−16	−30	N.W. „	„
30	−20	−20	W. strong	Blizzarding, very cold.
31	−12	−25	N.N.W. light	Fine, clear.
Feb.				
1	−23	−27	N.N.E. light	Cloudless.
2	−8	−26	E. mod.	Thick, clearing towards evening.
3	−15	−18	N.N.E. light	Cloudless.
4	−4	−19	E. strong	Blizzarding, warm.
5	0	−5	N.E. „	„
6	1	0	E. mod.	Blizzard, moderating.
7	−8	−15	N.W. light	Cloudless.
8	−9	−19	N.W. „	„
9	−7	−18	N.W. „	„
10	−2	−21	N. „	Light clouds.
11	−9	−15	N.W. „	Cloudless.
12	−9	−19	W. „	„
13	−2	−15	N.W. „	„
14	2	−10	N.W. „	„
15	−5	−14	N.W. „	„
16	...	−22	N.W. „	Cloudy early, cleared later.
17	...	−26	Calm	Cloudless.
18	...	−32	Calm	Cloudless.

Date.	Max. in Shade.	Min.	Wind.	Remarks.
1902. Feb.				
19	−30	−42	N.W. strong	Drifting, cold.
20	−30	−43	N.W. mod.	„ „
21	−33	−40	N.W. „	Cloudless, wind falling.
22	−15	−38	Variable, light	Cloudy, sun at times; maximum taken in sun.
23	−31	−31	N.W. light	Cloudless, cold.
24	−35	−42	N.W. strong	Drifting thick, cloudless above.
25	−25	−41	N.W. „	Blizzarding, drifting thick.
26	−30	−37	N.N.E. mod.	Cloudless, drifting; maximum taken in sun.
27	...	−39	N.W. „	Drifting a little.
28	−15	−39	N.W. very light	Cloudless, almost calm; maximum taken in sun.
Mar.				
1	...	−45	N.W. very light	Cloudless, almost calm.
2	−25	−51	N.E. „	Cloudless; maximum taken in sun.
3	−22	−35	W.N.W. „	Hazy in A.M., bright in afternoon; maximum in sun.
4	−30	−41	N.W. mod.	Cloudless, drifting, cool.
5	...	−43	N.W. light	„ cold.
6	−25	−52	Calm	Cloudless.
7	−25	−45	E. in evening	Calm, cloudless.
8	−29	−38	N.W. light	Cloudless.
9	...	−43	E.S.E. mod.	Hazy, drifting.
10	−5	−23	Calm	Cloudless.
11	...	−27	N. strong	Light snow early, wind rose in afternoon.
12	...	−42	N.W. light	Blizzard last night, cloudless, cool day.
13	...	−50	Variable	Hazy, light snow in afternoon.
14	−27	−32	N.W. strong	Blizzarding.
15	−36	−51	W. mod.	Cloudless, drifting, cold.
16	...	−51	W. light	„ cold.
17	−27	−49	E. strong in afternoon.	Cloudless, calm early, blizzard in afternoon.
18	−22	−33	N.W. light	Cloudless.
19	−24	−39	W. very light	Light clouds, fine.
20	3	−25	S.E. mod.	Hazy, drifting.
21	7	−7	S.E. „	Cloudless, drifting.
22	14	−1	S.E. strong	Blizzarding, drifting thick.
23	...	0	S.S.E. light	Cloudy, very warm.
24	...	11	S.E. „	Overcast, light snow at times.
25	...	4	S.E. „	Cloudless, warm.
26	27	12	...	Clear early, hazy and snow later; maximum in sun.
27	28	21	E. strong	Blizzarding, wet snow flying.
28	22	4	E. light	Blizzard last night, fine day.

Date.	Max. in Shade.	Min.	Wind.	Remarks.
1902.				
Mar.				
29	...	4	N.N.E. light	Light snow forenoon, cleared later.
30	−2	−21	N.N.W. mod.	Cloudless, drifting early, calming later.
31	...	−23	S.W. light	Cloudless.
Apr.				
1	...	−5	W. light	Cloudless forenoon, light snow in evening.
2	1	−24	W. „	Cloudless.
3	...	−31	Calm	„
4	−5	−35	N.W. light	„
5	−18	−33	N.W. „ then N.	Cloudless early, strong N. wind, drifting later.
6	...	−31	N.W. then S.E. light	Cloudless, clouded up in afternoon.
7	...	−25	Variable light	Cloudless.
8	...	−30	E. light	„
9	...	−21	N.E. light	„
10	...	−24	E.N.E. light	„
11	...	−27	E. then S. light	Cloudless forenoon, cloudy in afternoon.
12	0	−18	N.W. light	Cloudless.
13	−13	−30	N.W. strong	Cloudless and drifting.
14	...	−26	N.W. mod.	„ „ a little.
15	6	−25	Variable light	Cloudless.
16	...	−16	N. light	Thick and snowing.
17	32	3	S.	Light snow till noon, then clear.
18	...	−26	N.W. light	Thick foggy forenoon, cloudless afternoon.
19	30	3	N.W. then N.E.	Cloudy, thick, snow wet.
20	36	...	N. light	Cloudy, hazy, fog in evening.
21	39	8	Calm	Fine, hazy at times, warm.
22	22	12	N.W. light	Overcast.
23	−7	−28	N.W. „	Cloudless.
24	14	−17	N.W. „	Cloudy morning, cloudless afternoon.
25	−3	−29	W. „	Cloudless.
26	−11	−41	N.W. „	„
27	10	−25	N.W. strong	Blizzarding, drifting thick.
28	18	−3	N.W. „	Blizzarding.
29	20	5	N.W. „ then W. mod.	„ moderating in afternoon.
30	24	0	N.W. mod.	Unsettled, drifting at times.
May				
1	...	2	N.W. light	Hazy, clear at times.
2	27	1	N.W. light	Overcast, clear at times.

Date.	Max. in Shade.	Min.	Wind.	Remarks.
1902. May.				
3	20	3	N.W. „	Overcast.
4	14	5	E. „	Fine and clear.
5	9	-5	N.W. „	Overcast.
6	14	-7	W. „	„
7	12	-11	N.W. strong	Blizzarding.
8	16	-8	N.W. light	Overcast.
9	16	-1	N.W. „	„
10	21	2	N.W. „	„
11	13	4	N.W. mod.	„
12	24	4	S.W. „	Cloudless.
13	34	-3	S.W. then N.W. light	Light snowfall forenoon, cleared later.
14	26	-7	N.W. light	Overcast, clear in evening.
15	19	-10	N.W. „	Overcast.
16	23	0	S.E. „	Overcast in forenoon, cleared later.
17	33	1	E. mod.	Light clouds, fine.
18	36	2	S.S.E. mod.	Cloudless.
19	40	7	S.S.E. light	Cloudy, wind increasing in evening.
20	33	23	S.E. light, then N.E. strong	Rain and sleet forenoon, blizzard in afternoon.
21	27	14	W. strong, then calm	Blizzarding forenoon, then clear and calm.
22	18	0	N.W. mod.	Blizzarding at times.
23	26	0	N.W. strong, then calm	Blizzarding forenoon, then calm.
24	18	1	N.W. mod.	Cloudless, calm in evening.
25	34	0	N.W. then S.W. light	Cloudless, light winds.
26	29	4	E. light to mod.	Cloudless forenoon, cloudy later
27	22	15	N. light	Cloudless.
28	34	-2	N. „	„
29	39	4	N.W. light	„
30	37	20	N.W. „	Overcast.
31	35	13	N.W. „	Overcast, light snow at times.
June				
1	38	26	N.W. „	Cloudless.
2	43	22	S.W. „	Cloudless, very warm all day.
3	44	26	N.W. then N.E. light	Cloudless forenoon, cloudy later, winds light.
4	40	28	N.N.E. mod.	Overcast, light snow.
5	32	25	N. light to mod.	Unsettled.
6	33	21	N. „ „	Overcast, snow squalls at times.
7	34	25	N.E. light	Squally, sunny at times.
8	34	29	N.W. „	Overcast.
9	47	30	N.W. „	„ light snow at times.
10	43	29	N.E. „	Cloudy but fine.

Date.	Max. in Shade.	Min.	Wind.	Remarks.
1902. June				
11	42	29	N.W. light	Cloudy but fine.
12	46	31	N.N.W. „	2 in.snow forenoon, sleet in afternoon.
13	46	32	E. „	Cloudy but fine.
14	49	32	Variable light airs	Overcast, unsettled.
15	43	31	N. mod.	Squally.
16	45	30	N.W. light	Cloudless, hot.
17	52	33	S.E. „	Cloudless.
18	53	30	S.E. „	Cloudless, hot.
19	57	32	S.E. „	„ „
20	53	31	S.S.E. to N. light.	Cloudless.
21	56	34	E. light	Bright forenoon, rain-clouds in afternoon.
22	52	39	Variable	Cloudy but fine.
23	52	38	S.S.E. mod.	Cloudless.
24	52	35	S.E. light	Light clouds.
25	42	35	S.E. „	Cloudless.
26	47	34	S. mod.	„
27	50	37	S.S.E. mod.	„
28	52	41	Calm	Bright forenoon, clouds later.
29	55	35	N.N.E. light	Shower in night, overcast to-day.
30	...	36	N.W. „	Rain in night, unsettled to-day.
July				
1	49	31	W. light	Light clouds, fine.
2	...	31	W. „	Cloudless.
3	57	33	N. variable	Fine, one light shower.
4	44	37	W. fresh	Rain squalls, cleared late.
5	47	34	W. light	Cloudless.
6	48	30	W. „	„
7	43	...	W. „	„
8	...	...	W. „	„
9	58	...	W. „	„
10	52	36	N.W. mod.	Cloudless forenoon, cloudy later.
11	57	37	W. light	Cloudy, light shower, then cleared.
12	...	35	Calm, then E. strong	Overcast, calm early, strong E. wind later.
13	...	36	E., S.W., N.E.	Heavy rain in night, cloudless later.
14	52	39	N.E. mod.	Cloudless.
15	48	41	S. strong, then calm	Cloudless after strong puff from S.
16	55	31	E light.	Cloudless.
17	60	...	Variable light	„
18	62	...	S.E. light	Unsettled, thunder-shower in afternoon.
19	54	...	Variable light	Cloudless forenoon, cloudy later.

Date.	Max. in Shade.	Min.	Wind.	Remarks.
1902. July				
20	...	47	Variable light	Fine forenoon, thunder-shower in afternoon.
21	...	48	N. light	Dull forenoon, cloudless later.
22	48	42	N.W. light	Thick mist and rain.
23	...	45	Calm	Dull forenoon, clear later.
24	...	41	N. light	Cloudless.
25	56	38	N. „	„
26	...	39	N.W. light	Cloudless.
27	...	45	N.W. „	Cloudy but fine.
28	...	44	N.W. „	Dull forenoon, cloudless later.
29	65	31	W. „	Cloudless.
30	...	29	N. „	„
31	...	29	N.W. „	„
Aug.				
1	...	27	N. light	Cloudless.
2	58	26	N.E. to N. light	„
3	65	36	Variable light	„
4	...	44	N.N.E. strong	Dull, cloudy.
5	...	45	N. strong	„ heavy clouds.
6	...	38	Variable, calm	„ raining after 10 A.M.
7	...	42	N.E. mod.	„ cloudy, mist on hills.
8	48	40	N.N.W. „	„ „ light rain in afternoon.
9	...	41	N. light	Dull forenoon, cloudless later.
10	...	28	S.E. „	„ „ „ „
11	52	23	S.E. „	Cloudless.
12	...	26	Variable light	„
13	...	29	S.E. light	„
14	...	37	S.S.E. „	Cloudless day, light rain in evening.
15	...	44	S.W. mod.	Dull early, cleared later.
16	...	30	N.W. light	Sharp shower early, fine later.
17	...	30	Calm	Clear forenoon, heavy clouds in afternoon.
18	...	44	W. light	Rain in night, cloudless evening.
19	...	32	Calm	Cloudless.
20	...	36	„	Cloudless, clouds and E. wind at 8 P.M.
21	...	44	Variable	Dull but fine.
22	...	46	N.N.E. light	Heavy mist early, cleared later.
23	49	42	N.E. mod.	Dull.
24	...	...	N.E. „	„
25	...	...	Calm	Cloudless.
26	...	35	S.E. light	Overcast.
27	...	...	Calm	Cloudless.
28	...	32	„	„
29	...	30	N. light	„
30	...	22	N.E. light	Cloudless. Arrived at Fort Norman.
31	...	31	E. „	Fine and clear.

Date.	Max. in Shade.	Min.	Wind.	Remarks.
1902. Sept.				
1	...	37	Calm	Dull and cloudy.
2	...	35	S.E. mod.	„
3	...	47	S. light	Fine, clear. „
4	...	41	N. „	Overcast.
5	...	47	Calm	Rain all day.
6	...	45	N. light	Overcast, fog early.
7	...	43	S. „	Fine.
8	...	32	Variable	Fine at times, local showers.
9	...	41	N. mod.	Fine and clear.
10	...	31	S. light	Overcast.
11	...	34	S. „	Cloudless.
12	...	44	Calm	Rain, cleared, rain again.
13	...	35	N. mod.	Fine.
14	...	34	S. light	Overcast, light snow.
15	...	30	N. strong	Cloudy (at Fort Simpson).
16	...	25	N. light	Fine.
17	...	24	S. mod.	Cloudless.
18	...	23	Calm	„
19	froze	sharp	N.W. light	„
20	...	...	Calm	„
21	...	...	„	Fine and clear.
22	...	...	N.E. then S. mod.	„ „
23	...	...	S.E. strong	Rain squalls.

VI

LIST OF ARTICLES FOR TRADE, &c.,

Sent up in the Whaling Schooner "Francis Allyn"

Sheath knives . . . . 3 dozen.
Jack „ .. . . 4 „
12-inch „ . . . . 1½ „
Goggles . . . . 2 „ (assorted, some very dark smoke).

Tin ovens . . . . 2 „
Fish lines (33″ thread) . . . . 1 lb.
  „ hooks, 8/o . . . . . . 1 gross.
Hatchets (common) . . . . . ½ dozen.
  „ (shingling) . . . 1 „
26-inch saws (cross-cut) . . . 2.
  „ „ (splitting) . . . 2.
Thimbles . . . . 6 dozen (open top).
Needles (ordinary) (1 to 6) . . 2000.
  „ (glovers) (5 and 6) . . 3000.
Scissors . . . . 2 dozen (6 inch).
Buttons (assorted) . . . . . 10 „
Looking-glasses . . . . . . 2 „ (common).
Buttons (fancy gilt) . . . . 20 „
Combs . . . . 2 „
Steels (sharpening) . . . . . 1 „
Files (flat 10 inch) . . . . . 4 „
  „ (3 cornered) . . . . . 4 „
Wood rasps . . . . 6 (12 inch).
Axes (3 lbs.) . . . . 1 dozen.
Pants (overalls, 34 × 36) . . . 8 pairs.
Jumpers . . . . 8 „ (full size).
Thread (cotton) . . . . . ½ dozen boxes, assorted sizes.
  „ (linen) . . . . . . 6 lbs.
Matches (Vulcan) . . . . . 6 dozen.
  „ (Trade) . . . . . 1 case.
Traps (fox) . . . . 2 dozen (No. 1).
Shot . . . . 1 bag (No. 3).

Powder . . . . 3 (12½ lb. kegs), Dead sho
                                    Dupont, 2 F. G.
Lead . . . . 10 lbs.
Rifles . . . . 6 Remingtons (38 cal.).
Loading tools . . . . 6 sets.
Shells (loaded) . . . . . . 1000.
Primers . . . . 1000 (4 boxes) not sufficient.
Musket caps . . . . 1000.
Beads (3/0 white), 10 lbs. . . . (7 and 8), 5 lbs. of each.
Tobacco-boxes . . . . . . 2 dozen.
Match-boxes . . . . 2 ,,
Spy-glasses . . . . 6 (assorted).
Tent . . . . 1 (7 × 9).
Webbing harness . . . . . 100 yards.
Burning glasses . . . . . . 2 dozen.
Flint and steels . . . . . . Small bag (1 quart).
Finger-rings . . . . 4 dozen boxes.
Gimlets . . . . 4 ,, assorted.
Awls . . . . 6 ,, without handles.
Lead skillets . . . . 1 small.
Pots and pans . . . . . . 1 dozen pots; 1 dozen pans.
Pipes (clay) . . . . 1 box (2 gross).
  ,, (wooden) . . . . . 2 dozen (cheap).
Sheet-lead . . . . 5 feet 6 inches wide.
Shawls for women (cheap) . . . 1 dozen.
Cotton shirts (full size) . . . . ½ ,,
Duffel for socks . . . . . . 1 pair best California blank‹
                                    (largest size).
White lead . . . . 6 1 lb. tins.
Chocolate . . . . 50 lbs. (eating-sweet).
Ginger . . . . 5 lbs.

LIST OF FOOD AND TOBACCO SUPPLIES

Tobacco-plug for self, 50 lbs.
       ,, natives, two 12-lb. caddies, 24 lbs.
Oatmeal (coarse), 100 lbs.
Sugar in whiskey barrel, 330 lbs.
Biscuit (hard tack), 26 inch cask full, 600 lbs.
Salt, three 10 lb. boxes, 30 lbs.
Pepper (ground) in glass jars, 15 lbs.
Pork (clear), 1 barrel.
Tea (best), 10 lbs.
Cocoa, Van Houten's (1 lb. tins), 25 lbs.
Coffee (ground) in soldered tins, 25 lbs.

Patent sperm candles, 30 lbs.
Kerosene (160 grade), 50 gals. case oil.
Methylated spirits, 2 gallons (hermetically sealed).
Frying-pans, three, one large, two small, steel.
Butterine, in 10 lb. pails, 100 lbs.
Mosquito netting, 6 pieces.
Wire, brass and copper, half-dozen spools tacks.
Varnish for canoes (Smith's), 1½ gallons and a brush.

MEDICAL LIST

Iodoform.
Mercurial ointment (extra strong) for protection from lice.
Adhesive plaster.
Chlorodyne.
Opium.
Laudanum.
Cocaine.
Pills, purgative.
Ginger, Tincture of.
Liniment.
Dental forceps.
Mustard plasters.
Pyrethrium powder.   Persian insect powder and blower.
Mennens' Borated Talcum.
Vaseline.
Lint.
Absorbent cotton.
Phenacetine, 5 grains.
Quinine, 3 to 5 grains.

VII

MEASUREMENTS OF HUDSON BAY ESKIMO

Name.	Age.	Height.	Girth of Chest.	Extended Arm.	Length of Arm from Shoulder to Tips of Fingers.	Shoulder to Ground.	Hip to Ground.	Length of Hand.	Sex.	Children. Boys.	Children. Girls.
Ang-ĕ-ak	35	65½	40	68	27	53	36	7½	Male	1	2
Tĕr-en-iyah . . .	25	64½	36½	65¼	27	54½	35½	7	"	2	...
Ang-ĕ-lik	28	64½	36½	66	26¾	52½	35½	7¼	"	3	...
Ki-hi-hŭt-nark . .	26	62¾	39½	64	26½	50½	35½	7	"	1	...
Hik-kŭl-eyah . . .	40	61	37½	60½	25	49	33½	7	"	1	2
Keit-mi-ariŏk . . .	23	64¾	37½	66¾	27	53	36½	7½	"	1	1
Pig-li-nak	27	62	37	63½	26¾	50½	34½	7¼	"	2	1
Milŭk	40	63¾	40	65½	27	52½	34½	7	"	none	none
Ei-yar-renni . . .	32	65½	39	66½	27	54	35	7¼	"	...	3
Eg-jo	20	62½	38½	61	23½	51¼	35	6¾ (Biceps, 13½) (Forearm, 11)	"	2 wives No children	
Ŭlig-bŭk	28	65¾	37¾	65¾	28½	54	37¾	7¼	"	2	1

These measurements were taken at Fort Churchill in April 1899. These Eskimo belonged to the Hudson Bay.

Remarks.—Hudson Bay Coast Huskies—all married. Strongly built and of good physique. All had large stomachs and were generally fat. They were healthy and strong (muscularly); hair straight, black, and worn longish, except for a circular patch on crown which was cut short. Eyes dark brown. Complexion much the same as that of an Indian. Teeth of most very good. Ages were approximately ascertained from the old Hudson Bay employés at Fort Churchill.

MEASUREMENTS OF ARCTIC COAST ESKIMO

Height.	Girth of Chest.	Fathom.	Arm, Shoulder to Finger Tips.	Leg from Hip.	Length of Hand.	Length of Foot.	Sex.
5 feet 3⅝ inches.	37 inches.	62½ inches.	25 inches.	33 inches.	7 inches.	10 inches.	Male.
5 ,, 5½ ,,	38 ,,	62 ,,	25½ ,,	34½ ,,	6½ ,,	10 ,,	,,
5 ,, 6¼ ,,	38½ ,,	62 ,,	27 ,,	32½ ,,	7 ,,	10½ ,,	,,
5 ,, 5 ,,	39 ,,	62½ ,,	27 ,,	32½ ,,	7 ,,	10½ ,,	,,
5 ,, 6½ ,,	38½ ,,	66 ,,	29 ,,	34 ,,	7¼ ,,	9½ ,,	,,
5 ,, 1¼ ,,	36 ,,	61½ ,,	27 ,,	33½ ,,	7 ,,	10 ,,	,,
5 ,, 1 ,,	...	...	...	...	...	...	Female.
4 ,, 10½ ,,	...	...	...	...	...	...	,,
4 ,, 10 ,,	..	...	...	...	...	..	,,
5 ,, 1½ ,,	...	...	...	...	...	...	,,
4 ,, 10½ ,,	...	...	...	...	...	...	,,

Taken near Ogden Bay in May 1902.

VIII

ESKIMO WORDS AND PHRASES.

The following Eskimo words and phrases were taken down [from] the dictation of the Hudson Bay Company's interpreter at Churc[h], and represent the Eskimo language as spoken in the imme[diate] neighbourhood of the Bay. The vowel sounds are :—

ă	as in	. . . *at.*		ī as in	. . .	*eat.*
ā	,,	. . . *father.*		ŏ ,,	. . .	*hot.*
ĕ	,,	. . . *set.*		ō ,,	. . .	*boat.*
ē	,,	. . . *sate.*		ŭ ,,	. . .	*but.*
ĭ	,,	. . . *it.*		ū ,,	. . .	*boot.*

The diphthong *au* represents the vowel sounds in *how ; aw* [is to] be pronounced as in *haw ; ch* as in *church, g* hard, and *y* as in *y*[et;] *k* at the end of a word is faint. A vowel immediately followed [by a] consonant in the same syllable is to be pronounced short, unl[ess it] is marked long.

Persons.

Man	ăn-gūt.
Woman	armuk.
Father	attăr.
Mother	ănă.
Son	er-ning-a.
Daughter	pannik.
Infant	nu-tara-lark-nark.
Brother	nūk-kuk.
Sister	nei-yuk.
Boy	arn-nu-tĭk-nark.
Girl	arn-nak-nak.
Young man	i-nu-ūk-tŭk.
Old man	ūt-tŭk-kuk.
My wife	nūl-yet.
Twins	mul-reit-mut.
Eskimo (singular)	Innūk.
,, (plural)	Innuit.
Friend, partner	kut-ti-mĕ-ruptar.
Trader	ni-wa-kut-tau-hŭk-tŭk.
White man	kablu-năk.

Living Creatures.

Bear (polar)	nun-nok.
Caribou	tūk-tu.
Young buck caribou	angu-hullūk.
Older „ „	angu-hull-rah-ōk.
Full grown bull	pŭng-yuk.
Dog	keit-mek.
Bitch	arn-a-lŭk.
Fox	ter-i-en-i-uk
Hare (arctic)	u-kŭllik
Seal (small)	net-chŭk.
Seal (large)	ūg-yŭk.
Walrus	ai-vik.
Whale (white)	kul-er-lu-wik.
Wolf	a-mar-ŏk.
Wolverine (glutton)	kăk-wi.
Fish	ĕ-kŭl-lo.
Salmon	ĕ-kŭl-up-pik.
Red-fish (salmon out of season)	hi-wi-terro.
Trout	ikh-lōr-ak.
Whitefish	keki-yuak-tŭk.
Mosquito	kik-to-rĭak.
House-fly	kup-pel-rŏk.
Bird	ku-pen-wark.
Duck	kuk-klu-tu.
Goose	ting-mi-uk.
Loon (diver)	kark-kan (imitative).
Ptarmigan	ŭk-ked-juk.
Swan	kūg-gi-yŭk.

Pronouns.

I	a-wonga.
Mine	a-wonga-ūnar.
We	u-war-ūt.
Ours	u-ar-ūna.
Thou or you	ĭg-bik.
Yours	ĭl-bit-ūna.
He, she, this, that	ted-bă.
That	ta-kwa.
They	i-lip-shi.
Theirs	tap-kwa-ūnă.
Who	ki-tūk
All, every	hūmar-lūk-tah.

Any . . . . ti-tellig.
Many or much . . . . . . a-mi-hŭt.
Many . . . . kŭp-shĭn, or kup-shĭd.
No . . . . nāga.
None . . . . nauk.

Parts of the Body.

Head . . . . ne-ăk-ŭk.
Hair . . . . nŭt-tset.
Face . . . . ki-nŭt.
Eye . . . . i-ĭk.
Ear . . . . hi-u-tik.
Nose . . . . king-ak.
Mouth . . . . kun-nek.
Teeth . . . . ti-u-ti.
Neck . . . . kung-i-henŭk.
Arm . . . . tellŭk.
Fingers . . . . ŭd-gei-ĭ.
Hand . . . . ŭd-gei-ĭ.
Back . . . . pŭmmĕ-lŭk.
Chest . . . . hŭk-id-jet.
Belly . . . . ah-kĕr-rŭk.
Finger-nails . . . . . . ku-tik.
Leg . . . . ni-ŭk.
Foot . . . . i-ti-reit.
Toes . . . . keit-min-wăk-i-nu-rak.
Blood . . . . au.
Body . . . . kut-dig-kar.

Numerals.

The Eskimo have words for most numbers up to 100; bu
almost never use those beyond 10. In expressing numbers up t
10 they seldom use words, but use their fingers.

1. atau-jak.
2. mŭl-rŭk.
3. ping-a-hūt.
4. chit-a-mŭt.
5. tel-ĭ-mŭt.
6. arro-e-gnĭd-git.
7. mŭl-rŭk arro-e-gnĭd-git.
8. ping-a-hūt arro-e-gnĭd-git.
9. kŭling lŭark-tŭt.
10. kŭlĭk.

11. atd-kenīd-git.
12. mŭlrūnik atd-kenīd-git.
13. ping-a-hūt atd-kenīd-git.
14. chitamŭt atd-kenīd-git.
15. tel-ī-mŭt atd-kenīd-git.
16. arro-e gnīd-git atd-kenīd-git.
17. mŭl-rūk arro-e gnīd-git atdkenīd-git.
18. ping-a-hut arro-e-gnīd-git atdkenīd-git.
19. kūling luark-tūt atd-kenīd-git.
20. mŭlrūk adgē-ĭt.
30. ping-a-hūt adgē-ĭt.
100. kūlik adgē-ĭt.

Geographical and other Natural Conditions and Objects.

North	wauk-nŭk.
South	ping-nĕk-nŭk.
East	kŭn-nĕk-nĭk-neiyok.
West	wok-nei-rei-tūk.
Land, earth	nūna.
Barren ground	nut-tal-ĭk-nak.
Sun	hek-ken-nŭk.
Sunrise	hek-ken-nŭk-pūk.
Sunset	hek-nŭk-tellik-pūk.
Moon	tet-kŭt.
Star	ūb-blor-iak.
Sky	kei-lūk.
Wind	ŭn-orri.
Cloud	nu-yak.
Fog, mist	tekki-kūni.
Rain	ni-pŭl-lūk.
Snow	up-pūt.
Ice	shi-ku.
Frost	kek-ki-kūni.
Fire	u-kar.
Smoke	i-shuk.
A hill	king-ak.
Larger hill	king-ak-yuak.
Portage	ĭkĭ-wĭt-tūt.
Promontory	nu-wūk.
River	kūk.
River-mouth	ă-kok.
Rapid in a river	ko-nĭk-yu-āk.
Kazan River	kūn-wet-nark.
Stream	ku-ĕt-nāk.
Waterfalls	kūk-nek-yuāk.

Rock	kai-ĕk-tūk.
Stone	wi-yerra.
A large lake	immuk-angi-kūni.
Small lake	immŭk mik-i-kūni.
Doobaunt Lake	Tu-li-ma-lūg-yuăk.
Yath Kyed Lake	Hĕko-lig-yuăk.
Water	immŭk.
The sea, or salt	terri-ōk.
Flood-tide	ūling-u-yŏk.
Ebb-tide	tinning-u-yŏk.
Bay or inlet	kung-er-klŭk.
Shore	hig-yŭk.
Island	keki-ek-tak.
Marble Island	Ŭk-shor-riak.
Flower	ŭd-gi-kăk.
Moss	ting-au-yak.
Green grass	i-wĭk.
Willows	ok-pi.
Tree or wood	ni-park-tŭk.
Feather	mit-kawk.

Implements, Weapons, Dress, Food, &c.

Bow (for shooting)	pi-tek-chi.
Arrow	ka-re-ōk.
Gun	hek-kud-dĭd-jūt.
Gunpowder	ari-anig, or ariet.
Gun-caps	ik-nuk.
Gun-cover	pi-ti-ki-tuk.
Small shot	kar-i-ōk-wau-yet.
Rifle	kar-i-o-tuk-tok.
Bullet	kar-i-ōk.
Fishing-net	metsi-tōti.
Fishing-line	ippi-ūtah.
Fishing-hook	karri-ōk-kuk.
Sheath-knife	pil-laut.
Pocket-knife	ū-ku-tuk.
File	ug-i-ak.
Flint and steel	ik-nyŭk.
Iron kettle, or iron	hauik.
Stone kettle	ūt-kū-shik.
Spoon, dipper, ladle	kei-yu-tuk.
Axe, or spear	i-pu.
Needle	mĭt-kūt.
Beads	hung-au-yet.
Snow-shoes	tug-glu-yark.

Sleigh	kamu-u-ti.
Sail of boat	ting-el-rau-tuk.
Harness	annu.
Goggles	ig-uk.
Telescope	ken-rōk.
Pipe	pu-yu-let-chi.
My pipe	pu-yu-let-chi-tiga
Tobacco	tip-lĭ-terrōt.
Matches	ik-i-tit.
Wooden house	igloriah.
Snow-house	iglu.
Camp, or tent	tu-pek.
Pack	nut-muk-uk.
Cache (of supplies, &c.)	per-o-yak.
Meat	nekki.
Dried meat	nīp-ku.
Frozen meat (junk)	a-wit-tīt.
Marrow	put-tuk.
Heart	u-mek.
Meat of deer	tūk-tu-nekki.
Meat of musk-ox	ūm-ming-muk-nekki.
Tongue of deer	u-kok.
Deer's hair	mit-kok.
Deer's horns	nug-yōk.
Deer's bone	hau-nuk.
Whalebone	pĭl-rah.
Grease	pu-nĕr-nuk.
Biscuit	nuk-klus-wăk.
Gloves, mits	por-lūk.
Deerskin coat (outer)	ku-lĭk-tăk.
Deerskin coat (inner)	ūlu-păk.
Trousers	kar-lĕk.
Deerskin socks, or leggings	kum-mik-par.
Sealskin boots	ipper-au-chik.
Moccasins	kum-muk.
Deerskin blanket	kai-pik.
Parchment, skin	mit-ko-i-tūk.
Iron	hauik.
Copper (red iron)	au-pūl-uk-tuk hauik.
Mica	keb-lūk-keriak.

Times and Seasons.

Spring	ū-ping-kăk.
Summer	u-ping-lăk.
Autumn	au-yak.

Winter . . . . ûk-i-ûk.
To-day . . . . ûb-lumi.
Yesterday . . . . . . ip-kwûk-kûk.
Day before yesterday . . ip-kwûk-karni.
To-morrow . . . . . ûk-argo.
Day after to-morrow . . ûk-argo-argo.
Very early in the morning . u-bla-kût.
Dawn . . . . kau-yok.
Morning . . . . . . ûb-lark.
Daylight . . . . . . kauk-met.
Noon . . . . ûb-lûmi.
Evening . . . . . . u-nûk-pût.
Late evening, dusk . . . u-nûk-pûk.
Night . . . . ûn-wak.

Adjectives.

Alive . . . . u-mei-yok.
Bad . . . . pid-chuk-i-kûni.
Black . . . . ter-nek-tûk.
Blue . . . . tu-ok-tûk.
Broken . . . . . . hek-ă-mettûk.
Chief . . . . u-shu-muttuk.
Cold . . . . ikki, or nuk-kûni.
Correct, all right . . . . tai-metnă.
Dirty . . . . erming-ik-tok.
Dead . . . . tu-ku-kûni.
Deep . . . . ikki.
Enough . . . . . . nuk-muk-tûk.
Far . . . . kan-nōk, or ûnar-hek-kûni.
Fast, quick . . . . . pĕ-lā-kûni.
Fat (animal) . . . . . tu-nûk.
Fearless . . . . . . kup-pĕ-i-na-kûni.
Good . . . . pid-chuk.
Green . . . . u-kau-yak.
Hot . . . . ōnar-kûni.
Hungry . . . . kā-ă-kûni.
Lost . . . . tummuk-tûk.
Plentiful . . . . . . mīk-i-kûni.
Long . . . . tukki.
Red . . . . au-pûl-ûk-tûk.
Right (on right hand) . . a-wu-ta-rût.
Large . . . . ang-gi-kûni.
Shallow . . . . ik-ka-kûni.
Sick, sore . . . . . . ă-ă.
Sleepy . . . . sin-ni-tûk.

Sleep	sinni.
Slow	pe-lei-i-kūni.
Small	mĭk-i-kūni.
Strong (of men) . . .	pid-gu-kūni.
Strong (of materials) . .	pin-ni-kūni.
Thick	ibi-u-kūni.
Thin	sa-kūni.
Tired	men-ro-tūk-nă-pĭd, or men-wūn-a-kūni.
Weak (of men)	pid-gu-i-kūni.
Weak (of materials) . . .	pinni-i-kūni.
White	kuk-ok-tūk.
Yellow	kŭnnū-huk.

Verbs and Phrases.

Arrive	tik-ik-pu.
When shall we arrive? . .	kaku ted-benni tik ik-pu.
In two nights	mulrūk rhĭnĭ-hūlĭ.
Boil the kettle	ĭlĭ-lĕr-a-li.
Yes	tauka.
Bring	keilĭ, or lerig.
To carry a pack on back	nut-muk-tūtū-ak.
Clean (imperative) . . .	ulluk-terli.
Come	keilĭ.
I want you to come again .	a-te-lu keilĭ.
I am glad that the Eskimo have arrived	ka wenna kūni innuit-tik-ik-pu.
To chop with an axe . .	wūlu-mak-tūk.
Is it cold? or, Are you cold?	ikki-kūni.
To cry or weep	kē-ai-yūk.
To dance	mu-mek-tūk.
To drink	immi-lĕrĭg.
To eat	neri-lerig.
How far? (distance reckoned by time) . .	kanŏk-o-a-hi-tik-po.
To follow a person . . .	king-u-hi-kummar.
To fear.	kup-pe-na-kūni.
To kindle a fire	u-kar-hunnali.
Fetch that	uggĭ-a-rok.
To finish work	per-nik-tūk.
Give (imperative) . . .	keil-irrok.
I will give (in bartering) .	ei-tūk.
Give me some	ei-tūnga.
Go home	pi-hūk-tūk.
Go	ani-lawk-mi-langa-tūk.

Gone, departed	au-lek-tūk.
Go there! (imperative) . .	pŭka-taulĭ.
Have you any?	tei-tūk mennar.
Is that yours?	ĭl-bit-ūna.
Who is this man? . . .	ki-nau-na.
How long is the lake? . .	immuk kannok tukki kĭkkō.
How long is the river? . .	ko-kun-ōk-tukki kĭkko.
Killed	pi-tuk-pĭt.
To laugh	ĭg-luk-tūk.
Look!	tuk-koi.
Look for some willows . .	ok-pi-lūni kennĭ lerig.
Mend	kurrio-tak-tōk.
Make haste	tōbĭ.
Have you any matches? .	ik-i-tit hu-tē-tūk.
Are you ready?	at-ti.
Yet	hūlĭ.
Are you ready yet? . . . } Is everything packed up? . }	hūli-penning-i-lăhē.
Is it raining?	ni-pŭl-lūk-kūni.
Return (go back) . . .	i-ter-rit.
Speak, say, tell	ūk-ak-tūk.
Shoot	hek-kōk-tūk.
Snore	kum-nu-yok.
Sing, or make a song . .	pi-jek hunnali.
Sleep	khi-nik-tūk.
See the next Eskimo . .	nenni-eti-lūk innuit-tuk-u-yu.
Will it snow?	kunni-lik-na-le-rāmi.
I am starting (setting out) .	awonga-aulek-tūk.
We are starting . . .	ar-wurro.
Are you starting? . . .	aulek-păhi.
Let us start	aulē lek-tăhai.
When do you start? . .	kukka-wo-aular-o-mark-păhi.
Stop, wait	u-wot-chero
Shall we see?	tukkū-u-lū-bar.
Shall we see deer? . . .	tukku-tukku-u-lu-bar.
Sit down	innĭ-tik, or appi.
Stand up	nikku-wĭ-ti.
To smoke	pu-yu-let-chi-yok.
To steal	tig-lik-met.
To take, catch	tig-u.
Walk slow! (imperative) .	pe-la-ku-nūk-nŭk.
Walk faster	pe-lei-i-kuni-tō-bĭ.
To walk	pi-hu-la-erli.
Where did I put it? . .	mammu-ping-i-yak.
How do you do? . . .	tai-ma.
What is the name of this? .	hūna-ut-ka-ūna.
This is	ted-ba.

These are	ŭk-kwa.
Here	ted-binnĭ.
Near	kŭni-kūni.
On this side	mik-kăni.
On the other side, or be-	
yond	u-ut-tăni.
Over there	măni.
Is there open water? . . .	i-mei-tūk-hūli.
Is there any wood? (fuel) . .	kei-yūk-tŭk menna.
There is no wood	kei-yūk-tĕ-tŭk.
Where is my	nau . . .
Where is my pipe?	pu-yu-let-chi tĭga nau.
Where are my gloves? . . .	por-lūk-ker-nau.
Are you thirsty?	immuk-rŏg-na-kŭni.
Where did you get this	
from?	nŭki-nūna.
I don't know	ummē-er-hŭk.
To tell lies	hug-lu-au-wik.
Work, make, do	hun-e-yok.
Want to, wish to	pĕ-hwăk-tūk.
Tracks of deer	tu-ming-mek-kwa.
Here is a track	medja-tu-mit.
Sleigh track	in-nĭk.
At once	tĕd-bă-tĭd-bă.

The following Eskimo words and phrases are in use among the natives of the Baker Lake region.

Husband	ū-i.
Widow	wi-gar-năk.
Brother	nūka.
An Indian	un-ĕlik.
Deer without horns	kŭt-ē-nĕk.
Deer with broken leg . . .	nŭp-pi-yok.
Black bear	ŭk-lar.
Polar bear	nŭn-nŏk.
Female deer	no-kwei-lĕk.
Birds	ting-mĭ-ro-shŭk.
Wavey goose	kŭng-ak.
Goose	ting-mĭ-ŭk.
Duck	mĭt-tŭk.
Eider-duck	mi-tŭk.
Crane	tet-ĭg-yūk.
Arctic owl	ŭk-pĭt-yuak.
Gull	nau-ya.
Hawk	kĭd-gau-wik.
Hawk (another species) . . .	i-hiung-nŭk.

Snow-bird	kŭ-pen-wăk.
Lark	ŭm-mau-li-yŭk.
Lark (another species) . .	kŭ-pen-wăk-pa-yŭk.
Lark (red-poll)	ok-pi-miu-tŭk.
Butterfly	tŭk-ŭl-li-ti-kat.
Louse	ku-mŭk.
Lice	ku-meit.
Blackflies	mel-u-giak.
Foot (of man)	ik-ĭn-wrăk.
Feet	ik-in-wrōtik.
Nose	king-ak.
Eye	i-i.
Ear	hi-ūt.
Hair	nu-yak.
Leg	ni-u.
Arm	tellek.
North	kunneng-nŭk, or ta-wenni.
South	ping-ŭng-nŭk, or ta-renni.
East	ni-yĕk, or tau-nenni.
West	wawk-nŭk, or tŭk-păr-ni.
Weather	hī-lă.
Good weather	hĭlă kek-tūk.
Bad weather	pĕk-shĭ-kuni.
Fog	tŭk-tū.
Calm water	ok-sho-a-kūni.
Rough water	ăt-ko-na-kūni.
Swift current	nŭg-gi-kūni.
Snowing	kŭn-nek-tūk.
Drifting	pĕk-sĕk-tūk.
Kazan River	Sāka-wak-tūk.
Schultz Lake	Kŭmmen-nik.
Aberdeen Lake	Kŭmmen-nik.
Baker Lake	Kŭmmen-nik-yuak.
A small lake or pond . .	tesh-ek.
Deers' crossing-place . .	kĕn-rā-lĕn.
A portage	itti-wĭt-tūk.
A gulch	ĭt-ĕk-shŭk.
A hill	ik-hwa-rŏk.
A small hill	ik-hwa-rŏk-năk.
At the top of a hill . .	kūd-ba-ro.
At the foot of a hill . .	at-ba-ro.
A divide, watershed . .	ŭt-ten-nek.
Sand	hior-ŭk.
Gravel	tu-a-pŭk.
Mud	makh-ga, or mag-kŭk.
Slush of snow . . .	immŭk-tūk.

Rough ice	i-lau-yak.
Crack in ice	ei-yŏk-răk.
Thaw	au-ma-kūni.
Against the wind . . .	ud-got-it.
Down the wind	uku-miktūt.
A cairn	in-nūk-shūk.
Dwarf birch	au-a-lĕk-ĕ-āk.
Grass	i-wĭk.
Boiling-point	kid-jŭk-tūk, or tek-ti-tuk.
Sea-shell	tŭb-lū-yăk.

Kitchen (of snow-house) .	i-gar.
Door	păr.
Tent-pole	kŭn-ŭk.
Deer-hide	ŭmmĕk.
Birch twig layer for bed .	ki-lĕk-tĕt.
Skin for lying on . .	ŭd-bŭk.
Deerskin blanket . . .	kei-pik.
Stick for beating deer-skins	ti-lūk-tūt.
Babiche (deer-skin strips) .	kūni-yŏk.
Seal-skin	kei-thĭk.
Fuel	kei-yū-ĭt, or kei-yu-ĭk-tŏk.
Frying-pan	ip-o-ĕlik.
Cup	immo-shŭk, or immo-hū-yăk.
Deerskin pail for water . .	kŭt-tŭk.
Box	kei-yŏk-kūt.
Large bag	pu-er-ak.
Small bag	nŭk-mŭk-tŭk.
Bag for pipe, &c. . . .	ik-nyŭk-wĭ-ŭk.
Shovel	po-el-rĭk.
Candle	ikki-yŭk.
Oil lamp	kūl-ek.
Lamp wick	mŭn-nĕk.
Scissors	ti-bi-au-tūk.
Thread (European) . . .	u-ĕ-lū
Thimble	tik-et.
Nail, iron	kĕki-yak.
Lead	ā-kĕl-rōk.
Axe	u-lĭ-maut.
Ice-scoop (long-handled) .	i-laut.
Ice-chisel	tu-ok.
Stick for sounding snow .	sŭb-gūt.
Snow-knife, dag	pŭnnăr.
Driftwood	ti-bi-ok.
A plane	kai-ek-shau.

U

Ribs of deer	tu-lǐ-mǎk.
Sleigh runners	nǔp-pūt.
Ground lashing of runners	nǔkki-tǔk-pǐt.
Upper lashing of runners .	nukki-taro.
Saw (for cutting) . . .	ū-lūt.
Line (for hauling) . . .	ak-tū-nǎk.
Dog-whip	ipper-aw-tǔk.
Ship	ūmi-a-yūak.
Mast	nǔp-par-ōtǔk.
Paddle	po-tǐk, or pau-tǐk.
A smoothing-skin for wiping sleigh runners	bĕr-merk-chǐ.
A pitfall	kǔd-gi-tǔk.
Seal spear	ūn-ark.
Map, or chart. . . .	ik-sher-ak.
Hat	nǔsh-ǔk.
Deer-skin pants . . .	ūt-tǔk-tǎ.
Deer-skin sock (inner) .	ping-ĕ-rak.
Clothes (of white men) .	nu-ek-shǎ.
Raw meat (frozen) . .	nekkǐ-kwǎk.
Raw meat (not frozen) .	au-nar-kūni.
Unfrozen meat . . .	mi-ki-yǎk.
Entrails of deer . . .	in-ĕl-yu-ark, or ark-i-ǎr-ŏk.
Loins of deer	u-lǐ-u-shǐ-nĕk.
Rump of deer . . .	ūk-pǔttǐk.
Hair	mit-kŏk.
Oatmeal	immelli (Eskimo form of English word).
Cranberry leaf (for smoking)	ǔtting-mǔk-tǔk.
Long ago	it-chǔk.
Some time ago . . .	kǔng-er-shǔk, or tĕm-nǎ, or teipsh-marni.
Fall, autumn	au-yak.
Last fall	alrani.
Next winter	ūk-i-ūk-pǔt.
Two winters hence . .	ping-a-yū-ǎgo.
Three winters hence .	shitam-ǎgo.
Year after next . . .	kǔk-ū-waw.
Three years hence . . .	ping-a-yu-ǔng-ni.
Four years hence . .	shita-mǔng-ni.
Five years hence . .	telli-mǔng-ni.
Soon	shū-kēli, or ūbli-yūk.
Quick, or soon . . .	tū-ǎ-wǐ.
By-and-by, or wait a little	u-wat-tzarro.
All the time, always . .	kǔng-er-lūk-tǎ.
Every day	ip-kwǔk-helli-gǎmi.

The Eskimo seasons and months are: Ukiok, or winter, consisting of four months; Ug-lĭk-nak-tŭk (Dec. 10 to Jan. 10), Au-wŭt-ni-wik (to Feb. 10), Net-tĭ-yĕt (to March 10), the seal month, Terrig-lū-ĭt (to April 10).

U-ping-lark-ak, or spring, consisting of two months: Tet-ki-nŭk (to May 10), Au-wĭk-tŭk (to June 10).

U-ping-lark, or summer, consisting of two and a half months: Mŭnnĭt (June, or the egg month), Tū-wĕ-yak-wik (July), and half of Heg-yĕ-ei-wĭk.

Au-yak, or autumn, consisting of two and a half months: viz. half of Heg-yĕ-ei-wĭk, and the months Akū-lek-korgwĭk and Amer-ei-yak-wik.

Uki-ek-shark, a season with which we have none corresponding, consists of the month called Shik-ū-wik, or ice month.

Uki-yak, which also has no corresponding season here, consists of the month called Kettuk-rāk-rĭb-wĭk.

Few Eskimo know the names of all their months.

The same, or similar	i-lŭg-i.
Different	ŭl-lŭg-i.
The other one	iglua, or eiponga.
Good	pich-ak.
Better	pich-au-kūni.
Best	pich-et-yu-ak.
Narrow	tu-a-kūni.
Narrower	tu-art-tūk.
Narrowest	tu-art-tūt-yuak.
Long	tŭk-ki-kūni.
Longer	ŭk-u-let.
Longest	tŭkki-yor-yuak.
Light	kau-mar-kūni.
Dark	ta-kūni.
Deep	it-i-kūni.
Shallow	it-ka-kūni.
Broad	hil-i-kūni, or ĭk-ek-tu-kuni.
Narrow	tu-a-kūni.
Heavy	oka-mei-i-kuni.
Light	okei-kūni.
Short	nei-kūni.
Soft	a-ki-kuni.
Hard	shĭt-ti-kuni.
In, or on, the ground	nūna-mi.
On, or in, the water	im-mŭk-immănĕ.
In, or on, the ice	shi-ku-immănĕ.
Up hill	ku-barro.

Down hill	at-barro.
Precipitous	ŭn-nŭk.
Straight	tĭk-ok-tūk.
Crooked	tĭk-ū-i-kūni.
In front	hi-wŭl-ĭt.
Behind	king-rĭk-tŭk, or tau-nenni.
Opposite	tu-kī-lĕrig.
Old	ū-tŏk-kŭk.
Young	innu-hŭk-tūk.
Full	tĕt-tĕt-tūk.
Empty	tĕt-ten-nĭ-tūk.
All right	tai-met-nak, or hwo-o-nĭt.
Supple, pliant	kei-tu-kūni.
Stiff	kĕ-rāt-tĕ-yŏk.
Broken	nŭp-pi-yŏk.
Forgotten	po-i-yŏk-tūk.
Very near, close at hand .	kun-nĭt-na-mit.
Approaching	kei-yūt.
Going away	wawk-wawk-tūk.
Lost	nĕ-lū-na-kūni.
Hidden from view . . .	tel-ĭk-tūk.
Finished (food) . . .	nūng-ū-yūk.
Lazy	shĕr-pĕk-tūk.
Angry	ŭng-gū-tĭ-ı-yok.
Half	ko-pŭk.
Half way	igli-hŭk-tūk, or keit-ka.
Half way	ked-jer-rei-yŏk.
Between	ŭk-ı-nĕk.
Together	illuit-keit.
Alone	ted-bet-yūak
Both	tŭm-mā-mŭt.
Only one	kĕ-himi.
Outside	hi-la-mi.
Flat (land)	mun-i-kūni.
Slow	hullau-hu-kūni.
My (clothes) . . .	ker
Wet	kĕn-ni-pa-kūni.
Pulled tight	ăkūt.
Wounded in the paunch .	nĕr-rūk-kŭk.
Nearly boiling . . .	ai-pai-yok.
More	ŭt-ti-lŏ.
Some, or part of	i-lŭng-er.
To camp (in snow-houses)	tŭng-mark-tūk.
To stay in camp	u-bli-yūk.
To boil (water)	tĕk-i-tūk.
To boil meat	i-gŭlli.

To cook	u-yŏk.
To chop with an axe . .	u-li-măk-tūk.
To open with a knife . .	pi-lŭk-glu.
To tie up	kei-pi-li.
Tie it! (imperative) . .	kei-pĭg-li.
To unfasten	i-go-milli.
To take	ting-u-yūk.
Where are you going? . .	hūli-ăk-petik.
Where is he going? . . .	hūli-a-rŭmna.
To hunt	kei-nĕk-tūk.
To go to meet a deer . .	nar-yu-tok-tūk.
To follow a deer	mŭl-lig-tūk.
To follow a man	u-lek-tūk.
To go in front of dogs and sleigh	hi-wūl-ĕk-tūk.
To go behind dogs and sleigh	king-u-hik-tūk.
Behind (other things) . .	hi-wūl-ĭt.
In front of (other things) .	king-ūl-ĭt.
To accompany	pŭkka-tau-li.
Accompanied	pŭkka-tau-yūk.
To follow a river or shore .	ŭt-tŏk-tūk.
To follow tracks	ŭt-tūm-nĭd-tūk.
Fresh tracks	nū-tăk-tū-mit.
To go downstream . . .	shi-ti-yūk.
To go upstream	mei-yŭ-răk-tūk.
Where do you come from?	men-nĭp-p'hī.
Where does it (or, do they) come from?	nŭkki-nimna-pi-yūk.
Where?	nau-wimna, or nenni.
To forget	pŏï-yu-rămă.
Forgotten	pŏï-yŏk-tūk.
I will look	tĕk-ūli.
Will look, or see . . .	tŭkko-hwa-petkar.
I want to see one thing .	tŭkko-hwăk-părăr.
I want to see many things	tŭkko-hwăk-pŭtkar.
I will take a walk to look at the ice	awonga-pi-hūk-tūk shi-kū-tĕkuli.
To be able to see far . .	nĭp-tĕt-kĕt-tūk.
Not to be able to see far .	nĭp-te-tūk.
To want	pĭ-lŭg-o, or pi-hwa-rŭp-ko.
Not to want	pi-hwung-nĭ-nŭpkū.
To want	pĭt-ă-kă-kūni.
What do you want? . . .	hūmă-gŭ-ōk.
To bring	ŭg-gĭ-ak-tūk.
Fetch that	ŭg-gĭ-yūk.

Go and get (implying a journey)	ai-klĭk-tūk
Go and bring (a small article)	hi-aw-wĭk.
Find, or found	nŭn-i-yūk.
Will find	nūn-i-yūk-măk
To give	pi-yūk.
To take away	ŭshi-wawk-li.
To take away	nŭkka-tūk.
To take along	nŭk-sarlĭ.
Took along	nŭk-sark-tūk.
To go away (of persons) .	wawk-wawk-tūk.
Gone, departed	pi-tă-hŭngă-mŭn
To remain	nūt-kŭng-ai-yŏk.
To run (of persons) . . .	ak-pĕt-tūk.
Will start	au-lăr-ū-māk.
Will not start	au-lē-lŭng-nĭd-tūk.
To accompany, or travel together	pŭk-a-tauli.
Will come	kei-yu-măk.
Have not arrived . . .	tik-ing-nĭd-tūk.
To go quickly	pi-hūa-lĕt-yu-ămŭt.
To go slowly	pi-hūa-lei-tūk.
A sleigh goes quick . . .	shūk-kau-ūk-tūk.
A sleigh goes slowly . .	shūk-kei-tūk.
Dogs go quick . . ' .	pŭngă-lĭk-tūk.
Dogs go slowly . . .	nū-kŭt-tar-waw-yak-tūk.
To ascend a hill . . .	mei-yu-ark-tūk.
To descend a hill . . .	ŭmū-kok-tūk.
To ascend to top of hill .	nĕ-hĭk-pūk.
To fly away	wawk-tūk.
To lie down (of deer) . .	ako-pi-yūk.
To lie, or sit (of a man) .	ako-mei-tūk.
To run (of deer)	pŭnga-lĭk-tūk.
To cross a river	ki-pi-yu.
To swim (of deer) . . .	nŭl-lūk-tūk.
To dive (of a seal) . . .	ŭt-kak-tūk.
Gone to hunt	mok-kai-tūk.
To cover	u-lig-li.
To turn over (as a blanket)	mū-mig-li.
To place, to put . . .	il-lilli.
To cut up an animal . .	pi-lŭk-tŏk-tūk.
To sink	ki-wi-yŏk.
To float	pūk-tel-ei-yŏk.
To dry	pŭn-nĕg-sĕk-tūk.
To wet	kinni-ok-shŭk.
To divide amongst . . .	au-wĭk-tūk.

To possess	pi-ter-li, or kŭk-pi-hil-lī.
To steal	tĭg-līt-tūk.
Not to steal	tĭg-lī-nī-tūk.
To steal	tĭg-lu-i-kūni.
To tell lies	hŭglo-tu-kūni.
To melt in a pot . . .	auk-tūk.
To melt naturally (as ice, &c.)	tu-wĕ-yăk-tūk.
To grow (as grass) . . .	pĕr-rōk-shai-yok.
To die	tū-kū-kūni.
Dead	tork-kor-yūk.
Tied up (one dog) . . .	I-pĭl-ĭk.
„ (two dogs) . . .	I-pĭl-ĕk.
„ (three dogs) . .	I-pĭl-ĭt.
Killed instantaneously (as a deer shot)	ikki-wīt-tok.
It smells bad	mŭmmĕi-i-kūni.
It smells good	mŭmma-a-kūni.
To have	pĭ-tĕ-lĭk.
To meet	kŭt-ĭ-yū.
Wind rises	ŭn-norri-tu-yŏk.
Wind falls	ŭn-norri-gik-tor.
Shut the door	u-mĭg-lĭ.
Where are my moccasins or socks ?	kŭm-mĭk-păr ker-nau.
To shovel snow	ni-wŭk-tūk.
To use ice-chisel	tu-ŏk-tūk.
There is water below the ice	kunger-tei-yūk.
There is no water below the ice	put-ting-nŭk.
To shoot over an animal .	kŭl-ro-tūk.
To shoot under an animal .	ker-tu-tūk.
To dress a deer	a-tŏk-tūk.
To sew (boots)	mek-sok-tūk.
Will eat	nĕri-yu-măk.
To hear	hī-yu-tik.
Horns grow	nŭg-gi-hei-yok.
I told you	awonga-igbik ukak-tūk.
To understand	tū-hăk-pūnga.
Do you understand . .	tū-hŭk-pĭg.
I don't understand ? . .	tū-hŭng-i-tūk.
What ?	sū-a.
Why ?	hū-ŏk.
Is that correct ?	tai-mĕt-năk.
I do not know	kau-yu-mŭngi-tūt-yuăk.
Remember	pŏĭ-yu-nĭg-tūk.

I wonder where . . . . temna.
To think . . . . . . a-hiu-wimna.
Some men. . . . . . il-ă-nL
A little . . . . ei-yĕ.
For . . . . mŭn.
For Milŭk . . . . . Milŭk-mŭn.
A hole . . . . pŭ-tŭk.
On top of, up . . . . . kŭt-shĬ-kŭni.

INDEX

Printed by BALLANTYNE, HANSON & CO.
Edinburgh & London